INFANT PERCEPTION: FROM SENSATION TO COGNITION

volume II   Perception of Space, Speech, and Sound

THE CHILD PSYCHOLOGY SERIES

EXPERIMENTAL AND THEORETICAL ANALYSES OF CHILD BEHAVIOR

EDITOR
DAVID S. PALERMO

DEPARTMENT OF PSYCHOLOGY
THE PENNSYLVANIA STATE UNIVERSITY
UNIVERSITY PARK, PENNSYLVANIA

INFANT PERCEPTION: FROM SENSATION TO COGNITION

volume II Perception of Space, Speech, and Sound

Edited by

Leslie B. Cohen

Department of Psychology and
Institute for Child Behavior and Development
University of Illinois
Champaign, Illinois

Philip Salapatek

Institute of Child Development
University of Minnesota
Minneapolis, Minnesota

ACADEMIC PRESS   New York   San Francisco   London

A Subsidiary of Harcourt Brace Jovanovich, Publishers

ACADEMIC PRESS, INC.
111 Fifth Avenue, New York, New York 10003

United Kingdom Edition published by
ACADEMIC PRESS, INC. (LONDON) LTD.
24/28 Oval Road, London NW1

Library of Congress Cataloging in Publication Data
Main entry under title:

Infant perception.

    (Child psychology)
    Includes bibliographies and index.
    CONTENTS: v. 1. Basic visual processes.--v. 2. Per-
ception of space, speech, and sound.
    1.   Infant psychology.   2.   Visual perception.
3.   Auditory perception.   I.   Cohen, Leslie B.
II.   Salapatek, Philip.   [DNLM: 1.   Cognition—In
infancy and childhood.   2.   Perception—In infancy and
childhood.   3.   Sensation—In infancy and childhood.
WS105 141]
BF723.I6I53   155.4'22   75-3582
ISBN 0–12–178602–1 (v. 2)

Contents

List of Contributors

Numbers in parentheses indicate the pages on which the authors' contributions begin.

T. G. R. Bower (33), Department of Psychology, University of Edinburgh, Edinburgh, Scotland

Jeanne Brooks (101), Infant Laboratory, Institute for Research in Human Development, Educational Testing Service, Princeton, New Jersey

Peter D. Eimas (193), Department of Psychology, Brown University, Providence, Rhode Island

Gerald Gratch (51), Department of Psychology, University of Houston, Houston, Texas

Kurt Hecox* (151), Department of Neurosciences, University of California, San Diego, La Jolla, California

Michael Lewis (101), Infant Laboratory, Institute for Research in Human Development, Educational Testing Service, Princeton, New Jersey

Herbert L. Pick, Jr. (3), Institute of Child Development, University of Minnesota, Minneapolis, Minnesota

Albert Yonas (3), Institute of Child Development, University of Minnesota, Minneapolis, Minnesota

* Present address: Department of Pediatrics, University of Texas, Southwestern Medical School, Dallas, Texas.

Preface

Perceptual development has been one of the most rapidly expanding areas of investigation over the past two decades. A number of factors have converged to make this expansion possible: the dissemination of Piagetian theory and data, the application of ethology to human behavior, the redemonstration by Fantz (originally demonstrated by the German psychophysicists) that even the newborn can be cajoled into answering interesting research questions, improvements in both technology and methodology, and finally, striking recent advances in developmental neurophysiology.

The study of infant perception has experienced a particularly fruitful proliferation during this period. Although isolated reports of the infant's ability to see and hear date back to the nineteenth century, it has only been within the last few years that investigators have begun comprehensive programmatic examinations of early sensory, perceptual, and cognitive systems. The present volumes, which constitute the first synthesis of recent research and theorizing on infant perception, reflect this trend. The contributors do more than list what the infant is capable of perceiving; their approach is to organize the material in a cohesive, systematic framework. Several authors outdid themselves, summarizing large bodies of existing research, reporting in some detail previously unpublished data, and integrating the two into an original theoretical system. What has emerged is a view of the infant as a curious blend of neural–behavioral systems—reflex and voluntary, sensory and perceptual, sensorimotor and representational—who provides a likely bridge between advances in ethology, neurophysiology, and sensory systems on one hand, and the cognitive linguistic mature human on the other.

We did not feel compelled to include systematically all areas or modalities of infant perception in these two volumes. Our constant goal was to represent and analyze the flow of programmatic investigations, rather than isolated studies or pockets of research. The amount of research has been most pronounced in infant vision, and to a lesser extent in infant audition. For this reason the organization of the volumes reflects that emphasis with the first volume and most of the second devoted to infant visual perception. Although a search was made, we were unable to fulfill our goal in the "other" sensory systems, e.g., taste, smell, touch, the vestibular and kinesthetic senses. However, given the continuing proliferation of research in all areas of early perceptual development, we expect such chapters to be feasible in the very near future.

Volume I begins with a chapter by Maurer in which most of the major physiological and behavioral techniques used to measure infant vision are assessed. Each technique is critically evaluated in terms of the method employed, the type of data which can be obtained, and the anatomy of the visual system. In Chapter 2, Karmel and Maisel show how one of these techniques (measurement of visually evoked responses) can be used to assess infant visual preferences for patterns varying in amount of contour. They also propose a neuronal model to explain developmental changes in these preferences.

The value of the corneal reflection technique for the study of infant attention and visual scanning patterns is amply demonstrated by Salapatek in Chapter 3. Integrating considerable evidence from his own work as well as data from other laboratories, he provides answers to basic questions about the innate organization of perception, focal versus peripheral processing, and oculomotor involvement in perceptual learning. The evidence is also used as a basis for evaluating a variety of existing theories of perceptual development.

In Chapter 4, Fantz, Fagan, and Miranda examine both developmental changes and individual differences in early pattern perception. The authors present a large body of data, accumulated over a number of years, in order to trace the development of visual preferences for variations in form, pattern arrangement, size versus number of elements, and novelty versus familiarity. They show that most of these changes are a function of gestational age rather than age since birth, and that their techniques are also sensitive to differences between retarded and normal infants.

The final chapter in Volume I could be considered a continuation of the preceding one. Cohen and Gelber concentrate on evidence of infant visual preferences for novelty and on the implications of such evidence for models of early recognition memory. The pros and cons of habituation versus paired comparison techniques are discussed, and evidence from both is shown to be remarkably consistent on such issues as the type of visual information infants can remember, how long they can remember, and the conditions most likely to produce interference with that memory.

Volume II begins where Volume I leaves off. The chapters in Volume I are arranged along a continuum from basic sensory and neurophysiological functioning to information processing and memory. All of the chapters deal primarily with two-dimensional pattern perception. In Volume II the third dimension, depth, is added. The first chapter by Yonas and Pick discusses the difficulties prior research has had in assessing infant perception of depth or space. Two research strategies are proposed which would provide more powerful evidence of early space perception, and several specific experiments are suggested which employ these new strategies. The second chapter by Bower provides a link between infants' perception of space and their perception of objects. In the first half of the chapter he argues that occlusion information is critical to an infant's perception of depth, and in the second half he argues that the development of object permanence seems to require both an infant's perception of three-dimensional boundedness and his understanding of the transformation involved when one object goes inside another.

The development of object permanence is discussed further in the next chapter, by Gratch. After a brief description of Piaget's sensorimotor stages, Gratch critically evaluates both psychometric studies of object concept development and studies focusing specifically on Piaget's theory. The chapter closes with a comparison of "constructivist" (Piaget) versus "realist" (Gibson) theories, and the conclusion is reached that neither can provide a completely adequate account of all the data.

"Constructivist" versus "realist" theories are also compared in the chapter by Lewis and Brooks, but this time in reference to social perception. The authors reject the notion that theories constructed to explain infant nonsocial perception are also sufficient for social perception. Considerable emphasis is placed on the infant's development of the concept of self, and that concept is used to explain the infant's perception of other persons.

The theme changes in the final two chapters of Volume II, from infant vision to infant audition. Nevertheless, the organization of the chapters reflects the same continuum from basic sensory and neurophysiological functioning to information processing and social–linguistic ability. In Chapter 5 Hecox describes in detail the developmental anatomy of the auditory pathway. Major anatomical structures from the middle ear to the cortex are discussed in terms of both function and development. Next comes an examination of electrophysiological functioning, followed by the description of experiments in which one electrophysiological measure (the brainstem evoked response) is effectively used to assess infant auditory capacity.

In the concluding chapter of Volume II Eimas describes a series of studies on the infant's receptiveness for the segmental units of speech, his ability to perceive phonemic feature contrasts, and the manner in which this perception occurs. A theoretical mechanism for infant speech perception is also proposed, and an attempt is made to relate the findings on early speech perception to the development of the full linguistic competence.

The task of editing these two volumes was somewhat more difficult than we had anticipated but also considerably more rewarding. We became more and more pleased as one chapter after another appeared with original theoretical and methodological statements as well as reviews of research. We would like to express our appreciation to the authors for their obvious expenditure of time, effort, and thought on their contributions. We would also like to thank our students and colleagues for their help in editing manuscripts, and, in particular, Richard Aslin, Martin Banks, Ruth Pearl, Elliot Saltzman, and Robert Schwartz for preparation of the subject index.

Contents of Volume I

part A: OBJECTS AND SPACE

chapter 1: An Approach to the Study of Infant Space Perception

ALBERT YONAS
University of Minnesota

HERBERT L. PICK, JR.
University of Minnesota

I. INTRODUCTION

What does it mean to say that an infant perceives space? In intuitive terms it means that he can perceive where things are. He perceives which end is up. He registers how far away things are. He perceives whether they are straight ahead or to the side. He can tell which things are next to which other things. In more abstract terms he can identify the direction and distance of objects from himself and from each other. Operationally these questions are usually framed in the form of discrimination and identification. For discrimination one would want to know whether the infant is able to perceive that two directions or positions in space are different. For identification one would want to know whether he is able to make a unique response to any given distance or direction. This chapter will be concerned with an analysis of the ability of infants to perceive space, with how we know what it is an infant is perceiving, and with what we can infer about his perception.

This chapter will not be a traditional review of the classical cues for the perception of space and an assessment of an infant's sensitivity to them. An interested reader may avail himself of one of several reviews of such literature (e.g., Kessen, Haith, & Salapatek, 1970; Pick & Pick, 1970; cf. Chapter 2 by Bower and Chapter 3 by Gratch in this volume and Chapter 4 by Fantz, Fagan, & Miranda in Volume I). Rather this chapter will deal with the problem of making inferences about an infant's knowledge of space. We feel that the area of infant space perception is entering a period of extraordinary progress. For decades William James's view of the infant's perceptual world as a blooming buzzing confusion was held by most psychologists. Fantz, with his elegantly simple techniques of observation, was able to demonstrate that this was not true. Moreover he inspired numbers of other psychologists to use his methods and develop other methods of their own to assess the boundaries of infant perception. Thus, besides fixation preference (Fantz, 1961, 1963), these techniques now include conditioning of operant responses (Bower, 1964), habituation and dishabituation of ongoing behavior (Bartoshuk, 1962), orienting responses (Hruska & Yonas, 1971; Campos, Langer, & Krowitz, 1970), the use of ecologically meaningful responses such as locomotion (Walk & Gibson, 1961), reaching (Bruner & Koslowski, 1972), and surprise (Charlesworth, 1963). In recent years T. G. R. Bower, more than anyone else, has exploited these techniques in exciting ways for understanding infant space perception.

What does it mean to say that an infant perceives three-dimensional space? It could mean that the infant possesses an abstract three-dimensional cartesian representation of space in which information from various sense modalities is integrated. At the other extreme it could mean that the infant simply possesses a set of spatially specific responses, that is, reflexes triggered by specific sensory stimulation. An example of such a response might be a saccadic eye movement elicited by the onset of a stimulus at a given point on the retina.

Obviously any assertions about a child's representation of space rest on inferences and cannot be based on immediate information. But of course that is also true of assertions about any but one's own knowledge of space. The thesis of this chapter is that by making reasonable inferences, a parsimonious explanation of space perception may be found. We will try to analyze the circumstances under which these inferences are warranted and useful. For example many species have been found to avoid the deep side of a visual cliff (Walk, 1966). Some psychologists would infer that this behavior implies a knowledge or perception of depth and the concomitant danger of falling. Is this inference warranted? Zaporozhets (personal communications) has argued that 6-month-old infants' failure to crawl onto the deep side of the visual cliff was due to the cessation of activity that is part of a simple orienting response evoked by the deep side of the cliff. Another example is that 3-month-old infants, lying on their backs, blink when a disk falls toward their eyes (White, 1971). May we infer the perception of changing distance and of impending collision? It is possible that any very rapid motion of a contour over the retina will evoke the same response.

In the following discussion we will explore various kinds of evidence on the basis of which it might be possible to infer the degree of an infant's perception of space. We will suggest that two of the most powerful types of evidence for such inferences are stimulus convergence and response convergence. We mean by stimulus convergence the generalization of a particular response to two or more physically dissimilar stimuli that carry the same information. Take as an example a subject trained to select the nearer of two objects on the basis of linear perspective alone. If that subject generalized his response to the nearer of two objects defined only in terms of stereoscopic information we might infer perception of depth. We mean by response convergence the gener-alization to a given stimulus situation of different responses with the same outcome. Consider, for example, an infant reaching repeatedly for an object at a particular location in space. No two responses will be identical and yet an infant of 3 to 5 months of age will usually attain the object.

II. STIMULUS CONVERGENCE AND THE REPRESENTATION OF SPACE

Let us begin with an example—an experiment on perception of depth in newborns by Fantz (1961). He presented a disk and a sphere to infants of 1 to 6 months of age and observed the direction of their eye fixations. In different conditions textured and un-textured stimuli were presented monocularly and binocularly in direct and indirect lighting. The infants showed significant prefer-ence for fixating the sphere over the disk. This was interpreted as demonstrating depth perception in the young infant. The clearest preference for the sphere was found when it was highly textured and presented in direct lighting in such a way as to accentuate shading and brightness contrast. An alternative interpretation is that the preference was elicited by a specific stimulus variable—amount of contour, rather than depth. The texture and lighting combination generated a maximum difference in amount of high contrast contour between the disk and the sphere, and there is evidence (Karmel, 1969) that amount of contour is an important determiner of stimulus preference.

How might we be more certain of the interpretation of the results of such an experiment in terms of sensitivity to depth per se? Depth could be varied independently of amount of contour. That is, amount of contour could be held constant and degree of depth varied. If degree of depth still determined degree of preference we would be more willing to accept the depth interpretation. An interesting illustration of this approach could imply Julesz stereograms (Julesz, 1971). The depth information in these pairs of random dot figures, and indeed the identity of a form at all, are derived solely from the disparity between them and do not involve prior identification of a shape or contour on the basis of which depth is inferred. Thus, if an infant fixated such a stereoscopically generated shape, one might infer sensitivity to depth. And indeed, Bower (1970) has reported that 20 to 30% of infants show fixations using Julesz figures in a way similar to that suggested here. However, as has been pointed out before (Pick & Pick, 1970; Bower, 1972), such responses might be made specifically to retinal disparity rather than to the depth that such disparity generates. (Adults sometimes report seeing some unspecified vaguely defined shape before it "pops out" into depth.)

Is there any way we might be still more certain of the depth interpretation? Suppose that we had a number of experiments like the one employing Julesz figures in which preference is assessed. For example in one experiment a stereoscopically defined object would be paired with a flat projection of that object. In a second experiment a pair of stimuli consisting of dot patterns is presented monocularly to subjects whose heads are fixed in position. The dots of one pattern are at different distances from the subject, producing different degrees of blur depending on the accommodation of the lens of the eye. In a third experiment, the pair of stimuli differ only insofar as one has motion parallax specifying solidity or depth and the other does not. (This could be done by presenting, for one stimulus, an array of lights such that they translated uniformly across the retina as the subject moved his head and a second stimulus such that the motion across the retina specified the motion parallax of two surfaces at different distances. Such motion parallax has been shown to be effective with adults. Cf. Gibson & Gibson, 1957.)

Let us further suppose that in all these three experiments the infant showed a fixation preference for the solid or three-dimensional object. What could account for this set of stimulus preferences? There might be separate independent explanations for each of these preferences. It is difficult to see what these would be and it would certainly be more parsimonious to seek a unified explanation for all these preferences. One property common to all three preferred stimuli is that they each have more stimulus variation than the nonpreferred stimuli. Thus preference might be simply a function of amount of stimulus variation. Suppose, however, similar experiments were added with other depth cues, for example, pictorial depth cues such as texture gradients. In such displays (Figure 1.1, parts a and b) stimulus variation can be equated while maintaining differences in three dimensionality. If infants continued to prefer the three-dimensional members we ought to be more willing to accept the depth interpretation.

In short, if independent explanations are required to account for all such preferences we have a rather unparsimonious state of affairs. All these displays vary with depth, and if the three-dimensional member of the pair is preferred it is appealing to infer a mapping of each of these into a common representation of space. Thus the argument is one of parsimony and simplicity rather than logical necessity.

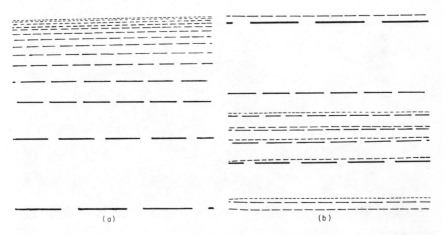

(a)   (b)

Figure 1.1. (a) and (b).   Two displays approximately equal in complexity but differing in degree of portrayed depth.

Psychologists have long been dissatisfied with the limitations of the discrimination or preference experiments because, as Bower (1972) points out, it is difficult on the basis of a simple discrimination to identify the effective stimulus variables. Psychologists with an associationist viewpoint have typically argued that the effective stimuli were low level sensory variables. In the preceding discussion, it has been argued in essence that a *pattern* of discriminations or preferences rather than a single one may indeed help identify the effective stimulus variables and these may be higher order meaningful dimensions.

Consider the phenomenon illustrated in Figure 1.2. This photograph of convexities and concavities as described by von Fieandt (1949) will reverse its depth relations when inverted. The convexities will become concavities and vice versa. The information for direction of depth is contained in the relationship between the shadow or shading information and a spatial reference system. In viewing photographs the relevant spatial reference system seems to be based on assumption that light comes from above. If Figure 1.2 is rotated 90° the spatial direction in depth of the forms is no longer seen as different by most observers. However the complexity and variation within the visual display itself is, of course, equivalent. The difference in the display in the two orientations is only in the relationship which specifies depth. If infants were to show more discrimination when the patterns were oriented in a way in which adults see depth rather than in other orientations it would again be

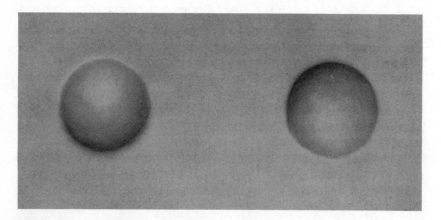

Figure 1.2.   The only information within this picture for the difference between the convexity and concavity is shading.

unparsimonious to say that infants are responding to low order sensory information. Such a pattern of results might be obtained from infants if they showed a consistent preference for the convexity or concavity when oriented as in Figure 1.2 but no preference when the shapes were rotated 90°.

Although it has been argued that patterns of discrimination can be informative about the underlying stimulus dimensions involved in space perception there is a still more powerful paradigm for studying the development of an infant's responsiveness to space—the transfer experiment (cf. Pick & Pick, 1970, p. 776). Again using the example of depth perception, a large number of cues provide redundant information about separation in the third dimension. Suppose it were possible to produce a preference for a given member of a pair of identical objects at different distances when the only information for distinguishing their distance was provided by a single depth cue. Then a test for preference could be conducted when their distance was distinguished by different depth cues. Positive transfer would be powerful evidence for an assertion that there was mediation by some sort of spatial representation. This paradigm is illustrated by an experiment (Yonas, 1973). Infants were habituated to a pair of actual convexities or concavities. After this habituation period they were tested for fixation preference with a photograph like that of Figure 1.2. Significant preference was shown for the pictorial representation of the novel object. During habituation shading provided no relevant information. The fact that the infants preferred the novel stimulus suggests that they were responding on the basis of depth relations within the distal stimulus. This result should be accepted with some caution since an attempt at replication was unsuccessful when less habituation was obtained. Results are clearer in the case of older children. In a similar experiment (Benson & Yonas, 1973) 3-year-olds were trained to select either a convexity or concavity from a pair on the basis of stereoscopic information or on the basis of tactual information. In both cases they showed positive transfer to photographs like Figure 1.2 in which shading provided the relevant depth information.

If a program of research, in principle similar to this example, established that there was transfer from each specific depth cue to every other, the most reasonable interpretation would be that a common spatial representation mediated the transfer. While it would be possible that such a transfer could be mediated by separate associations, either learned or innate, the parsimony of an interpretation in terms of a common representation is obvious. If, on the other hand, all these cues do not converge in early infancy, and previous work suggests that such is the case, the way the different cues cluster together may suggest important insights into the nature of perceptual development (cf. Chapter 4 by Fantz *et al.* in Volume I; Bower, 1966; Walk & Gibson, 1961).

The beginning of such a program can be illustrated by the work of Bower (1965) who trained 40- to 60-day-old infants to turn their heads when presented with a cube of a specific size and at a specific distance. In a transfer test they showed most generalization to a cube of the same size at a different distance. A larger cube farther away projecting the same size retinal image elicited less generalization, as did a larger cube at the same distance as the original training cube. Thus the infants seem to be responding in terms of size-at-a-distance. However, in a replication in which infants were trained and tested with two-dimensional pictures of the displays, most generalization occurred when the retinal size of the stimulus was invariant. The implication is that motion parallax provides infants with information for depth but pictorial cues do not (cf. Chapter 4 by Fantz *et al.* in Volume I; Walk & Gibson, 1961, for other cases where pictorial depth information is less effective in early development). However, the interpretation that pictorial cues are different must be made with caution since there was actually conflicting information present in the pictorial situation. The pictorial cues specified distance but the other cues such as motion parallax would specify a flat surface at a specific distance. Older children have been found to be more responsive to pictorial depth when conflicting information is reduced (Yonas & Hagen, 1973).

The possibility that infants respond in terms of size-at-a-distance or in terms of the relation between shading information and direction of light suggest sensitivity to higher order stimulus variables which have been suggested by J. J. Gibson to form the basis of our perception (J. J. Gibson, 1966). He has argued that analysis of stimulation at a biologically relevant level is more appropriate for perception than the reductionistic analysis of physics. Higher order stimulus variables include information for movement and change of objects, motion of the observer, layout of the environment, properties of rigidity, elasticity, animateness, etc. For example, when the whole visual field transforms, motion of the observer is specified. When there is symmetrical expansion of a closed contour in the visual field the approach of an object is specified. When this expansion is a hyperbolic function of time the approach is specified as being constant in velocity. Sensitivity to such variables has been studied in infants (Lee & Aronson, 1974; Bower, 1965; Ball & Tronick, 1971; Hruska & Yonas, 1971) and will be discussed later.

III. RESPONSE CONVERGENCE AND THE REPRESENTATION OF SPACE

The second very general class of evidence on the basis of which representation of space might be attributed to infants involves analysis of responses. An example of a response from which one might infer a spatial representation is provided by Engen, Lipsitt, and Kaye (1963). They presented newborns with intense odors by holding Q-tips saturated with various substances 5 mm from their noses. Infants responded to some of these odors with general activity, including head movement, leg withdrawal, and respiration change not unlike a mild startle. With repeated presentation the response became much more abbreviated and approximated "simple retraction or turning of the head from the locus of the odorant . . . [p. 77]." One explanation of such behavior, perhaps implied by the author's purposive description, would be: (a) that the infant knows the location of the door, (b) wants to get away from it, and (c) knows how to move his head in order to increase the distance between his nose and the odor source. An alternate interpretation could be based on the infant's sensitivity simply to the intensity of stimulation and not to its spatial properties. When the intense stimulus was first presented the infant responded with general diffuse movement. Upon repeated application the unconditioned startle response became less diffuse with only the head movement components remaining. The authors suggest that this refinement may be a form of learning by means of differential reinforcement. The point is that on the basis of this evidence it would be unwarranted to attribute elaborate spatial knowledge to the newborn infant. The convergence of a number of different responses, on the other hand, could convince us that a single spatial description most economically accounts for the behavior. If the infant turned to the left when the odor was presented on the right and to the right when the odorant was presented on the left, if he moved up when it was presented below the nose, down when presented above, we would have a number of different responses with a common spatial result. Since in the Engen *et al.* (1963) study, the position of the odorant always was in front of the infant, any head movement would turn the head from the locus of the odorant.

Another example of a response slightly more encouraging of a spatial interpretation is the lens accommodation of an infant to targets of varying distances. Haynes, White, and Held (1965) showed that the ability to accommodate or focus the lens of the eye to different distances develops gradually with age over the first 2 to 3 months. During the first month the infant maintains fixed accommodation for a distance of about 18 cm in spite of changes of target distance, while the 3-month-old finely adjusts his accommodation to the target distance. One explanation of such behavior would be that the infant registers the distance of the object and adjusts the accommodation of the lens accordingly. However, again, an alternative explanation is that the blur of an unfocused image elicits a random search for an accommodation of maximum clarity.

Just as in the case of stimulus convergence, we must both be on guard not to assume that spatially specific responses necessarily require spatial perception and at the same time remain open to the possibility that they do when such interpretation is more reasonable. An interpretation of this second example of accommodation in terms of perception of space is more compelling than in the case of the newborns' response to odors. However, it is still not entirely satisfactory. While lens accommodation may be finely spatially graded it may be that no other response system shows appropriate spatial specificity, that is, there is no response convergence.

In this section we wish to discuss the conditions under which explanations of responses to spatial properties in terms of perception of space are more or less reasonable. In analyzing responses in this section we will exclude the class of arbitrary conditional responses, some of which were mentioned previously. That is, we will not consider responses such as head turning when this has been conditioned to a stimulus situation unrelated to spatial discrimination. In such cases, investigation of space perception does not depend so much on the arbitrary response which has been conditioned but rather on the cleverness with which stimulus conditions can be manipulated.

In making this analysis it may be useful to consider a sequence that might be termed a perceptual act. The infant is presented with a stimulus situation. He may make some adjustments; perhaps he may mobilize himself for an instrumental response, then make the instrumental response itself.

The eye adjustments that infants make include fixation of station-
ary and moving targets, vergence movements, and accommodation.
We want to examine the extent to which these responses imply
space perception. (We are not examining the possibility that they
themselves provide information about space. That is, arguments
have been made that the proprioceptive feedback from the eyes
when they converge at targets of different distances provides
information about distance or that proprioceptive sensitivity to eye
position provides information about the azimuth of a stimulus. Such
cues do not seem to be especially important or effective even for
adults.) There are a number of studies which demonstrate the
ability of neonates and very young infants to bring their line of sight
to a particular direction in space (Wertheimer, 1961; Turkewitz *et
al.*, 1966; Gorman, Cogan, and Gillis, 1957; Fantz, 1958; Salapatek &
Kessen, 1966; Aslin & Salapatek, 1973). Some of these show that
neonates will selectively fixate a portion of the field depending on
the nature of the stimuli. The ability of an infant to bring his eyes to
a given direction in space is potentially evidence for the existence of
spatial perception. Of course such coordination might be achieved
on the basis of random correction of error. That is, an infant might
detect that there is a discrepancy between a given direction of gaze
and a target, then simply move at random noting whether movements increased or decreased the discrepancy. He could then
simply persist in movements which decreased the discrepancy.
Such a capacity—being able to detect discrepancies of position and
increases or decreases of discrepancy—would be a primitive kind of
space perception. A high probability of changing the direction of
fixation initially in such a way as to decrease the discrepancy would
be evidence of a more refined kind of space perception—one in
which relative directions are registered. The most refined kind of
space perception would be specified by initial ballistic or saccadic
eye movements to a target. Such movements would imply that the
infant had some kind of information about his own starting
position, the target position, and the relation between the two. Of
course, as with most indices of perception, failure to obtain a
behavior may not mean failure of perception but failure of motor
capacity. Furthermore, such indices assume that an infant is trying
to reduce the discrepancy between target and present eye fixation.
Kessen, Salapatek, and Haith (1972) found that neonates tended to
concentrate their eye positions in the direction of single vertical
contours in the field of view but not in the direction of single
horizontal contours. While these authors did not describe in detail

how subjects brought their eyes to the relevant position they did observe a "positive relation between the proximity of eye and edge and the probability of the next eye movement being toward or crossing the edge . . . [Kessen, Salapatek, & Haith, 1972, p. 17]." This observation is the kind of nonrandom change of eye position that would be expected in a differentiated space. On the other hand, neonates in this study as in previous ones (Salapatek & Kessen, 1966; Salapatek, 1968) scanned more in the horizontal direction than in the vertical even in blank field control conditions. The authors use this fact in conjunction with the hypothesis that the eye is attracted to a place where frequent changes in intensity occur to explain why vertical contours are fixated more than horizontal. Specifically, intensity changes do not happen very often with the small number of vertical eye movements occurring in the presence of a horizontal contour: hence, no concentration of fixations. This interpretation of their data suggests a pattern of eye movements more like what has been called here discrepancy reduction. In any case the pattern does not seem to be typical of precise ballistic movements. A final point about an infant's ability to bring his line of sight to a given direction concerns the lack of convergence in the newborn. Wickelgren (1967) found little evidence of convergence. This would suggest that eye positioning at best would be an unreliable index of space perception.

From such analysis, at this time it must be concluded that no precise definition of an eye-position-defined azimuth space has been demonstrated for neonates. Older children and adults clearly are able to move their eyes ballistically to a given direction and to do it with a high degree of accuracy. When does this ability develop? Aslin (cf. Chapter 3 by Salapatek, in Volume I) demonstrated that infants as young as 1 month show directionally appropriate eye movements to presentations of targets at new positions in the field of view. The eye moved in a series of small saccades rather than in a single large saccade. This method should be extended to both younger and older infants so as to ascertain the developmental course of both directional and magnitude components of eye movements.

Although there is no highly certain evidence for the perception or representation of spatial direction at birth, evidence from cataract patients suggests it may not require visual experience. These patients, blind from birth, whose sight had been restored in later years (von Senden, 1960) have not been reported to have any difficulty in identifying the visual direction of objects. For example, it usually was quite clear to the patient what objects he was being questioned about. There was some mention of a disturbing nystagmus but this seems to have been more of a bother for the patient's maintenance of fixation rather than inability to position the eye at all. In the most carefully researched case (Gregory & Wallace, 1963) the patient was even able to recognize visually letters of the alphabet that he had known previously only by touch. This is explicable if eye position mapped directly into tactual–motor perception without prior visual experience.

The reader should keep in mind that studies of fixation are relevant primarily to representation of azimuth. As implied by Hochberg (1974) saccadic eye movements must be responsive to retinal position and cannot be responsive to the distal stimulus. When looking at another person from head to toes, for example, responding to the constant size of a person with changing distance would clearly be maladaptive. On the other hand, there is another kind of preplanned change of direction of eye fixation that might provide information about an infant's sensitivity to depth. Hochberg (1974) made the insightful suggestion that compensatory eye movements made with change of head position should be tied to the distance of the target. As the head rotates, a higher rate of compensatory eye motion is required to maintain fixation on near targets than on distant ones. These compensatory eye movements may be preprogrammed and not depend on feedback since they begin simultaneously with the movement of the head. The existence of such compensatory eye movements coordinated with the distance of a target would provide evidence for the existence of sensitivity to three-dimensional space in infants. If compensatory eye movements appropriately graded to the distance of an object and appropriate lens accommodation developed in parallel, there would be greater probability that a common spatial representation was involved.

A second class of responses which has recently been used to index perception of spatial variables involves the mobilization of the organism to act. These are measures of the autonomic nervous system and were first investigated systematically by Sokolov (1960). He distinguished between two general types of response to change of stimulation. One characterized by heart rate deceleration he termed the "orienting reflex" and it typically followed a moderate change in stimulation. The other, characterized by heart rate acceleration, he termed a "defense reflex" and it typically followed a large change of stimulation.

Graham and her colleagues (Graham & Clifton, 1966; Graham & Jackson, 1970) have adduced a good deal of evidence confirming that heart rate response is a good index in the adult human of two different kinds of arousal. Heart rate acceleration seems to be characteristic of intense, possibly alarming, stimuli and can be characterized as part of what Sokolov described as a defense reflex. Heart rate deceleration, on the other hand, seems to be characteristic of novel, possibly interesting, stimuli and can be characterized as part of Sokolov's orienting reflex. It is not clear (Graham & Jackson, 1970) that heart rate can serve to distinguish two such states in neonates. The typical heart rate response to much stimulus change in neonates is acceleration. Heart rate deceleration may be difficult to elicit at all. However, deceleration has been reliably elicited in older infants, certainly in those between 1 and 6 months of age.

The use of these responses as indices of depth perception can be illustrated by the work of Campos and his colleagues and Hruska and Yonas (1971). In one experiment (Campos, Langer, & Krowitz, 1970) infants of 2 months of age were placed face down alternately on the shallow and deep side of a visual cliff. With 2-month-olds greater heart deceleration occurred on the deep side. Campos interpreted this as evidence that these infants discriminate between the two sides of the visual cliff but aren't sensitive to the possible "dangerous" implication of the stimulus situation. By the age of 9 months (Schwartz, Campos, & Baisel, 1972) the deep side elicited a heart rate acceleration, while the shallow side continued to elicit deceleration. This result would be consistent with an interpretation that between 2 and 9 months lack of optical support becomes aversive to infants. In quite a different experiment on depth perception the development of the heart rate response showed a similar trend (Hruska & Yonas, 1971). Young infants (2 months old) showed a heart rate deceleration to both the expansion and contraction of a silhouette in their visual field. Many older infants (6 months old) on the other hand, showed a heart rate acceleration to the expansion of the silhouette while continuing to show a deceleration to its contraction. As noted earlier, the rate of expansion might provide information about impending collision. The response of the older infants could indicate sensitivity to such information. It is interesting to note that in these heart rate studies the younger infants did not produce an *appropriate* defensive response to the situation which might have been considered dangerous.

Appropriateness is a new criterion for inferring sensitivity to depth. In these studies it depends on the application to infants of

Sokolov's distinction between orienting and defensive reflexes. That interpretation gains its power from the biological adaptiveness of the defense response in a dangerous situation. Such an interpretation would be most compelling if the two different responses could be demonstrated to the same proximal stimulation in one case when the situation was dangerous and in the other case when it was not. Such a demonstration might be accomplished using the orienting response infants make to an object receding from them. Would the same infants make a defensive response to that same proximal stimulation if the object receding from them was a surface on which they were lying (or at least the optical specification of that surface as might be accomplished by dropping the surface out from under the glass plate of a visual cliff)?

Appropriateness as one criterion for inferring sensitivity to depth is potentially very useful but fraught with difficulties. White (1971) used the eyeblink as an index of sensitivity to impending collision. He arranged to drop a disk toward the face of a prone infant in such a way that neither vibration nor air pressure accompanied the visual stimulation. The first consistent evidence of blinking appeared at about 2 months of age. After that the response developed rapidly over the next 8 to 10 weeks and seemed to be complete by 4 months of age. If this is a response to an approaching stimulus and not simply to rapid motion of a contour across the retina it would seem to be biologically adaptive. On the other hand, such an interpretation of blinking was rejected by Bower in analyzing the results of his own studies. Bower, Broughton, and Moore (1970a) also examined the responses of young infants to approaching objects. Infants of 6–20 days of age responded to the approach of real objects by interposing their hands between the objects and their faces and withdrawing their heads. When the object was replaced by an expanding shadow projection there was a smaller but still significant response which was absent in the presence of a contracting shadow projection. In his interpretation of these results Bower stressed the importance of the hand movements as an adaptive response while rejecting the adaptive value of the eyeblink. Ball and Tronick (1971) reported a similar study with infants from 2 to 11 weeks of age. They found infants reacting to both real and optical approach with complex coordinated movement of the hands and raising of the head. This behavior was interpreted as defensive.

It is not necessary to interpret the behavior of the infants in either the Bower, Broughton, and Moore study or the Ball and Tronick studies as appropriate avoidance responses. Just as Bower rejected the eyeblink as an adaptive response for analysis by White, it would be possible to question whether head raising is an adaptive response to impending collision. An alternative interpretation raised by Ball (1970) is that the infant is following the movement of the upper part of the shadow projection. Ball did not feel this was an adequate account of the head movement, but support for this interpretation is provided by an unpublished study by Yonas, Frankel, Bechtold, and Gordon. This study compares responses to an approaching real object, an expanding shadow projection, and a control shadow condition. In this condition the screen was masked off except for a vertical column that presented a nonexpanding, rising contour. Infants from 3 to 9 weeks of age withdrew their heads further from the display when only the rising contour was presented than they did in either of the other two conditions. In attempting to visually track the contour the infants frequently rotated their heads up and back. Arm raising and blinking were equally frequent in all conditions with these young infants. On the other hand, older infants, 8 and 9 months of age, blinked and withdrew from the screen on half the expanding shadow trials, while these responses occurred significantly less frequently when the rising contour was presented. Although these findings argue that by 8 months infants avoid appropriately a looming object by withdrawing and blinking, such a conclusion may not be warranted for 1- and 2-month-olds. Great care should be used in inferring the intentions of young infants from rather ambiguous behavior.

Another potential index of space perception is surprise. Surprise might be a variant of the orienting reflex. However, orienting typically occurs as a response to novelty while surprise occurs as a response to an unexpected stimulus. Though novelty and unexpectedness are related concepts, they have been distinguished by Charlesworth (1963). Charlesworth (personal communication) also has reported considerable difficulty in identifying surprise in infants. It is very difficult to obtain reliable judgments of surprise in infants on the basis of movies and videotape records. Charlesworth and Sroufe (personal communication) have been investigating the possible use of combinations of automatic and behavioral measures as indices of surprise. In spite of these difficulties several interesting studies of space perception have classified responses as surprise, inferring that an infant's expectations have been violated. In one instance a conflict between the location of a visual and an auditory source was presented to young infants (Aronson & Rosenbloom,

1971). The mother sat looking at the infant through a soundproof window and loudspeakers were arranged so as to make her voice appear to come either from her mouth or from the side of the room. When the voice location was moved from the mother's mouth to the side, the infants became very distressed. This was interpreted as evidence that the infant's expectancy that voices come from mouths had been violated. Another interpretation is that the visual stimulus of the mother and her voice in a different location elicit incompatible orienting responses. This interpretation could be tested by presenting pairs of highly attention attracting stimuli of various kinds at different locations. The pairs of stimuli could be comprised of the same or different sense modalities. Even if this alternative explanation is true, the study does demonstrate a degree of directionally specific visual and auditory behavior in the young infant.

Disruption of expectation was also employed in a study of depth perception (Bower, Broughton, & Moore, 1970b, c) in which infants were presented a virtual object by means of a stereoscopic display. The presence of stereopsis in infants would be particularly unexpected since they have poor convergence (Wickelgren, 1967). Infants as young as 7 days of age were reported to show upset when they reached out and failed to make contact with the presumably expected object. This is an extremely exciting finding as it demonstrates not only the presence of stereoscopic depth perception in the newborn but also the presence of a finely tuned motor–proprioceptive sensitivity and the coordination of vision and proprioception. The importance of this result does not depend on whether the response is truly one of surprise but rather on the fact that the behavior is distinctive and specific to the relation between the motor behavior and visual system.

An implication of this work of Bower and his colleagues is that there is an innate unity of the senses. This idea is developed more fully elsewhere by Bower (1974). With an interest in studying the development of visually guided reaching in infants Lasky (1973) created a conflict situation analogous to Bower's. Rather than presenting an infant with an ungraspable object he made the infant's limb invisible. Infants reached for objects under two conditions. In one, an infant could reach for an object while viewing both it and his hand through a transparent plastic sheet placed under his chin. In a second condition the original object was still present but the plastic sheet was replaced with a mirror giving the infant an identical view of the reflection of a second object. Now of course his hand and arm were no longer visible during a reach. At 6 months of age the reaching was disrupted by the absence of the visual hand. Younger infants showed no effect of the absence of the visual hand. This result would suggest that the coordination of visual and kinesthetic–motor space is not innate but follows a developmental course. The divergence between Bower's and Lasky's results might be due to many factors—their situations were quite different. However, this general technique of putting one modality in conflict with another seems to be a very promising method for investigating the development of spatial behavior. Lee and Aronson (1974), in another example of this technique, pitted visual and gravitational information of upright posture against each other in a study of infants' use of information in maintaining posture. Infants of 15 months of age stood facing the wall of a large roomlike cube. This cube was suspended from the ceiling of a large room and was open at the bottom so that the infants were actually standing on the floor. The cube could be swung back and forth several feet. If the cube was swung forward the optical stimulation was similar to that which would occur if the infant were falling backward (and vice versa). An appropriate response might be for the infant to lean forward. All seven infants tested showed such appropriate responding even to the point of falling. Thus at this age optical stimulation seems to be dominant over vestibular and proprioceptive information for maintaining posture.

Both Lasky's and Bower's observations of an infant's surprise about conflict in space depended on the reaction of an infant to the results of his own reaching. Reaching and grasping would seem to be excellent indices of the sensitivity of an infant to three-dimensional space. Of course we would not want to infer sensitivity to space if an infant randomly thrashed his arms and contacted and even retrieved an object. However, consider the reach of a normal 6-month-old. The hand rapidly extends in an azimuth appropriate to the direction of the object. This will occur almost exclusively when the object is within reach. This directionally specific response persists for long periods of time. When he fails to attain the object he will reach again. The response will cease when the object is reached, grasped, and retrieved. The behavior is flexible. He can get to the same spatial location along an indefinitely large number of paths and he can attain targets placed at an indefinitely large number of places. No one would describe behavior with these properties as random thrashing. Rather one would be likely to call it intentional. If an infant can intentionally move his hand from any place in space to any other place, especially if he can do it ballistically, he must have some sort of internal representation of space. The study of the development of reaching would thus seem to be an especially fruitful place to gain information about the development of sensitivity to space. Of course, again the absence of differential reaching behavior cannot be unequivocally interpreted as the absence of sensitivity. It could reflect purely development of the motor system or lack of interest in attaining the object.

Eye–hand coordination in infants has been carefully studied by Piaget (1952), by White (1971), and by Bruner and Koslowski (1972) among others. Interest in the development of such coordination has not for the most part been motivated by a desire to understand the development of space perception. One gains the impression, indeed, that these investigators view the infant as being able to perceive the position of the target. The critical problem is getting the hand to that position. For Piaget there is reciprocal assimilation between the hand and visual schemata and between the eye and manual schemata. The eye attempts to follow everything the hand does (second stage), and the hand attempts to grasp whatever the eye observes (fourth stage) (Piaget, 1952). For Bruner the orientation of the eye and head and body toward objects has already been perfected as has coordination between vision and the mouth when eye–hand coordination is perfected (Bruner, 1969). Whatever the case, numerous observations indicate that the hand can reach a visually apprehended target from almost any starting position by the age of 6 months.

Many investigators have reported that for young infants a close object can evoke an undifferentiated high level of activity. This gradually evolves into a highly differentiated spatially specific reach from which a refined spatial representation might be inferred. Frankel (1972) has reported from careful longitudinal case studies of two infants what might be interpreted as an intermediate spatial representation. These observations reminiscent of Bruner's concept of the mouth as a tertium quid (Bruner, 1971) concern how an infant is able to get his thumb into his mouth. At first, up to about $1\frac{1}{2}$ months of age, the thumb seemed only to reach the mouth on the basis of random movement. Indeed, even if the back of the hand hit the mouth or the thumb hit the upper gum, it was not oriented appropriately so as to get into the mouth at about $1\frac{1}{2}$ months, the mouth would move toward the thumb if it hit the face close to the mouth, or the hand would move to the mouth if it made contact as far away as the cheek. Gradually the directedness of the hand and mouth improved to the point that they would get together by means of the shortest route no matter where initial contact between them was made—the thumb tracing across the face in the appropriate direction. One gets the impression of the development of a polar coordinate system with the mouth as origin but one in which the origin can move.

Piaget and White both observed a later stage in development of hand–eye coordination that involved the infant's looking back and forth between his hand and the target. This would suggest that an error correction process of the type described previously (p. 13) might fit early eye–hand coordination. Bruner also reports coordination becoming more efficient under visual surveillance up to about 6 months of age. However Lasky (1973) found reaching quite common with infants as young as 3½ months of age even when visual feedback from their hands was precluded by a mirror as described previously. Also Frankel (1972) in his longitudinal studies failed to observe any sustained hand regard. Apparently such regard is not *necessary* for the development of reaching. In addition Lasky's observations suggest that ballistic movement of the hand is possible at a very early age, implying sensitivity to visual location of a target, starting position of one's own hand, and a representation that contains information about how to get from the starting position to the target location.

Exactly when this behavior becomes functional is very difficult to define. Many observers report that infants can be aroused by a visual stimulus into thrashing activity (or that their visual attention may be captured and general activity inhibited). The arm thrashing could result in contacts with the stimulus if it is close enough. Such contacts seem to get more frequent with age and thus imply a kind of directedness. At some point an observer is willing to judge the thrashing to have enough directedness to be considered swiping. Swiping consisting of quite accurate ballistic movements that do not result in prehension is typically reported to first appear at about 2½ months (White, 1971). Assuming that the movements are ballistic and accurate, they certainly imply visual localization. Their ballistic nature could be verified by moving the object after the swiping motion has started. Bruner and Koslowski (1972) studied infants between 10 and 22 weeks of age. They noted that, before infants were capable of reaching, they made differential hand movements to two sizes of objects. In contrast with these reports of gradual development, Bower, Broughton, and Moore (1970b) have reported spatially specific reaching by 6- to 11-day-old infants to targets presented from 60° to the left of midline to 60° to the right. Seventy percent of the reaches were within 5° of the target. He also has reported that there is adjustment of the finger–thumb separation of the hand during reaching just prior to contact in infants from 7 to 15 days of age (Bower, 1972). He suggests the possibility that such precocious responses may subsequently be extinguished if not reinforced appropriately. This possibility might explain why other investigators have failed to find such responses in older infants.

In the presence of an object, a 6-month-old infant will not only reach for it, if it is close enough, but will also locomote appropriately if the object is out of reach. Walk and Gibson (1961) took advantage of this fact in their now classical visual cliff studies. Walk's subsequent parametric investigations have demonstrated increasing sensitivity to depth as a function of age (Walk, 1966). The latest model of the visual cliff employs a gradually narrowing runway along which the infant is induced to crawl. At some point the runway is too narrow and the infant goes off to one side or the other. This technique reduces the proportion of infants who fail to respond at all in the visual cliff situation.

More recently Walters and Walk (1974) have studied infants' response to depth by means of a placing response. This response consists of an infant putting his hands out in front of himself as he is brought slowly down to a surface. A group of 15 infants between $8\frac{1}{2}$ and 11 months of age were tested by bringing them down to the deep or shallow side of a visual cliff. Of the trials to the shallow side 91% elicited placing responses while only 31% of the trials to the deep side did. Also avoidance of the deep side of the visual cliff in the traditional test seemed correlated with consistency of the placement response.

There is little doubt that the 6-month-old infant has spatial sensitivity. The convergence of such responses as spatially specific reaching and spatially appropriate behavior on the visual cliff (and a bit later the placing response) is very compelling. The explanation of such behavior on the basis of individual stimulus–response couplings would be incredibly complex and unparsimonious. If such an explanation is extended within the domain of reaching at an age when the infant can move his hand from any place to any other, the number of stimulus–response couplings would necessarily be enormous. On the other hand, it is difficult to conclude with equal confidence that younger infants can perceive depth, as the experiments of Ball and Tronick suggest, in view of the negative results of Yonas and Hruska and Campos in which other responses were employed. This is not a matter simply of difference in sensitivity of the method—Campos showed differential sensitivity to the two sides of the visual cliff. Rather it is, indeed, a matter of interpretation of the meaningfulness of the response. And that is the place where response convergence is most helpful.

IV. SUMMARY AND CONCLUSIONS

Throughout this chapter we have used the terms *spatial representation* and *perception of space* without providing any explicit definition. In the case of perception of space we attempted to imply quite specifically that we meant registration of the properties of three-dimensional space as we adults know it. We did not mean simply discrimination of cues normally associated with space to which spatial meaning must somehow become associated. Our use of spatial representation was even more vague. However, we have in mind a concept even further along the same dimension. That is, we have in mind attributing to infants, to some degree, a knowledge of spatial layout in three dimensions which is something like an adult's knowledge of spatial layout of his nearby environment. In various parts of the chapter we have pointed to evidence that in one way or another seems to us to point in that direction. However, there are a number of metatheoretical aspects of this idea we would like to discuss in this concluding section.

How could we possibly know that an infant has the sort of knowledge implied by this concept of spatial representation? How, for that matter, can we know that an adult has such knowledge? Of course it is possible to ask an adult about his experience of space and if properly questioned he will respond about an extended arrangement of objects and their directions and distances relative to each other in his perceptual experiences. Although there are philosophical problems in interpreting these verbal reports of talking subjects, we certainly can get a feeling that they experience space in the way we do. Furthermore, when this introspective report also corresponds with spatially appropriate behavior by a number of different response systems under conditions when the spatial position of an object is defined by a number of different types of stimulus information, we are convinced of the usefulness of asserting the presence of a spatial representation. [This correspondence should not be taken as a complete given with adults. Consider, for example, what happens with adults when they are subjected to an artificial disjunction of sensory information by wedge prisms. First of all, when a subject initially views his hand through prism spectacles that optically displace their apparent position he does not experience any disjunction of proprioceptive and visual information. Second, if he is asked to point with the other hand out of sight under a table at either the visual position of his hand or its felt position, the pointing is invariably a compromise between the visual and proprioceptive positions that he would point to in the absence of the disjunction (Pick, Warren, & Hay, 1969). Third, after wearing such prisms for several days if he is asked to point straight ahead and to indicate a visual target that lies straight ahead, the two directions will typically be different inasmuch as the two response systems have adjusted differently to the prism distortion (Hay & Pick, 1966). Thus we have a situation in which adults' introspective reports of their spatial experience and two other response systems do not correspond and yet the adult is not aware of any discrepancy. In such a case, even with adults, we would not be able to account for their behavior in terms of a unitary spatial representation.]

Of course with infants the possibility of introspective reports is immediately ruled out and the availability of response systems is severely limited. Our thesis has been to suggest that if there is stimulus and response convergence we should infer the existence of a spatial representation. However, what is the nature of this spatial representation? It could be a set of motor commands about how to reach certain positions in space when one could see or feel the position of part of his body, such as his hand. That is, it could be a set of stimulus–response associations. Such an idea has been proposed for adults by Taylor (1962) and he suggests that perceptual development may well consist of a building up of these large sets of associations. Of course, response convergence would require that different sets of stimulus–response associations get built up for different systems so that, for example, the hand and the eye could both get to a particular position. Such an idea would seem to imply that changing part of one set of stimulus–response commands would transfer to the remainder of the set and to other sets on the basis of generalization gradients. Another type of spatial representation might consist of a set of motor responses that would get the hand out to a particular place in space, for example: lift hand, move it to right, extend it, etc. This would be a sort of dead reckoning system and would require that the person know his original starting position and keep track of what he had done. It would not require that the person have any of the general representative features we noted previously. This, in fact, is somewhat reminiscent of Piaget's primary circular reaction where an infant accidentally achieves a particular effect, e.g., hitting a mobile, and then simply repeats that response. However, *repeating that response* contains more than traditionally meets the eye. As Bernstein (1967) and also MacNeilage (1970) have pointed out, if an infant can indeed do this he is achieving more than a simple sequencing of the same muscle contractions. The effects of specific muscle contractions depend a great deal on the initial position and state of the limb and body. Thus to achieve the same spatial position time after time requires rather different muscle commands depending on the specific position and state of motion of the limb at the beginning of the movement. Bernstein argues cogently that the motor commands must be coded in relation, not to muscles, but to ultimate target positions. The same argument is true for Taylor's set of stimulus–response commands. Even these primitive kinds of behavior may require rather abstract spatial representation. Both these types of stimulus–response command systems might initially be very specific to particular initial positions in space and to a small number of goal positions.

A more refined and complete spatial representation would be a system of interrelated spatial positions with the following properties: (1) reversibility; for every position A and B, knowing how to go from A to B implies knowing how to go from B to A; (2) transitivity for every position A, B, and C, knowing how to get from A to B and B to C implies knowing how to get from A to C; (3) given any two positions A and B, knowing how to get from A to B by one route implies being able to get from A to B by other possible routes. There have been no systematic investigations of such knowledge even within the close reaching space of young infants. Bruner (1971) and others have observed the frequent retrieval of objects to the mouth by infants. This would imply an ability of the infant to go from one specific place to a variety of other places and get back to the mouth, that is at least the beginning of the first of the preceding properties. The third property would best be exemplified by detour behavior. However, there have been no systematic investigations of detour behavior in young infants. Neither have there been studies of the second (transitivity) property described in young infants. Maier (1936) conducted a maze study employing this principle with children between 3 and 8 years of age. The youngest children showed some ability to combine two separate experiences in the maze in a way appropriate to that second transitivity principle.

In trying to specify the degree of refinement of spatial representation one might consider its metric characteristics. Indeed one could apply Stevens's measure theoretic classification to such systems— i.e., nominal, ordinal, and interval properties (Stevens, 1951). Thus a spatial representation might be considered to have nominal properties when an infant could tell whether two objects were in the same or different places and nothing more. That is simply an ability to discriminate. In general we have not considered just ability to discriminate as implying by itself a spatial representation. However, recall that if there were stimulus convergence in a discrimination experiment we would be more willing to infer a spatial representation. Consider an instance in which an infant responded identically to the same distance even though defined by two quite different stimulus cues and, conversely, responded differently to two different distances when defined by the same type of stimulus information. Or, more radically, consider an infant making same–different discriminations to stimuli presented in different sense modalities. Bryant, Jones, Claxton, and Perkins (1972) have demonstrated such an ability in 8-month-old infants. These infants selected the one of two stimuli shown visually that had previously been presented to them tactually. During the tactual presentation the stimulus had emitted a sound that presumably made the stimulus more interesting for the baby. Although this was an object discrimination experiment one could adapt it to study cross-modal transfer of azimuth or distance discriminations.

A spatial representation with ordinal properties would be one which had properties such as adjacency and betweenness and perhaps direction as well as the nominal properties mentioned previously. Again it would seem possible to set up various kinds of tests for such properties in infants. Finally, interval properties could be tested for as well, by habituation and transfer of generalization tests. Of course the occurrence in older infants of precise ballistic hand movements (and in younger infants of precise saccadic eye movements) implies a kind of metric spatial representation.

Finally, no matter what the form of a spatial representation, it is important to consider the frame of reference for that spatial representation. A spatial representation as a set of motor commands implies either an object reference system or a set of sequential responses. However, frames of reference can be analyzed much more finely even for infants. Frankel's case study observations described earlier of an infant learning to get his thumb into his mouth suggest the development of a polar coordinate system with the mouth as origin. That is, the infant develops a sensitivity to where his hand is when it first contacts his face and can track his thumb across the face toward the mouth. The mouth also anticipates and moves toward the thumb.

The question of what frames of reference infants use for their perception has never been seriously asked. It seems likely that infants by 1 year of age would use external reference systems. For example, if one asks, if Mommy is coming, an infant might look at the door from any place in his room. Again it would seem easy to conduct discrimination experiments with even younger infants analogous to the old place-versus-response experiments with rats. That is, one could teach an infant a left–right discrimination, then shift the apparatus in the room to see if he continued with the same egocentric response or the same place response. If he made a place response it would be possible to vary the external frame in various ways so as to determine what the effective reference system was.

Overall then we feel there are meaningful questions to be asked about infants' spatial representation. With adults we can be convinced about the usefulness of this concept because of the happy coincidence of stimulus convergence, response convergence, and introspective reports. With infants we of course cannot obtain introspective reports. However, to the extent that we can obtain stimulus and response convergence we assert the usefulness of the concept of spatial representation with infants as well.

REFERENCES

Aronson, E, & Rosenbloom, S. Space perception in early infancy: Perception within a common auditory–visual space. *Science*, 1971, *172*, 1161–1163.

Aslin, R. N., & Salapatek, P. Saccadic localization of visual targets by the very young human infant. Paper presented at the meeting of Psychonomic Society, St. Louis, Missouri, 1973.

Ball, W. A. Infant responses to looming objects and shadows. Honors thesis, Harvard College, Cambridge, Massachusetts, 1970.

Ball, W., & Tronick, E. Infant responses to impending collision: Optical and real. *Science*, 1971, *171*, 818–820.

Bartoshuk, A. K. Response decrement with repeated elicitation of human cardiac acceleration to sound. *Journal of Comparative and Physiological Psychology*, 1962, *55*, 9–13.

Benson, K., & Yonas, A. Development of sensitivity to static pictorial depth information. *Perception and Psychophysics*, 1973, *13*, 361–366.

Bernstein, N. *The coordination and regulation of movement.* New York: Pergamon Press, 1967.

Bower, T. G. R. Discrimination of depth in premotor infants. *Psychonomic Science*, 1964, *1*, 368.

Bower, T. G. R. Stimulus variables determining space perception in infants. *Science*, 1965, *149*, 88–89.

Bower, T. G. R. The visual world of infants. *Scientific American*, December, 1966, *215*, 80–92.

Bower, T. G. R. Morphogenetic problems in space perception. In D. A. Hamburg, K. H. Pribram, & A. J. Stunkard (Eds.), *Perception and its disorders.* Research Publications Association for Research in Nervous and Mental Disease. Vol. 48. Baltimore, Maryland: Williams & Wilkins, 1970.

Bower, T. G. R. Object perception in infants. *Perception*, 1972, *1*, 15–30.

Bower, T. G. R. *Development in infancy.* San Francisco: Freemon, 1974.

Bower, T. G. R., Broughton, J. M., & Moore, M. K. Infant responses to approaching objects. *Perception and Psychophysics*, 1970, *9*, 193–196. (a)

Bower, T. G. R., Broughton, J. M., & Moore, M. K. Demonstration of intention in the reaching behavior of neonate humans. *Nature*, 1970, *228*, 679–681. (b)

Bower, T. G. R., Broughton, J. M., & Moore, M. K. The coordination of visual and tactual input in infants. *Perception and Psychophysics*, 1970, *8*, 51–53. (c)

Bruner, J. S. Origins of problem solving strategies in skill acquisition. In R. Rudner, & I. Scheffler (Eds.), *Logic and art: Essays in honor of Nelson Goodman.* Indianapolis, Indiana: Bobbs-Merrill, 1969.

Bruner, J. S. Origins of mind in infancy. Paper presented at meetings of American Psychological Association, Washington, D.C., 1971.

Bruner, J. S., & Koslowski, B. Visually preadapted constituents of manipulatory action. *Perception*, 1972, *1*, 3–14.

Bryant, P. E., Jones, P. E., Claxton, V., & Perkins, G. M. Recognition of shapes across modalities by infants. *Nature*, 1972, *240*, 303–304.

Campos, J. J., Langer, A., & Krowitz, A. Cardiac responses on the visual cliff in prelocomotor human infants. *Science*, 1970, *170*, 196–197.

Charlesworth, W. R. The role of surprise or novelty in the motivation of curiosity behavior. Paper read at SRCD meetings, Berkeley, California, 1963.

Engen, T., Lipsitt, L. P., & Kaye, H. Olfactory responses and adaptation in the human neonate. *Journal of Comparative and Physiological Psychology*, 1963, *56*, 73–77.

Fantz, R. L. Pattern vision in young infants. *Psychological Record*, 1958, *8*, 43–47.

Fantz, R. L. A method for studying depth perception in infants under six months of age. *Psychological Record*, 1961, *11*, 27–32.

Fantz, R. L. Visual perception from birth as shown by pattern sensitivity. *Annals of the New York Academy of Sciences*, 1963, *118*, 793–814.

Frankel, D. A longitudinal case study of the development of reaching. Unpublished manuscript, Institute of Child Development, Univ. of Minnesota, 1972.

Gibson, J. J. *The senses considered as perceptual systems.* Boston: Houghton-Mifflin, 1966.

Gibson, J. J., & Gibson, E. J. Continuous perspective transformations and the perception of rigid motion. *Journal of Experimental Psychology*, 1957, *54*, 129–138.

Gorman, J. J., Cogan, D. G., & Gillis, S. S. An apparatus for grading the visual acuity of infants on the basis of opticokinetic nystagmus. *Pediatrics*, 1957, *19*, 108–1092.

Graham, F. K., & Clifton, R. K. Heart-rate change as a component of the orienting response. *Psychological Bulletin*, 1966, *65*, 305–320.

Graham, F. K., & Jackson, J. C. Arousal systems and infant heart rate responses. In H. W. Reese, & Lipsitt, L. P. (Eds.), *Advances in child development and behavior.* Vol. 5. New York: Academic Press, 1970.

Gregory, R. L., & Wallace, J. G. Recovery from early blindness: A case study. *Experimental Psychology Society Monographs*, No. 2, Cambridge, Massachusetts: Heffer, 1963.

Hay, J. C., & Pick, H. L., Jr. Visual and proprioceptive adaptation to optical displacement of the visual stimulus. *Journal of Experimental Psychology*, 1966, *71*, 150–158.

Haynes, H., White, B. L., & Held, R. Visual accommodation in human infants. *Science*, 1965, *148*, 528–530.

Hochberg, J. Higher-order stimuli and inter-response coupling in the perception of the visual world. In R. B. MacLeod, & H. L. Pick, Jr. (Eds.), *Perception: Essays in honor of James J. Gibson.* Ithaca, New York: Cornell Univ. Press, 1974.

Hruska, K., & Yonas, A. Developmental changes in cardiac responses to the optical stimulus of impending collision. Paper presented at Meeting of Society for Psychophysiological Research. St. Louis, Missouri, 1971.

Julesz, B. *Foundations of cyclopean vision*, Chicago: Univ. of Chicago Press, 1971.

Karmel, B. Z. The effect of age, complexity, and amount of contour on pattern preferences in human infants. *Journal of Experimental Child Psychology*, 1969, *7*, 339–354.

Kessen, W., Haith, M. M., & Salapatek, P. H. Infancy. In P. H. Mussen (Ed.), *Carmichael's manual of child psychology.* (3rd ed.) New York: Wiley, 1970.

Kessen, W., Salapatek, P., Haith, M. The visual response of the human newborn to linear contour. *Journal of Experimental Child Psychology*, 1972, *13*, 9–20.

Lasky, R. E. The effect of visual feedback on the reaching of young infants. Unpublished Ph.D. dissertation, Univ. of Minnesota, 1973.

Lee, D. N., & Aronson, E. Visual proprioceptive control of standing in human infants. *Perception and Psychophysics*, 1974.

MacNeilage, P. F. Motor control of serial ordering of speech. *Psychological Review*, 1970, *77*, 182–196.

Maier, N. R. F. Reasoning in children. *Journal of Comparative Psychology*, 1936, *21*, 357–366.

Piaget, J. *The origins of intelligence in children.* New York: International Universities Press, 1952.

Pick, H. L., Jr., & Pick, A. D. Sensory and perceptual development. In P. H. Mussen (Ed.), *Carmichael's manual of child psychology.* (3rd ed.) New York: Wiley, 1970.

Pick, H. L. Jr., Warren, D. H., & Hay, J. C. Sensory conflict in judgments of spatial direction. *Perception and Psychophysics*, 1969, *6*, 203–205.

Salapatek, P. Visual scanning of geometric figures by the human newborn. *Journal of Comparative and Physiological Psychology*, 1968, *66*, 247–258.

Salapatek, P., & Kessen, W. Visual scanning of triangles by the human newborn. *Journal of Experimental Child Psychology*, 1966, *3*, 155–167.

Schwartz, A. N., Campos, J. J., & Baisel, E. J. The visual cliff: Cardiac and behavioral responses on the deep and shallow sides at five and nine months of age. Paper presented at meetings of Eastern Psychological Association, Boston, Massachusetts, April, 1972.

Sokolov, E. N. *Perception and the conditioned reflex.* New York: Macmillan, 1960.

Stevens, S. S. Mathematics, measurement, and psychophysics. In S. S. Stevens (Ed.), *Handbook of experimental psychology.* New York: Wiley, 1951. Pp. 1–49.

Taylor, J. G. *The behavioral basis of perception.* New Haven, Connecticut: Yale Univ. Press, 1962.

Turkewitz, G., Birch, H. G., Moreau, T., Levy, L., & Cornwell, A. C. Effect of intensity of auditory stimulation on directional eye movements in the human neonate. *Animal Behavior,* 1966, *14,* 93–101.

von Fieandt, L. Das phönomenologische Problem von Licht und Schatten. *Acta Psychologica,* 1949, *6,* 337–357.

von Senden, M. *Space and sight* (1932) (Transl. P. Heath) London: Methuen, 1960.

Walk, R. D. The development of depth perception in animals and human infants. In H. W. Stevenson (Ed.), *Concept of development.* Monograph of Society for Research in Child Development, 1966, *31* (5, Serial No. 107), 82–108.

Walk, R. D., & Gibson, E. J. A comparative and analytic study of visual depth perception. *Psychological Monographs,* 1961, *75* (15, Whole No. 519).

Walters, C. P., & Walk, R. D. Visual placing by human infants. *Journal of Experimental Child Psychology,* 1974, *18,* 34–40.

Wertheimer, M. Psychomotor co-ordination of auditory-visual space to birth. *Science,* 1961, *134,* 1692.

White, B. L. *Human infants: Experience and psychological development.* Englewood Cliffs, New Jersey: Prentice-Hall, Inc., 1971.

Wickelgren, L. W. Convergence in the human newborn. *Journal of Experimental Child Psychology,* 1967, *5,* 74–85.

Yonas, A. Development of spatial reference systems in the perception of shading information for depth. Paper presented at Society for Research in Child Development Meetings. Philadelphia, Pennsylvania, 1973.

Yonas, A., & Hagen, M. Effects of static and motion parallax information on perception of size in children and adults. *Journal of Experimental Child Psychology,* 1973, *15,* 254–266.

chapter 2: Infant Perception of the Third Dimension and Object Concept Development

T. G. R. BOWER
University of Edinburgh

I. INTRODUCTION

In this chapter I am going to try to link two traditional psychological problems, the problem of the third dimension and the problem of object permanence. There is a conceptual link between the two problems, at least as traditionally stated, since both are problems of how organisms come to make systematic responses to stimuli that are not "there" to be responded to; at least in traditional thinking there is no stimulus specifying distance or depth, while object permanence as traditionally tested requires the organism to locate objects that have gone out of sight and cannot, therefore, be a source of stimulation. I intend to argue in this chapter that perception of the third dimension is impossible unless the perceiving organism knows that objects that have gone out of sight still exist. In other words "out of sight—out of mind" cannot possibly characterize any organism that can perceive the third dimension. As a corollary to this, I intend to argue, as I must, that the problem of object permanence has been misconstrued. Disappearance is not the problem in object permanence. "Out of sight" is largely irrelevant to the "out of mind" behavior displayed by infants.

33

II. PERCEPTION OF THE THIRD DIMENSION

The third dimension of visual space has been a source of controversy among students of human development for many years. The basic question is whether or not infants can perceive depth, the third dimension of space. If the answer is yes, the next question is how do they do it. These two questions are related since the main argument of those who contend that infants cannot perceive space is that there is no stimulus system that could specify position in space to infants; this argument has a great deal of force. It is sufficient to vitiate several experiments that have purported to show that young infants can perceive depth.

These experiments are all discrimination experiments. They all show that infants can discriminate between two layouts that differ in their arrangement in the third dimension. However none of them show whether the basis of the discrimination is the distal variable, arrangement in the third dimension, or the proximal variables that would necessarily mediate such a discrimination. As Rock (1968), I think, was the first to point out, an organism could perfectly well discriminate between values on all of the proximal variables that specify position in the third dimension and yet have no awareness of position in the third dimension per se. This argument gains its main force from the inherent ambiguity of the proximal variables that specify position in the third dimension. Consider one of the classic specifying variables, motion parallax. If an eye is displaced laterally, e.g., by moving the head, remaining fixed on one object point, the picture plane projections of objects nearer than that object will be displaced in a direction opposite to that of the movement; the picture plane projections of objects further away will be displaced in the same direction as the movement (see Figure 2.1). Direction, speed, and extent of movement specify distance perfectly. However there is no obvious a priori reason why this pattern of change would yield perception of distance rather than perception of movements. Indeed there is evidence that this can happen, even in adults. Thus if one looks at Mach's book and perceives the wrong spatial arrangement of the edges of the stimuli in the field, head movements generating motion parallax need not correct the percept; instead a moving array may be seen. Gibson, Gibson, Smith, and Flock, (1959) found that a display simulating motion parallax changes did not yield the perceptual impression of an arrangement in depth, but rather perception of movements. Since motion parallax can thus be ambiguous, yielding either

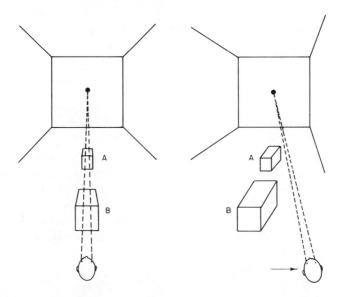

Figure 2.1.   Demonstration of motion parallax. When the head moves to the right and the eyes are kept fixed on a distant point, the nearer object, B, appears to move farther and faster to the left than does the distant object, A.

perception of depth or perception of movement, even to the adult eye, the argument that the variable can specify depth innately to the infant eye is necessarily weakened. The same ambiguity character-izes optical expansion and binocular parallax, the other major stimulus systems that can specify depth.

This problem is not disposed of by experiments that seemingly demonstrate space perception in very young infants (e.g., Bower, Broughton, & Moore, 1970a; Ball & Tronick, 1971). There remains the problem of just what stimuli could specify position in depth to the infant eye. Initially I myself was tempted to suppose that visual stimuli alone did not specify position in depth to young infants unless supported by some nonvisual, unambiguous stimulus. The source of this idea was the body of data on infants' responses to approaching objects. Many psychologists (e.g., White, 1963), using experimental setups in which only visual stimuli were available to specify the change of position of an object, had found that infants under 2 months showed no detectable responses to the approach of an object. On the other hand Sheridan, a pediatrician, informed me that response to an approaching object, a real object producing visual changes and changes in air pressure at the face, reliably differentiated blind from seeing infants. Since the air movement was common to both, presumably the visual changes were important in eliciting the response, although it seemed from the studies mentioned before that the visual changes alone did not elicit any response. It thus seemed possible that the visual changes plus the air movement change acted synergistically to produce a response that neither alone could produce. It could have been the case that the air movement was required to specify that the visual change signified approach rather than expansion while the visual change was required to specify direction and rate of approach. Given the rapid learning of the newborn (Lipsitt, 1969), it seemed possible that the visual change alone could come to specify approach. As I have argued elsewhere (Bower, 1970), once one visual variable can specify position or change of position in the third dimension, it can serve to calibrate the others that necessarily co-vary with it in the real world. Attempts to test this idea showed that responses to an approaching real object, producing air movement, could indeed be elicited from young infants; similar but much weaker responses could be elicited in the absence of air movement; air movement by itself produced no response, a set of results that fitted quite well with the original hypothesis.

Although such an account of the development of visual space perception would have been hard to verify experimentally, it seemed to fit the available data quite well. Unfortunately for the hypothesis, there are now data that invalidate it. Walk (personal communication) has shown that visual placing does not develop until quite late. The test for visual placing involves moving the infant toward a surface, in which situation the infant will typically bring up his hands between his face and the surface. In this situation there is air movement against the face plus expansion within the whole optical array, neither of which suffices to produce a placing response. It is not a behavioral deficit since the placing response resembles the defensive response found when an object approaches the infant (Bower et al., 1970a) and can in any case be elicited by mechanical contact with hand or foot. At first sight it would seem that the only difference between the approach situation and the placing situation is that it is the infant that moves in the placing situation. It seems hardly plausible that the addition of vestibular stimulation inhibits a response that would be elicited by visual stimulation and air movement by themselves. However, a closer analysis of the two stimulus situations shows a possibly critical stimulus difference. In the approaching object situation the looming object expands to fill the visual field and, as it does so, it progressively occludes the background stimulus array. In the placing situation every object in the field expands but there is no progressive occlusion. Gibson (1966) has argued that kinetic occlusion provides the most valid stimulus information that one object is in front of another. If one object moves to conceal another, it must be in front of the other. This information was present in those looming experiments that found a defensive response. It is absent in the placing situation and it was absent in those experiments that found no response to an approaching object (White, 1963). Progressive occlusion could thus be the stimulus that disambiguates expansion pattern information. There may be no need to invoke air movement at all. It is perfectly possible that the visual stimulation alone carries all of the information necessary to specify position and change of position in the third dimension. Occlusion is an unambiguous stimulus. It seems to be critical for the operation of binocular parallax (Figures 2.2 and 2.3) and motion parallax. Occlusion in-

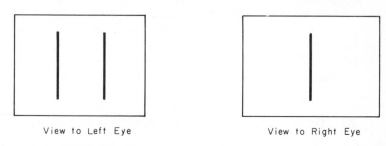

View to Left Eye   View to Right Eye

Figure 2.2.   Panum's limiting case of binocular stereopsis. The visual system seems to assume that the difference between these two views results from occlusion, producing an unambiguous percept, something that would be completely impossible on the geometry of the situation.

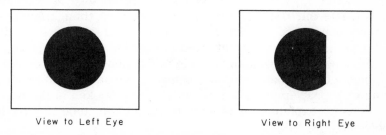

View to Left Eye   View to Right Eye

Figure 2.3.   Stereopsis without disparity. Again, as seen in Figure 2.2 the stable percept depends upon an assumption of occlusion.

formation could disambiguate these stimuli, so that the progressive learning theory proposed before might turn out to be unnecessary. If this hypothesis is correct, infants should show a defensive response to an optical expansion pattern provided that the expansion is accompanied by progressive occlusion of a textured background. This experiment has not yet been done. However, there is one experiment by Harris, Cassel, and Bamborough (1974) that points directly to the importance of occlusion information in the perceptual world of infants. Harris *et al.* have found that the tracking of radial movement is greatly disrupted if the moving object does not progressively occlude and then uncover a background. The lack of occlusion information significantly reduced the probability of tracking in infants as old as 20 weeks.

There is of course one obvious flaw in this attempt to make occlusion information the key stimulus for perception of the third dimension in young infants. Occlusion as a stimulus requires that an organism know that an object which has been occluded by another has gone *behind* its occluder; it also seems to require some memory of the characteristics of the occluded object or background (Kaplan, 1969). There is a large body of opinion in psychology that would deny these capacities to the young infant. The common interpretation of data on object permanence (Piaget, 1954) would seemingly knock this hypothesis out of court.

III. DEVELOPMENT OF THE OBJECT CONCEPT

The development of the object concept is one of the most fascinating aspects of cognitive growth in infancy. I would hazard a guess that the object concept is the most studied problem in infancy, bar smiling, perhaps. Certainly, everyone seems to have read Chapter 1 of Piaget's *Construction of Reality in the Child* (1954) where the basic phenomena are described, though few seem to have penetrated to the second and third chapters of that masterpiece. Despite the great attention paid to the development of the object concept, I wish to argue in this paper that the problem of the object has been misconstrued; we have misunderstood the infant's problem with objects and so have looked in the wrong directions for explanations of how the infant can come to solve his problems.

As it is usually presented, the problem in the development of the object concept is the problem of object permanence, the problem—

for the infant—of how to cope with objects that have vanished from sight. An infant of 5, 6, or even 7 months, if presented with an attractive toy, will reach out, take the toy, and play with it; if, however, one drops a cloth over the toy, so that the toy itself is no longer visible, the baby will act as if the toy no longer existed, making no attempt to remove the cloth, hardly even maintaining an orientation toward the cloth, and often manifesting facial and vocal signs of surprise if the cloth is removed to reveal the toy. Anyone observing this performance is almost compelled to believe that, for the baby, out of sight is out of mind. The object, once out of sight, seems to no longer exist, for the infant; indeed it would seem from the surprise one observes on reappearance of the object that the baby had thought that the object had genuinely been destroyed or annihilated by the covering cloth. Even after this early stage, when the infant will remove a cloth to get at an object, there seems to be no comprehension of what has happened to the object, as evidenced by the systematic errors that persist in the object permanence situation.

Most attempts to explain the baby's difficulty with standard simple covering have utilized the concept of representation; the baby has no way of representing an object once the object is out of sight; there is no "trace" left that could control behavior; the infant has no way of remembering that there is an interesting toy under that rather dull cloth. According to this view the young infant is a slave to immediate stimulus impact, with no way of responding to a stimulus that is no longer present. Only the immediately visible can control behavior. The word *visible* must be emphasized. There seems to be ample evidence that auditory or tactual inputs cannot replace visual input, at least in the earliest phases of coping with the problem. If the toy that is covered emits a noise, this continuing auditory input does not suffice to elicit search behavior. In fact even if the child has the toy in his hand before the cloth is tossed over it, this concurrent tactual input does not suffice to maintain any attempt to manipulate the toy, in the absence of visual input. These odd performances have suggested to several authors that lack of development of intersensory coordination is a cause of lack of object permanence, the development of intersensory coordination in some fashion making representation possible. The root idea here seems to be that the sensory systems themselves do not retain "traces" of past stimulus events; when one sensory system is linked with another via an association area, the association area can carry a trace, serving to represent the terminated event.

It is possible to use the general idea of representation as specifically mediated by the development of intersensory coordination to explain the development of the object concept. Indeed one can use the same kind of theory to encompass data from social development as well. However, the price of such a theory is also quite high in terms of data that must be ignored. For example there is ample evidence that intersensory coordination is present well before it is manifested in object permanence situations. Auditory–visual coordination is present at birth (Wertheimer, 1961; Aronson & Rosenbloom, 1971) and visual–tactual coordination seems to be present very early (Bower, Broughton, & Moore, 1970b). More relevant to the problem of object permanence are observations indicating the presence of auditory–manual coordination in situations that seem formally similar to the object permanence situation. If one places an infant in a totally dark room, then presents the infant with an audible object, that cannot be seen of course, infants who can reach at all—from the age of about 16 weeks in our sample—are able to reach out and seize the object (Bower & Wishart, unpublished manuscript). These same infants were totally unable to cope with the covering of an audible object in the standard object permanence situation until about 8 weeks later. Similar results have been obtained by Urwin (1973) working with a congenitally blind infant; that infant could reach and grasp audible objects at the age of 14 weeks, never having seen an object. This would seem to argue that whatever the problem in the object permanence situation, it does not stem solely or totally from a lack of intersensory coordination.

More damaging perhaps to the argument that success in object permanence reflects the development of intersensory coordination is the seeming anomaly that intersensory coordination wanes as object permanence waxes. All of the coordinations I have mentioned seem to fade away during the second half of the first year (Bower, 1973). Thus auditory–manual coordination measured in the way described above disappears during the second 6 months of life. An infant of 12 months is quite unlikely to reach for an audible object presented in darkness, whereas such an infant will almost certainly pass the equivalent object permanence test. It seems to me in the highest degree unlikely that two processes with such different developmental histories could be linked in a single causal sequence.

The role of intersensory coordination in the theory I am attacking is a minor one. The major point of that theory is that the infant has difficulty in the object permanence situation because he cannot represent objects that have gone out of sight. This fits data derived in the object permanence situation but again contradicts data derived from other situations. For example, there is now, I think, ample evidence that infants as young as 4 months can represent the path of objects that have gone behind a screen, even when that path must be inferred and cannot be tracked by continuing an ongoing movement (Bower, Broughton, & Moore, 1971). The most impressive experiments are those of Mundy-Castle and Anglin (1969). The experimental setup is shown in Figure 2.4. Two rectangular portholes cut out of a screen allowed the infant to see an object appear at position 1, move to position 2 and disappear, to reappear at position 5 and move to position 6. The time interval between disappearance at 2 and reappearance at 5 could be varied. The infants presented with this display were, by the age of 16 weeks, able to infer with their eyes the path of the object while it was out of sight, interpolating a curvilinear trajectory between the disappearance and reappearance points, whose height was proportional to the time interval between disappearance and reappearance. This degree of awareness is certainly not reflected in the object perma-

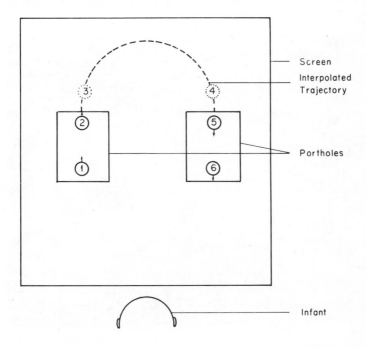

Figure 2.4. Experimental setup used by Mundy-Castle and Anglin (1969) where object is seen to move from 1 to 2 and then reappear at 5 and move to 6.

nence situation. One could argue that the eye and the head are controlled by different cognitive subsystems, as Schaeffer has tried to do (1971). However this line of argument cannot be sustained either. One has only to look at the reaching behavior of infants of 4–5 months to see that they manifest representation of invisible surfaces in their manual behavior. Differential hand-shaping is quite well developed in such infants, and would not be possible without some mechanism for inferring information about the invisible side of an object (Figure 2.5) (Bower *et al.*, 1970b). The situation of normal grasping is formally no different from the partial occlusion situation in which an object is partially covered by a cloth or other cover. Babies who show that they "know" where and what shape the invisible back surface of an object is will nonetheless make no attempt to get at an object that has been partially occluded in the standard object permanence situation. The point that infants do not fail the standard object permanence test because they cannot represent an object that has gone out of sight is made perhaps more forcefully by an experiment conducted by Bower and Wishart (1972). In that experiment the babies were shown a silent toy. Before they could begin to reach for it, the room was plunged into

Figure 2.5.   Differential hand-shaping of a 16-week-old infant.

darkness, so that the toy, baby, and all were invisible to the baby. (The experimenters could observe what went on via an infrared television system.) All of the babies in that experiment were able to reach out and take the toy with no difficulty, in total darkness; none of them made any attempt to get at a toy hidden in the standard object permanence situation. In both cases the toy was out of sight; only in the case of occlusion by covering did "out of sight" produce any difficulties. I would therefore contend that the difficulty in the standard covering situation must result from something other than the fact that at the end of the covering the toy is out of sight.

Further evidence relative to this point can be derived from situations that elicit lack of object permanence behavior with the lure object in full view. One of these was described by Piaget in the second chapter of *Construction of Reality*. If one presents an infant of about 5 months in our sample—older according to Piaget—with a toy to reach for, checking that the infant will in fact reach for it, and then places the toy on another large object, or even on a full foreplane surface, such as a tabletop, the infant will abort his attempts to grasp the object, pull away from it, and act indeed as if the object no longer existed, even though it is fully visible, sitting in front of him on top of another object. Bower and Wishart (1973) have recently replicated Piaget's original observations with every possible control to ensure equivalence of response requirements in the "on top of" and "dangling free" situations. There can be no doubt that an object placed upon another object seems to cease to exist at that moment, for a baby of 5 months, in just the same way as an object covered by a cloth seems to cease to exist for the same baby.

There are similar parallel phenomena—in sight situations that elicit the same behavior as the out-of-sight object permanence situation—right through the development of the object concept. Consider the behavior of a baby at Piaget's Stage IV of the object concept. If one presents an infant in this stage with an object that is hidden under one of two simultaneously visible opaque cups, the infant can remove the opaque cup to get the object; he will succeed again if the toy is hidden again under the same cup; if however the toy is hidden again under the other cup, this infant will typically fail, going to the cup under which he had found the object before. This performance can be explained as the result of a defect in representation, but representation need not be invoked at all. Exactly the same pattern of behavior can be produced if one uses transparent cups (Brown & Bower, 1973), where the object is not hidden at all but is rather perfectly visible inside the transparent cup. Despite this, behavior in the two situations is quite identical, both quantitatively (Butterworth, personal communication) and qualitatively (Brown & Bower, 1973).

Similar results are obtained with the Stage V test diagrammed in Figure 2.6. It does not matter if the test is done with transparent or opaque cups. The babies make the same typical errors.

Results like these have stimulated some investigators—including the writer—to speculate that the infant's true problem is in the organization of motor responses. This position is now, I think, untenable (Bower & Wishart, 1972).

What then is the infant's problem in this situation? I do not think that it is a problem in representation. If the same behavior results with an object that is fully in view, it is hardly parsimonious to look for special explanations of the opaque situation. What we require is an explanation that will handle all of the situations, and an explanation in terms of representation will hardly suffice for the transparent cup or "placed upon" situations. The infant's problem, I

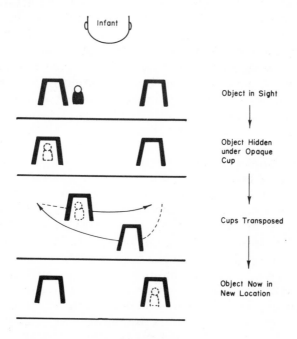

The Object Has Undergone an Invisible Displacement

Figure 2.6.   Diagram of the Stage V object permanence test.

wish to argue, stems from his concept of an object and the possible spatial relations between objects that are permitted by that concept. To explain this oversimple statement it will be necessary to backtrack to look at some other experiments that help to define the infant's concept of an object. The infant's most primitive definition of an object goes as follows: An object is a bounded volume of space in a place or on a path of movement. By a bounded volume of space I mean a volume with a top and bottom, a back and front, and a right bound and a left bound. If any of these bounds are missing, the infant does not treat the presented element as an object. The differences show up in looking behavior, patterns of discriminative responding (Bower, 1966) and, most crucially, in reaching itself. An infant who will reach for an object that is dangling in free space will not reach for an object placed upon, under, or against another object. This behavior indicates most clearly that the object no longer exists as an individual unique entity once it has lost one of its boundaries; rather the object becomes part of the object it is placed upon, so that both lose their identity, becoming a single object for the young infant. I am thus arguing that perception of three-dimensional boundedness is the first criterion used by an infant in deciding whether or not some static display element is an object, a surface, or a pattern on an object or surface. The infant does not realize that two objects can be in the same place if one is on top of the other. The infant is not entirely alone in the use of this criterion. Michotte (1962) has argued that adults use three-dimensional boundedness as a criterion of the reality of objects. The difference between the young infant and adult is that the adult can suspend this criterion to accord with prior information about the reality and identity of an object. The infant seems unable to do this.

Throughout the preceding discussion I have used the term *identity* without defining it. By identity I mean literally sameness. By a concept of identity I mean the rules that an organism uses to specify that an object seen at one time is the same object when seen at a different time or else is a replica of that object. I have argued elsewhere that the young infant has a rather simple concept of identity. For the young infant an object is the same object if it is in the same place or on the same path of movement (Bower & Paterson, 1973). As corollaries, the infant seems to have rules that state that two objects cannot occupy the same place or the same path of movement and hence that all objects seen in the same place or on the same path of movement are the same object. The evidence for this massive cognitive structure that I am imputing to the infant is not, I admit, overwhelming. The indicator behaviors are few. Specifically, if one presents an infant with an object that is mysteriously replaced by another object the infant will give no sign of search for the original object, even though the eye movements required are within the infant's repertoire; if by contrast one displaces an object the infant will look back to the place where the object was as if searching for the object, when the object is fully visible in a new place (Bower & Paterson, 1973). If one similarly transforms an object in motion, the young infant will continue to track the object, seemingly accepting it as the same object; if, by contrast, the motion track is changed, one can observe alternating glances between the visible object on its motion track and the prior motion track, indicating, I would argue, search for another object than that currently visible. Alternating looking is thus within the behavioral repertoire of these infants; that it is not shown where the motion track remains invariant and the object changes indicates, I would argue, that it is the motion that defines the identity of the object. Sameness is thus equated with place or motion identity. Replacement is equated with transformation, so long as place or motion remain unchanged. In this the infant is not so different from the adult (Michotte, 1962) who is subject to the same constraints but can bring in other information to overrule these constraints. Indeed by 5 months the infant seems to have introduced some new constraints himself to the effect that he is beginning to identify objects by their features (Bower et al., 1971) so that he can now identify an object that has changed position; place and movement are becoming coordinated. This last step represents a monumental advance, but an advance that is severely restricting as far as the object permanence situation is concerned. Consider what an organism with the cognitive structures just described will make of the object permanence test. The infant is shown a toy which is placed on a tabletop. A cup, say, is then placed over the toy. The sequence of events to the baby is toy in place A, then, cup in place A, in the same place. The infant can only interpret this sequence as either transformation of the toy into the cup, or, if he is more advanced, as replacement of the toy with the cup, with no explanation of what has happened to the toy. Until the infant can comprehend that two objects can be in the same place at the same time, if one is inside the other, the object permanence presentation must be totally mysterious, just as the relationship "placed upon" must be equally mysterious to the younger child. In other words it is not the fact of disappearance itself but the nature of the transformation involved in one object going *inside* another that perplexes the infant. That is why disappearance in darkness is no problem for the infant. That is why one object inside another is a problem, even when a transparent cup is used so that disappearance is not involved. That is why reappearance of an object that has been inside another seems to perplex the infant who goes so far as to pick up the enclosing cup and examine it.

Further evidence that it is the inside relation that produces the infant's difficulties comes from a study showing that infants who fail to cope with inside relations will nonetheless cope with the same problems if posed using "behind relations" to produce disappearances (Brown, 1973). Thus an infant who shows the typical loss of existence constancy behavior when shown a toy that is placed inside a cup will happily reach round or remove a screen behind which a toy has been placed. Out of sight behind is thus no more of a problem than out of sight in darkness and much less of a problem than inside, whether out of sight inside or in sight inside.

If I am right that the infant's problem with the object permanence test is to comprehend the relationship "inside," we need a new theory to account for the development of competence in the situation. Piaget (1954) himself has noted that comprehension of "inside" relations is a late development but has not, so far as I can see, proposed a theory of how the relations are discovered. One hypothesis that immediately suggests itself is that the infant could discover inside relations by observing objects in his own hands or in his mouth, perhaps. Brown (1973) has found that the relation inside is a problem even if it refers to an object that is inside the infant's own hand; if one places a small object on the palm of an infant of about 7 months, the infant will close his hand over the object, so that the object is out of sight inside the infant's own hand; the infant will then act as if the object no longer existed, usually eventually dropping the object. "Inside" is thus a problem even when it is inside the infant's own hand. Is it possible that the solution to this problem provides a model for the solution of the whole problem? While such a line of argument seems initially tempting, I do not think it can be sustained. In the first place, infants in our sample actually succeed in removing a single cup to get at an object *before* they succeed with objects that disappear inside their own hands. After they succeed with an object inside one hand, they will show characteristic Stage IV errors if an object is placed twice in one hand and then in the other hand, inspecting the hand which had previously held the object. The more advanced tests, "invisible" displacements and so on, are not possible with the infant's own hands. However, it would seem reasonable to conclude that the hand is no more privileged a container than any other, which it would have to be if it were to serve as the model for the solution of all inside problems. Second, such a model would be quite at sea in attempting to explain how armless and handless infants can come to develop a normal object concept more or less on schedule, as they seemingly do (Décarie, 1965). Finally, such a model would imply that the errors associated with inside relations are unique in development and are not causally connected with the developmentally prior and formally similar errors associated with place and movement relations, an implication that seems to be invalid (Bower & Paterson, 1972).

The last-mentioned study indicated that intensive tracking experience facilitated the emergence of competence with inside relations. If "inside" were a unique developmental attainment, this facilitation would not have occurred.

The development of competence with inside relations seems to be a saltatory process (Bower & Paterson, 1972). The pattern of development has the characteristics of a sudden deduction rather than a gradual discovery. A theory of the process would in such a case consist of the specification of premises or information on which the deduction is based plus a description of the rules which guide the deduction. From an experimental point of view attempts to discover the relevant information are a more feasible line of investigation than attempts to analyze the deductive rules in vacuo without knowing the information upon which they operate. If the process does operate by deduction from information given, one can presumably feed in different types of information to discover just what information will produce an acceleration in development. Unfortunately for this chapter there is no vast range of data on inputs that will or will not produce acceleration of the attainment of the object concept. Bower and Paterson (1972) found that early tracking experience facilitated emergence of the mature concept. Brown and Bower (1973) found that practice with transparent cups and covers, where the relation was manifest to the eye, did not produce acceleration. They also found that mixed practice with screens and cups did produce acceleration. This is not the sort of empirical foundation on which one would wish to construct a theory. The failure of experience with transparent cups to do anything to the rate of development would indicate, I think, that the relation inside cannot simply be read off from perceptual input; the relation must be constructed or deduced. The two studies that did produce acceleration by themselves do not tell us in any simple way what inputs produce development. Inasmuch as the infant's problem in tracking studies has to do with his definition of identity in terms of features rather than place or movement, it would seem that an advanced set of identity definitions will accelerate the object concept. This is in accord with the model for development of the object concept proposed by Bower (1967); the infant sees an object disappear mysteriously, so that it no longer has a location, an existence; removal of cloth or cover reveals an object that the infant cannot but recognize as the *same* object, same features, same place, etc.; there is thus a contradiction between the infant's comprehension of the disappearance and his comprehension of the reappearance and, on general grounds, we would expect contradiction to produce development. The other example is more complicated and cannot be readily fitted into the contradiction model. Nonetheless it seems to me that it is acceleration studies of this sort that are required if we are to analyze the conditions that precipitate development of the object concept. Without an understanding of the precipitating conditions we will never have enough data for us to work out the deductive rules that operate on the precipitating conditions. While it is likely that we will find as many precipitating conditions as there are embryological triggers, we need to know more than two of them if we are ever to work out a common factor that will specify a deductive mechanism. Only if we can specify such a deductive mechanism will we have a theory of the development of the object concept.

REFERENCES

Aronson, E., & Rosenbloom, S. Space perception in early infancy: Perception within a common auditory–visual space. *Science,* 1971, *172,* 1161–1163.

Ball, W. & Tronick, E. Infant responses to impending collision: Optical and real. *Science,* 1971, *171,* 818–820.

Bower, T. G. R. The visual world of infants. *Scientific American,* 1966, *215,* 80–92.

Bower, T. G. R. Morphogenetic problems in space perception. In D. A. Hamburg, K. H. Pribram, & A. J. Stunkard (Eds.), *Perception and its disorders.* Research Publications Association for Research in Nervous and Mental Disease. Vol. 48. Baltimore, Maryland: Williams & Wilkins, 1970. Pp. 193–200.

Bower, T. G. R. The development of object permanence. Some studies of existence constancy. *Perception and Psychophysics,* 1967, *2,* 411–418.

Bower, T. G. R. Unpublished data, 1973.

Bower, T. G. R., Broughton, J. M., & Moore, M. K. Infant responses to approaching objects: An indicator of response to distal variables. *Perception and Psychophysics*, 1970, *9*, 193–196. (a)

Bower, T. G. R., Broughton, J. M., & Moore, M. K. The coordination of visual and tactual input in infants. *Perception and Psychophysics*, 1970, *8*, 51–53. (b)

Bower, T. G. R., Broughton, J. M., & Moore, M. K. Development of the object concept as manifested in changes in the tracking behaviour of infants between 7 and 20 weeks of age. *Journal of Experimental Child Psychology*, 1971, *11*, 182–193.

Bower, T. G. R., & Paterson, J. G. Stages in the development of the object concept. *Cognition*, 1972, *1*, 47–55.

Bower, T. G. R., & Paterson, J. G. The separation of place, movement, and object in the world of the infant. *Journal of Experimental Child Psychology*, 1973, *15*, 161–168.

Bower, T. G. R., & Wishart, J. G. The effects of motor skill on object permanence. *Cognition*, 1972, *1*, 165–172.

Bower. T. G. R., & Wishart, J. G. Unpublished data, 1973.

Bower, T. G. R., & Wishart, J. G. Unpublished manuscript.

Brown, I. A study of object permanence. Unpublished Honours Thesis, Edinburgh University, 1973.

Brown, I., & Bower, T. G. R. Unpublished data, 1973.

Décarie, T. G. A study of the mental and emotional development of the Thalidomide child, 1965. In B. M. Foss (Ed.), *Determinants of infant behavior*. Vol. IV. London: Methuen, 1969. Pp. 167–187.

Harris, P. L., Cassel, T. Z., & Bamborough, P. Tracking by young infants. *British Journal of Psychology*, 1974, *65*, 345–349.

Gibson, J. J., Gibson, E. J., Smith, O. W., & Flock, H. Motion parallax as a determinant of perceived depth. *Journal of Experimental Psychology*, 1959, *58*, 40–51.

Gibson, J. J. *The senses considered as perceptual systems*. Boston: Houghton-Mifflin, 1966.

Kaplan, G. A. Kinetic disruption of optical texture: The perception of depth at an edge. *Perception and Psychophysics*, 1969, *16*, 193–198.

Lipsitt, L. P. Learning capacities in the human infant. In R. J. Robinson (Ed.), *Brain and early behaviour*. New York: Academic Press, 1969. Pp. 227–249.

Michotte, A. *Causalité permanence et realité phenomenales*. Belgium: Publications Universitaires, 1962.

Mundy-Castle, A. C., & Anglin, J. The development of looking in infancy. Paper read at the meetings of the Society for Research in Child Development, Santa Monica, California, April 1969.

Piaget, J. *The construction of reality in the child*. New York: Basic, 1954. (Original French edition, 1937.)

Rock, I. When the world is tilt. *Psychology Today*, July, 1968, 211–231.

Schaeffer, H. R. *The growth of sociability*. Baltimore, Maryland: Penguin Books, 1971.

Urwin, K. Paper read at Edinburgh University, January, 1973.

Wertheimer, M. Psychomotor coordination of auditory-visual space at birth. *Science*, 1961, *134*, 1692.

White, B. L. The development of perception during the first six months. Paper read at the American Association for the Advancement of Science, Cleveland, Ohio, 1963.

chapter 3: Recent Studies Based on Piaget's View of Object Concept Development

GERALD GRATCH
University of Houston, Texas

. . . the object is known because of conformity to a prior conception . . . an idea is tentative. . . . It controls an action to be performed, but the consequences of the operation determine the worth of the directive idea, the directive idea does not fix the nature of the object [Dewey, 1960, p. 288].

I. INTRODUCTION

Piaget, like two giants of another generation, John Dewey and George Herbert Mead (1934), has tried to frame a conception of how men know which is lodged in the activity of the knower. Reality never presents itself directly to the knower, ". . . original perception furnishes the *problem* for knowing; it is something *to be* known, not an object of knowing [Dewey, 1960, p. 179]." When the actor imposes a point of view upon events, then the events take on coherence in terms of the perspective. When events are not assimilated into a framework, awareness of events is fragmented, partial, episodic. However, there are many perspectives that can be taken on events, each affording a different and limited ordering. To know reality, the actor must develop a higher level of perspective, must look at events from multiple perspectives which themselves are lodged in a larger perspective that permits the various looks to be ordered.

The wellspring of the view of knowing of Dewey, Mead, and Piaget is their characterization of the scientist as one who uses theory and experiment to construct views of the world that compel belief and guide action and yet are corrigible. For every man, as well as the scientist, knowing the world is a selective process guided by concepts which in turn are reconstructed in the light of experiences in the world. Such a concept-contingent view of the nature of knowledge is contained in the analyses of scientific knowledge offered by Kuhn (1970) and Polanyi (1964).

Piaget's particular contribution has lain largely in his attempt to show how the child becomes the "scientist," the systematic construer of events. Piaget has charted a developmental sequence of increasingly complex notions of the world that the child constructs and he has provided an account of how the child acts at each level and how such activity leads to the next level. His myriad observations of children have been primarily keyed to the problem of diagnosing these general notions of the world.

The present chapter will focus on the earliest general level, the sensorimotor. The focus is on the growth of object knowledge (Piaget, 1954), and Piaget sees the infant construct six successive points of view about his experience with objects. Piaget views the newborn as a reflexive creature who encounters the world about him in William James's terms, as a "buzzing, blooming confusion." The infant's reflexive reactions to objects lead him ultimately to construct a notion, the concept of the object, which notion permits him to perceive objects rather than pictures, develop and appreciate symbols, and enter into stable relations with objects such as people.

The importance of Piaget's account of the development of the object concept in infancy has been widely sensed. He addresses himself to major epistemological issues, attacking both empiricist and nativist positions. He argues that the infant does not enter the world able to perceive objects in an ordered spatiotemporal field. He argues that the achievement of such an ordered view of objects does not result from repeated exposures to the world; it is neither the result of repeated perceptual experiences nor of response-reinforcement history. Rather, object knowledge grows out of the transaction between the infant's actions and things. Before the notion of the permanence of objects is formed, the infant confuses changes in his activity and the object's position with changes in object states. The achievement of object permanence provides a basis for unconfounding these factors and provides a fixed point in terms of which the infant can construct notions of space and time and cause.

However, Piaget's theory has not been well understood or well evaluated. In part, the reasons for the confusions surrounding the theory are easy to understand. His concepts, like those of Dewey and Mead, have not fitted into the mainstream of American psychology; he has been less than clear in presenting his views; his observations have been limited and unsystematic. Recently, this picture has begun to change. A goodly number of psychologists have begun to key their explorations of infant development to Piaget's object concept theory. But the work is highly variable in character. Some investigators have used his situations as takeoff points for the development of psychometric measures of object concept achievement as a means of exploring other aspects of infantile development. Some investigators have used his observations or speculations as bases for developing alternative views of how infants come to know objects, and some researchers have attempted to evaluate specific aspects of his observations and argument.

In this chapter, I shall try to give the reader a sense of these developments and what they portend. My plan is as follows. I shall begin by reviewing Piaget's theory. Then, I shall review current research relevant to the theory. Two main categories of work will be considered. First, the work that essentially has applied aspects of the theory in a psychometric sense. Second, the work that is addressed to the theoretical questions that Piaget has raised. I shall close with some provisional conclusions about the status of this developing literature. In carrying out this plan, I shall devote the bulk of the chapter to a detailed summary of and commentary on current research. I do this in part because this literature is relatively recent and not well known and in part to communicate concretely the open-ended status of the work sparked by Piaget's theory.

II. PIAGET'S THEORY OF THE CONSTRUCTION OF THE OBJECT CONCEPT

A. Introduction

To begin the discussion of Piaget's theory, I shall paraphrase the six stages of object concept development that Piaget lists in the

table of contents of *The Construction of Reality in the Child* (1954).
I begin in this way because this aspect of Piaget's theory has been
widely popularized by Piaget and his commentators. The stages are
indexed in terms of how infants respond to objects when the
manner and place of disappearance of the objects is varied. In the
first two stages, infants show "no special behavior related to
vanished objects." In the third stage, infants are able to find a
partially hidden object, but fail when the object is completely
covered. In the fourth stage, the infant can find a completely
covered object but cannot find it when, in view of the infant, it is
hidden in another place. In the fifth stage, the infant can find the
object wherever it is hidden so long as he observes the place of
hiding. In the sixth stage, the infant can find the toy even when the
object is "invisibly" displaced, e.g., the covered object is placed
under another cover, and only then does Piaget claim that the infant
knows the object as such.

Piaget's description of the growth of object knowledge may well
seem strange to the reader. He appears to be describing how infants
come to represent space rather than the growth of object knowledge. His stages seem to ignore such hallmarks of object knowing
as shape and size. Further, his description implicitly suggests that
an infant does not know an object if he can recognize it but cannot
search for it, and this in fact is what Piaget claims.

However, Piaget's view need not seem strange. His approach can
be clarified by focusing on what he means by an object and how he
describes levels of awareness of it. He focuses on common,
everyday objects and holds that such objects are substantial,
permanent, and constant in form. They are solid, three-dimensional
forms located in space–time frameworks, and they do not change
their nature as a function of changes in their location or their
relation to the viewer. This is a view of objects which is easily
shared. One can easily see why Piaget concludes that if an infant
perceives an object in this sense, as opposed to a picture, then the
infant should act as if the object is still present when it disappears
and should orient to its reappearance as if it is the same object as
opposed to a replica of the original object or a different object
entirely. Similarly, one can see why Piaget argues that the infant
who looks at the bottom of his feeding bottle and then orients it so
that the nipple comes into view sees a solid, three-dimensional form
whereas, the infant who focuses only on the bottom of the bottle is
aware only of some kind of pattern. Hochberg (1971) adopted a
similar line of reasoning in his evaluation of studies of infant

perception. He pointed out that one cannot conclude that infants see objects just because they attend to them differentially. Not only must the investigator specify features that the infant is attending to, but the investigator must be at pains to indicate that the infant manifests a variety of object-appropriate actions before there is warrant for concluding that the infant perceives objects as such.

Piaget's approach to the problem of object knowing can be further clarified by dwelling on the distinction he has made between the figurative and operative aspects of knowing. This distinction was not clear in his initial report, *The Construction of Reality in the Child*, but he (e.g., 1969) and Furth (1969) have since clarified the point. Piaget argues that each common object has a particular physical structure and information about it can be "extracted" by repeatedly looking at it. Through such a process, the child can come to form a copy of the object, a kind of schema which permits recognition and/or imagery of the particular object. This is figurative knowledge, and it affords only a limited sense of objects, what at times Piaget refers to as physical experience.

Object knowledge in the larger sense of the object in relation to other objects in space–time systems, e.g., object permanence, derives from operative knowing, from patterns of activity with respect to things. Just as things have a structure that can come to be observed, so too, Piaget argues, do activities. In acting on things, in putting them here and in putting them there, the infant creates the opportunity to witness things in relation to other things and to his activities. The dwelling upon such activities leads the infant to reorganize the schemes that underlie his activities, and the reorganized schemes provide the perspective within which the infant can perceive relations among things and a distinction between the actor and the object acted on. The permanence of things, their constancy of shape and size, their location in space, these are not "abstracted" from things but from the patterns of activity with respect to things. For example, the infant develops a sense of the constant size of objects through repeatedly moving objects close to him and far from him and becoming aware of the invariant relation between the variable appearances of the objects and his reversible actions.

The concept of the object is the result of such constructive processes, and the concept makes both object perception and object representation possible. It is a general scheme of an object. It does not refer to any particular object but makes the perception of particular objects possible. When the infant has the concept of the object, then he can perceive objects as such because he assimilates events into a framework which goes "beyond the perceptual field, anticipating relations which are to be perceived subsequently and reconstructing those which are perceived previously [Piaget, 1950, p. 112]."

Thus, Piaget's empirical emphasis, studying infants' search for hidden objects, is underlain by a theory which stresses that the problem of object perception is more than the problem of pattern recognition. It is a theory which explains the orderliness of the world of object perception, as opposed to the disorderliness of the world of "picture" perception, in terms of the "conforming" of the stimulus array to the prior conception. Piaget's stress on object search has led him to underemphasize, but not ignore, what he refers to as the "figurative" aspects of object knowing in infancy. This failure in emphasis will be a major theme in some of the studies to be reviewed. Further, Piaget's early presentation of his view, where he did not distinguish clearly between the figurative and operative facets of knowing, created an ambiguity about the relation of object conception to object representation and object perception. He seemed to imply that higher levels of object aware- ness always involved overt reflection, representational thought. However, it is clear now that he meant to say that the achievement of the object concept provides the framework which permits both the perception of objects as such and their representation. The concept permits both types of activity but they need not occur in concert.

Piaget's theory will now be presented in greater detail. The aim of this section is to provide the reader with a sense of the theory rather than a formal understanding of it. I assume that the reader is familiar, from other sources, with such technical concepts as assimilation-accommodation and equilibration. Further, I assume that the time is not yet ripe for a formal analysis of the theory. The latter assumption is based in part on the literature to be reviewed in subsequent sections and in part on what I feel is the value of Piaget's theory, namely, its heuristic promise for the study of infant knowing. Thus, though Piaget only observed his own three infants, his vision led him to discover a wide array of relatively novel age-ordered facts. Though Piaget's line of reasoning has precedents in figures such as Dewey and Mead, his six stages and his manner of interpreting facts in terms of these stage hypotheses have a unique character. In what follows, I shall try to communicate a sense of the facts he describes and the way in which he interprets them.

B.   The Stages in the Construction of the Object Concept

1.   THE EARLY STAGES (STAGES I–III)

Piaget views the infant in early infancy as developing three successive points of view or stages of object awareness. Through his interactions with objects, the infant shifts from reflex schemes (Stage I), to reflex-based habits (Stage II), to habit schemes that enable him "to make interesting sights last," the secondary circular reactions (Stage III). The infant's increasingly more flexible and coordinated ways of acting on and perceiving objects lead him to shift from showing "no special behavior related to vanishing objects" to the "beginning of permanence extending the movements of accommodation."

More concretely, Piaget notes that in the first month of life the infant moves from neonatal rooting for the lost breast to groping with his hand in the immediate area where he lost contact with the object formerly in hand and to visually following a moving object. The development of visual tracking is especially important for Piaget and provides an opportunity to make plain what Piaget believes is the orientation of Stage III infants to vanished objects. When the object moves behind a screen, he notes a progression. The 3-month-old infant will not anticipate where the object will appear but rather looks back to the place where it disappeared or the place where it first appeared. The infant is seen as localizing the object in a special place and his glance is viewed as an act that will make the object reappear. The infant's ability to turn back to the toy from which his attention has wandered is viewed in a comparable light. Later, the infant is able to anticipate the reappearance beyond the screen of the moving object. However, Piaget does not view the infant as being aware of the object in its absence. Instead, he interprets the achievement as evidence of the infant's ability to look in new places, of being able to anticipate trajectories rather than objects. The infant is still trying to prolong "the interesting sight" by extending his movements. In support of his interpretation, Piaget notes that the infant will not anticipate the reappearance of the object beyond the screen if the screen is very long or if the speed of the object's movement is so rapid that the infant cannot follow the entire trajectory of the object before it goes behind the screen.

Piaget points to several other observations as evidence for the existence of a Stage III point of view in infants of about 6 to 7 months of age. In playing peek-a-boo, he notes that an infant will quickly remove the cover if its own face is covered, but will not remove the cover from the adult's face. The absent object is not sought, rather looking is freed. As evidence that the infant is becoming aware of a more articulated object existing in an articulated near space, he notes that infants will recognize the feeding bottle when it is presented in a variety of orientations and will rotate the bottle so that the nipple is presented to the mouth so long as the nipple is in view. However, when the bottle is presented so that the nipple is not in view, the infant does not seek the nipple. Further, when a desirable object is covered in view of the infants, they will not remove the cover. But if the object is partially covered, the infants will seize the object if a familiar part is exposed and will be likely to ignore it if an unfamiliar part is in view (Piaget, 1954, Observation 22, p. 28). Moreover, the infants will pull the object out from under the cover rather than take the cover off the object, indicating that they do not comprehend that a whole object is beneath a cover. Finally, toward the end of Stage III, the infants will remove the cover from a totally occluded object if they begin reaching for the object before it is covered but will not do so if the object is covered before they begin reaching. Like Hunter's dogs (1913), they succeed because they "point," and they cease to search if the action is disrupted.

2. The Middle Stages (Stages IV and V)

The coordination of secondary schemes, particularly of vision and reaching, leads the infant to a new level of awareness of things, Stage IV. The ability of the infant to deploy his skills, so that some acts serve as means for others, and his increasing mobility lead him to be better able to observe and comprehend the polysensory nature of objects and such events as the various appearances and disappearances of objects. Piaget argues that the infant achieves a significant measure of size constancy because he discovers that the apparent changes in the size of the object that he moves to and fro are associated with the object sensed through having it in hand. The infant now comes to be able to find the nipple irrespective of the bottle's orientation in space when it is presented.

Piaget believes the infants' sense of the constancy of object shape and size precedes and sets the stage for the infants' principal achievement in Stage IV, namely "active search for the vanished object." The infants now will watch an object being covered and will uncover the object when they are given the opportunity to do so. But the infants do not yet know the object in its absence. They still have a "subjective" point of view, they still confound the object with their activity. That such is the orientation of Stage IV infants to vanished objects is indexed by the Stage IV error. Piaget notes that if, in full view of the infants, he hides the toy in a second place, they will immediately search for it in the first place, the place where they previously found it. Piaget argues the error is not due to forgetting. Rather the infants interpret the object as the thing-of-that-place-where-the-object-was-found, and therefore, magically, expect their action to produce it there.

Piaget seems to attribute to the Stage IV infant an expectation of finding the particular object that is hidden. He argues they have shape and size constancy, and he notes that Laurent, in Stage V, refused to accept a number of objects which were different from the one that was covered (Piaget, 1954, Observation 54, p. 67). However, the particularity of objects lies only in their featural characteristics. The infant still only knows objects figuratively, not operationally. Piaget believes the infant cannot distinguish the self-same object from many replicas of it, i.e., the objects are many similar things-of-many-different-places. Moreover, the infant's search is not guided by a representation of the absent object. Rather, his behavior is still on a practical level, guided by a series of probabilistically related indices. The cover indexes the toy and maintains the infant's object-expectant attitude. The infant does not image the toy in its absence.

The infants shift to a new level of sensorimotor organization in Stage V, tertiary circular reactions. They now initiate systematic investigations of the properties of actions and objects. They systematically study such events as the appearance of objects under various rotations and changes in locations. Such activities lead them to come to be able to find the toy wherever they see it hidden. At first, they find things at either of two places but repeat the Stage IV error when a third place is introduced. But then they come increasingly to handle any number of places. Their sense of space is broadened, articulated, and coordinated. They come to be able to take many routes to the same goal. But they still lack a true notion of the object and space. On the one hand, they still fail to realize the object is substantial in the sense of being in one-and-only-one place at a given time. If they fail to find the object in the place where they saw it disappear, they show "residual reactions," they will search in places where the object was located previously. On the other hand, they are not able to search out the object if the specific place at which it disappears is subsequently obscured. They still cannot represent the object in space.

3. STAGE VI

In this stage, the infant's action-schemes are organized into a reversible system which permits the child to enact courses of action prior to carrying them out. The infant can now represent himself and objects in a common space, and this permits the infant to seek out the object even when he does not see exactly where it disappears. Piaget argues the infant goes through a "vertical decalage" on this new level of activity. The infant recapitulates the Stage IV and Stage V errors with respect to hiding things out of view at multiple places. Piaget is careful to point out that achievement of the object concept does not imply that the infant knows "all about" objects. The infant does not know about the moon for example. In the preschool years, the child will have to learn that the moon does not follow him. In infancy, the concept of objects is egocentric and is limited to objects that can be experienced tangibly. The child's concept of objects will have to change systematically in later life to take account of distant objects such as the moon and objects that undergo metamorphoses over time. Further, the child's concept will have to change so that the child can appreciate the perspective of others on objects as well as his own.

III. PSYCHOMETRIC STUDIES OF OBJECT CONCEPT DEVELOPMENT

There have been several issues embedded in my presentation of Piaget's theory. One has been whether the newborn or the very young infant is aware of the orderliness of objects, e.g., their persistence in space and time, their invariant form and size. A second has been whether awareness of such order derived from perceptual activity or from extended courses of sensorimotor activity, i.e., is the information about order present in the proximal stimulus array or must the infant add information. A third has been whether there is evidence that the infant goes through stages, actively constructs systematically different general views of the order in the world during the course of infancy. A fourth has been the presentation of an array of relatively novel age-ordered facts that emerged from Piaget's development and deployment of his vision of infancy.

The studies to be reviewed in this section seem primarily to have been inspired by the fourth issue. The investigators have asked whether Piaget's facts about object concept development can be replicated, particularly those gross facts about search for hidden objects that Piaget uses to index the major stages that he argues underlie them. The work has been conducted in the hope that psychometric scales of object concept development can be formulated. The focus has not been so much on evaluating Piaget's theory as on the possibility of generating an index of the development of representational ability, an index which will be useful in clarifying the nature of early social attachment and the bearing of varying life circumstances on intellectual development. Because these issues are currently of such concern to many psychologists and because of Piaget's present stature, work along this line has been vigorously pursued and widely cited. For these reasons, this literature will be reviewed first.

A. Object Concept Scales

The principal workers in developing object concept scales have been Décarie (1965), Corman and Escalona (1969), and Uzgiris and Hunt (1966). Their scales have been keyed to the variations on the delayed response tasks described in Section II-A. In other words, can the infant find a toy hidden in one place, two places, three places? Can the infant find it when the object is invisibly displaced, at one place, at one of two places, at one of three places? Corman and Escalona and Uzgiris and Hunt have constructed elaborate scales designed for widespread use and have provided evidence of the ordinality of their scales in both cross-sectional and longitudinal studies.

Uzgiris and Hunt sought to develop a set of items that formed an ordinal scale in the Guttman sense. They focused on identifying levels, landmarks inspired by Piaget, rather than stages. Corman and Escalona have adopted a somewhat different approach. They take seriously Piaget's claim that stages are real, are general points of view, and that, within a stage of development, an infant may have encountered and assimilated a wide variety of situations or only a small number of them. Unlike Uzgiris and Hunt, Corman and Escalona constructed a set of items to represent each stage. They identify the infant as being in a particular stage in terms of whether he passes some of the items relevant to a particular stage and none of the items relevant to the next stage. They expect the stages to be ordinal, but they do not expect all the items within a stage to fall into an ordinal scale of difficulty. They anticipate that this strategy will permit them to evaluate whether poverty-youngsters lag in terms of their stage of intellectual development or the breadth of their experience. Their associates, Golden and Birns (1968), have modified the scale so that all items form an ordinal scale of difficulty, the scale being similar to the Uzgiris and Hunt Scale.

Miller, Cohen, and Hill (1970) question whether the Uzgiris and Hunt Scale in fact indexes levels of object concept development. They compared 6- to 18-month-old infants' responses to 15 scale items when the items were administered in the standard order, from least to most difficult, and when the item order was varied. They found that varying the item order produced different responses. They interpret their data as indicating that the scale could be reduced to three basic levels of difficulty, i.e., find a partially hidden object, find a totally covered object, find an invisibly displaced object. They argue that the relative difficulty of the other items was highly dependent on such task-order determined events as comprehension of and familiarity with the task to be performed.

The findings of Miller, Cohen, and Hill (1970) make a certain degree of sense in terms of Piaget's stage notions, and their comments on task order should have some bearing on the Corman and Escalona Scale. But the approach of Miller *et al.*, as well as that of Uzgiris and Hunt, implicitly does not assume that the many subtle variations on basic tasks that Piaget introduced contribute meaningfully to the diagnosis of an infant's stage of object concept development. Corman and Escalona do take Piaget seriously in this regard. But questions can also be raised about their approach to Piaget's views on both psychometric and theoretical grounds. At present, the number of items in each stage pool differ and, therefore, there is a question whether they can effectively assess the breadth of competence in each stage.

The theoretical objection has been developed by Broughton (1970). The scale constructors that have been discussed are, in good measure, aware of the objection, but it still stands as a caution to them and all other investigators who develop object scales and use them to illuminate other facets of infantile life. While such scales can be very useful, their "landmark" nature raises the danger of reifying the indices. Fundamentally such scales only describe the fact that infants pass or fail certain specific tasks. They do not indicate clearly how infants do this nor whether the performance is task-specific or general. However, the test items may put the investigator into the position of studying the "how" by the clinical methods that Piaget has employed, and all of the just-mentioned authors have set good examples of how this can be done and also have urged users of their scales to follow their example. Yet just as Hunter reified the delayed response task into an index of representational processes (see Fletcher, 1965; Munn, 1955), so too there is a very real danger that Piaget's use of it to diagnose intellectual development may lead the present generation of investigators to mistake the index for the reality. Seeking a hidden object, here or there, may occur for a variety of reasons, only some of which have to do with object representation. The studies reviewed in Sections III and IV are, in large part, addressed to articulating this claim, but before taking them up, the applications of object concept scales will be discussed.

B.   The Role of General Experience

A number of investigators have attempted to assess the influence of growing up in institutions or in lower-class families on the development of representational abilities through the use of Piaget-based object concept scales. Some interesting trends and some puzzles have emerged. Décarie (1965) studied infants from three environments: an institution, foster homes where the foster parents were going to adopt the infants, and natural homes. There were 90 infants, five from each environment at six age levels, i.e., 3, 6, 9, 12, 16, and 20 months. She found that type of environment was associated with object concept score, using a multiple regression procedure to show the degree of association. Her mode of analysis did not involve a direct examination of the relation between environment, age, and score. Inspection of her data (Figure 3, p. 156) indicates that: (a) The infants from institutions generally perform more poorly than infants from the other environments. (b) At the two oldest ages the foster home infants seem to behave more like the institution-reared infants than the home-reared infants whereas they appear more like the home-reared infants at younger ages. (c) There may be other interactions. She also administered the Griffith's Mental Development Scale, and performance on the two scales was highly correlated (as described later).

Paraskevopoulos and Hunt (1971) found a related trend in their large-scale study of Greek children. They compared infants from two orphanages and working-class families (most of whom were cared for in day-care centers during the day) in terms of their performance on selected items from the Uzgiris and Hunt object permanence scale. In one orphanage, there was a large infant-to-caretaker ratio (about 10 to 1), whereas in the other the ratio was about 3 to 1. The infants from the relatively understaffed orphanage succeeded on each object permanence item at a considerably later mean age than did the infants from the other orphanage, who tended to perform much like the infants from working-class families.

These studies of the relation between environmental variation and level of object concept development in Canadian and Greek infants are in general accord with the trends found for intelligence by such investigators as Dennis and Najarian (1957), but it must be recalled that the latter investigators found such differences no longer evident in the preschool years.

Moreover, comparisons between lower- and middle-class home-reared infants in the United States have yielded equivocal results. Golden and Birns have conducted three related studies of black children in which the parents either were on welfare, were employed as unskilled workers, or were employed in skilled or professional capacities. They used a modification of the Corman and Escalona Scale and the Cattell infancy schedule. In their first study (Golden & Birns, 1968), they raised the question of whether socioeconomic (SES) differences might indicate performance rather than capacity differences, that the poor infants might perform more poorly because they were less oriented to the tasks. Therefore, they administered the items in a manner calculated to maximize the infants' interest and opportunity to succeed. They studied infants at 12, 18, and 24 months of age. They found no differences between the performances of the three types of infants on the two kinds of tests at any of the ages studied. In the second study (Golden & Birns, 1971), they again compared infants from the three types of families on the two scales. Infants of 18 and 24 months of age were given the tests under standard test conditions and under the "optimizing" condition 1 week later. Performance improved in the second testing, but once again, they found no important SES differences. The children in the second study were given the Stanford-Binet at 3 years of age (Birns & Golden, 1972). The correlation between object concept or Cattell scores at 18 months and the Stanford-Binet scores at 3 years were not significant. The comparable correlations for the 24-month group were significant, the Cattell scores being more highly related to the Stanford-Binet scores than were the object concept scores.

Birns and Golden (in press) note the similarity between their results and those of Bayley (1965) and suggest that the "average expectable environment" of poor, home-reared infants is sufficient for object concept and general intellectual development during the period of infancy. Wachs, Uzgiris, and Hunt (1971), however, reach a different conclusion about object concept development from their comparison of 7-, 11-, 15-, 18-, and 22-month-old middle-class (white) and lower-class (primarily black) infants. They administered the Uzirgis and Hunt object permanence scale, several other scales from that schedule, and used the Caldwell Home Stimulation Scale to characterize the home environment. While they found relatively consistent SES differences in performance on other scales, the poor children performed less adequately than the middle-class children on the object permanence scale only at 11 months. Moreover, the difference seems attributable primarily to the fact that the lower-class infants needed more trials than middle-class infants on items that they both succeeded on. There were some correlations between items from the Caldwell Scale and performance on the object permanence scale, but the relations were not consistent. Thus, it is unclear why the authors emphasize that SES background is associated with performance on the object permanence scale.

However, a study by Bell (1971) suggests that the 11-month finding of Wachs *et al.* (1971) may not be artifactual. Bell compared lower-class black and middle-class white infants. She assessed the same infants at 8½ and 11 months of age in terms of an object permanence scale much like the scales used in the previous studies. Toys and a person (the examiner) were hidden. At 8½ months, the middle-class infants were more advanced in the person permanence task, but there was no difference between the two groups on the object permanence task. At 11 months, the lower-class infants did more poorly on both tasks.

Thus, Bell's results provide support for the conclusion that Wachs, Uzgiris, and Hunt arrived at, but it is clear that there are no unequivocal statements that can be made about the relation of social class to performance on object concept scales. Moreover, the longitudinal study of Lewis and McGurk (1972) raises questions about the utility of using object concept scales and infant test batteries to study these issues. They did not find that object concept scale scores were correlated at different ages of testing nor did they find that such scores were correlated with the Bayley schedule or with scores on a test of language production and comprehension at 24 months.

C. The Role of Experience with Persons

There is a long-standing tradition of viewing infants' ability to seek out absent persons as a sign that the infant has developed the ability to represent persons and is capable of forming "true" attachments to them (Bowlby, 1969). A number of investigators have sought to explore social development in terms of object concept scales. Décarie (1965) conducted one of the first. She introduced her study by very thoughtfully discussing object concept development from Piaget's point of view and discussing the development of objectal relations, feelings toward others, from a psychoanalytic point of view. She explored the relation empirically by constructing two relatively crude indices of the two lines of development, i.e., an eight-item object concept scale and a seven-item objectal relations scale. The latter involved such items as evidences of discriminative smiling at persons and appropriate responses to facial gestures and verbal commands. As indicated previously, she administered the scales to 90 infants from three environments and six age levels—3, 6, 9, 12, 16, 20 months of age. In general, performance improved with age on the object concept scale, and the home-reared infants performed best and the institution-reared infants performed worst. The objectal relations items did not fall into as clear a developmental order as did the object concept items, but in general, comparable results were found. The two scores were highly correlated with one another and with scores on the Griffith's Mental Development Scale. All scores were highly associated with age. Thus, Décarie identified a gross relation between object concept development and the growth of social feeling. The relation is gross because of the crude nature of the scales and because performance on both scales is highly associated with chronological age.

Bell (1970) sought to determine whether the frequent comings and goings of such salient objects as persons would lead infants to form a conception of their permanence before other objects. She constructed a permanence scale much like that of Corman and Escalona and Uzgiris and Hunt, and administered it once with a toy as the object and once with an examiner as the person. The schedule was administered to the same infants twice at 8½ months and once at 11 months. Most infants performed more ably with the person than with the toy (positive decalage). More interestingly, she found that a minority of the infants did as well or better with toys than with persons in some or all of the sessions (negative decalage). Their performance with toys tended to be comparable to that of the other infants, but their performance with persons was inferior. The babies also were observed at 11 months in a strange situation involving their interacting in various ways with their mothers and an examiner. They were classified as having one of three types of social relation on the basis of their behavior in the strange situations: (a) babies who actively tried to relate or be close to their mothers after brief separations and used them as a base of support during exploration and infants who either (b) tended to ignore their mothers or (c) were ambivalent toward them. Interestingly, the children who showed a negative decalage had either b or c types of social relations whereas, the infants who showed a positive decalage manifested the a type of social relation. Moreover, interviews with the mothers revealed that the mothers of positive decalage infants had more positive attitudes toward them, were more perceptive and responsive, and spent more time with them.

Bell (1971) repeated the study with lower-class black infants and found comparable results. The principal difference between the two samples was that a greater number of poor black infants showed the negative decalage and b and c types of social relations. Thus, Bell has shown that a very interesting pattern of relations exists between the way in which mothers act toward their children at home, how their babies orient to them and strangers in strange situations, and how ably the infants go about finding persons or toys when they disappear in various ways.

Serafica and Uzgiris (1971) approached the problem somewhat differently from Bell and Décarie. They proposed to examine how the infant–mother relationship evolves and how the development of the object concept relates to this process. They compared 4- to 12-month-olds in two situations. One was a 17-scene situation involving such incidents as giving and getting toys, being fed, and being left. Both the mother and an examiner went through the scenes with the infant. In each scene, infants received a score if they showed positive or negative affect, approached the person, and expected the next thing the person would do. To examine the evolution of the mother–child relationship, a Wernerian framework was used to seek evidence of both differentiation between persons and hierarchic integration. Infants were found to act differently toward the mother than toward the stranger with respect to each of the components—affect, approach, and expectancy. There were significant increases with age in the differentiation scores for two of the three components, i.e., approach and expectancy. As an indication of hierarchic integration, the authors counted as evidence of integrative activity each scene with the mother in which the infant showed all of the following: affect, approach, expectation, and responding differently to the mother than to the stranger. There was a significant increase in integration with age. The scores on the object concept scale were significantly correlated with the interpersonal relationship scores, age being held constant. Focusing on particular age periods, Serafica and Uzgiris found that there was little association between the two types of scores at ages 4–6 and 10–12 months, but there was some correlation at 7–9 months. In particular, the affect and approach scores tended to be associated with the object concept scores.

Thus, the three studies reviewed point to interesting relations between social development and performance on object concept scales. But, the nature of the relations needs clarification. Décarie's study indicates that a gross relation exists. Bell's work introduces some clarification. Infants who live with parents who are perceptive and responsive to them will be better able to cope with strange circumstances in which their mothers and others disappear and reappear. The link is interesting but general, and the relation to performance on the object permanence tests also is ambiguous. The more able searching of some infants for persons relative to objects may indicate that they have more advanced concepts of the permanence of persons or may indicate that they have more interest in persons. The Serafica and Uzgiris study also provides only gross indicators. However, as they note, it is interesting to observe that the greatest association between object concept scale performance and social relationships occurred in that period when infants are becoming active in keeping track of their mother and things, i.e., at the age of 7 to 9 months.

Moreover, Serafica and Uzgiris provide a valuable framework within which to locate future investigations. They argue that the mother–child relationship and object concept development should be looked upon as reciprocally evolving events. The direction for study should be to focus upon such important events as person and object disappearances–reappearances and evidence that the infant is or is not comprehending them in terms of a scheme that posits permanence and distinctions between self and other.

The work on object concept scales has been reviewed at some length because it appears to be the most vigorous tradition spawned by Piaget's theory. However, it appears to me to be a premature development. It is founded on an acceptance of Piaget's arguments and focuses on the correlates of infants' object search achievements rather than on an exploration of the problem-solving processes involved in object search. The leap would be warranted if object concept scale performance were found to have important correlates, but at present, no compelling correlations have been found. Work in this direction contains the danger that Broughton (1970) has signaled, namely, the reification of Piaget's ideas in terms of the scales. However, the scales can be used to explore the theory, and this theme will be picked up again, in Section IV-C, when other aspects of Uzgiris's work are considered.

IV. STUDIES FOCUSED ON PIAGET'S THEORY

The studies to be reviewed in this section primarily have been addressed to the issue of evaluating Piaget's explanations or facts, as opposed to applying them. This literature is organized in terms of four focal issues. The first is an attempt to refute Piaget's most general claim, namely, that infants construct the object concept. A number of studies have been conducted in an attempt to demonstrate that very young infants perceive the permanence of objects, that infants need not go through a long process of acting on objects in order to become aware that they exist even when out of view. The second issue has to do with older infants, 6 or more months of age, and their ability to localize occluded objects in space. The third issue revolves around the role of activity in object localization. Two general themes are included here. One has to do with the question of whether looking and doing play different roles in promoting search for occluded objects. The second has to do with whether there are stages of activity, and whether such stages are the precondition for different levels of object search. The fourth issue is that of figurative knowledge. Studies focused on figurative knowledge raise the question of whether infants have particular objects in mind when they search for hidden objects.

A.   Is Object Permanence Perceived by Very Young Infants?

Bower has seriously challenged Piaget's notions. On the one hand, he has tried to find evidence that the infantile world is not the chaos that Piaget presents, that the infant enters the world as a highly complex processor of object information. On the other hand, he has tried to show that the infant does not process the information as Piaget would have us believe. Bower believes that the orderly relations among objects are present in the stimulus array and that the young infant gains such information perceptually, through attending to the relevant features of the array. The infant, in Bower's view, need not construct such knowledge through actions on objects.

Bower (1966) has shown that infants within the first 2 months of life have a significant measure of awareness of size and shape constancy and depth. He and his associates, Broughton and Moore, have conducted an impressive array of studies indicating that infants see the solidity of objects within the first 2 weeks of life, a time when they show little ability to derive object information through touch (Bower, Broughton, & Moore, 1970a, b, c). Their studies indicate that such infants reach for objects and intend to grasp them because they mold their fingers appropriately while they direct their arms toward various objects, although they grasp various objects in a stereotyped fashion. Perhaps even more impressively, these infants became very distressed when they searched for a virtual image and contacted empty air where the object should have been.

These studies on the relation of touch and vision suggest that Piaget's ingenious account of how touch educates vision to achieve size constancy is in error (see Section II-B-2). Further support for Bower, Broughton, and Moore's view is provided by studies of 6-month-old infants conducted by Gratch and Landers (1971), and by Gratch (1972). Gratch and Landers found that such infants will fail to remove covers from their hands when they have seen and grasped toys and then have their hands covered. Gratch subsequently showed such infants would remove transparent covers from their hands under these circumstances, suggesting that their failure was due to an inability to appreciate what they had in hand.

More central to the theme of this chapter is Bower's attempt to show that very young infants see that objects are permanent. In one series of studies, he ingeniously adapted Michotte's analysis of the psychophysics of existence constancy for use with infants (Bower,

1967). Michotte concluded that certain stimulus arrays lead adults to see and immediately report, the continued existence or the nonexistence of occluded objects whereas other displays lead adults to such judgments only after reflection, in which case they know but do not see. A display leading to the perception of continued existence would be the slow covering of an object. Displays leading to conceptual, rather than perceptual, judgments would be the sudden darkening of the whole visual field, where adults know the object continues to exist, and the dissolving into thin air of an object, where adults know it ceases to exist. Bower reasoned that if infants responded appropriately to displays that lead adults to see existence and did not respond to other types of displays, then he could conclude that they were aware of existence on a perceptual basis.

In the first study in the series, 50-day-old infants were shaped to suck in order to produce a recording of a woman's voice, and a bull's-eye patterned sphere was present in the infants' visual field. Then the object was occluded in various ways and sucking no longer produced the voice. Under these conditions, infants tended to suck when the toy was occluded by slowly covering it. However, they did not tend to suck when the toy disappeared in the ways that do not lead adults to see object permanence, e.g., instant disappearance. Bower viewed these results as indicating that very young infants have object permanence on a perceptual level, that they continue to suck in the object's absence because they see it as present but covered.

Because of the difficulties in using the conditioning procedure, Bower used another method in a second study. The object disappeared in various ways, and he evaluated sucking behavior and heart rate for evidence of object permanence. He found that infants who witnessed a slow covering of the object would suppress sucking when the object disappeared and would quickly resume sucking when the screen moved on to expose the object. Heart rate increased at both of these points. On the other hand, the other occlusion conditions led the infants to suppress sucking when the sphere disappeared and to resume sucking shortly after it disappeared. They did not appreciably alter their rate when the object reappeared. Bower concluded once again that the slow covering led the infants to see that the object was still there, their suppression of sucking indicating that they were waiting for it to reappear.

However, given the results of the first study, it is not at all clear why they did not continue to suck. Presumably in Study 1, they sucked because they saw the object as a sign that sucking would produce the voice. But why were they sucking in Study 2? Is it because they were looking at the object or because it was something to do until there was something interesting to observe? Bower did not explore the difficulty, and it will be discussed later at greater length. Instead, he conducted several more studies with the same method. He varied the rate at which a screen moved past the object, the length of time the screen remained in view, and the age of the infants. He found that, with increasing age, infants showed the pattern of suck-suppression and suck-recurrence when the object disappeared and reappeared at faster rates of occlusion and over longer durations of object occlusion. Moreover, at 50 weeks of age, he found the infants showing the pattern even when the object "instantaneously" disappeared and remained out of view for as long as 9 min. He concluded the older infants were aware of object permanence on a conceptual as well as perceptual level.

These ingenious studies, unfortunately, bear in a very equivocal way on Bower's contention. Earlier, we noted that the infants might have been reacting to varying perceptual displays rather than to disappearing objects. We say this for several reasons. On the one hand, aspects of the data suggest that the very rapid screenings of the object led the very young infants to startle and withdraw from the scene. On the other hand, the object was large relative to the alleyway which contained it, and the infants may have been responding to it and the object alley as a whole rather than to an object in the alley. One can argue that the slowly changing scene created by the slow covering of the object captured the infants' attention in a way that the other changing scenes did not, and this, rather than object disappearance, was responsible for their conduct. Given these difficulties, one can only conclude that Bower's line of argument and investigation warrants clarification and replication.

Unfortunately, Bower turned away from these studies and took a different tack. He seems to have done this for reasons such as the ones advanced in the preceding paragraph. He, Broughton, and Moore introduce the next series of studies to be considered by stating their agreement with a comment by Piaget that Bower may have been varying displays and not object disappearance (Bower, Broughton, & Moore, 1971). In the new line of studies, Bower *et al.* investigated how infants follow moving objects. In their first two studies, they exposed 8-week-old infants to an object moving on a linear or a circular trajectory. During the series of trials, they would sometimes stop the object behind a screen and sometimes they would stop the object before it went behind the screen. When the object went behind the screen, the infants would look past the screen, as if anticipating its reappearance. But they would also do this when the object stopped before the screen. Thus, they nicely confirmed Piaget's line of reasoning about what young infants are tracking when they look past screens, i.e., they are not anticipating object reappearances, rather, they are following trajectories and/or are continuing action paths (see Section II-B-1).

Given these results, they posed two questions. With development, do the infants come to expect that the object that disappears will reappear, i.e., do they pay attention to object features or only to movement? Second, do the infants follow the track or are they only learning the contingency between the place of disappearance and the place of reappearance? To study these questions, they created four situations. In one, the object moved behind a screen and then reappeared. In another, the object moved behind the screen and then a markedly different object appeared. In the other two, the object moved behind the screen, and at the same instant, the same or the different object appeared at the other end of the screen. Groups of infants, at varying ages, 8 weeks to 20 weeks, experienced a trial series under one of these four conditions. During the trial series, at specified times, the object would remain behind the screen or would stop before it went behind the screen. The authors do not report what the infants did on the initial trials, when the object behaved in either a "normal" or abnormal manner. For some unknown reason, they failed to focus on these most interesting trials. Instead, they report on what the infants did when the object stopped out of view or in view. These trials, unfortunately, are ambiguous because one cannot know whether conduct on them is a function of the infants' ideas about objects or is a function of their having learned, somehow, to cope with these strange circumstances. Thus, in the instantaneous appearance condition, when the object stopped behind the screen, the 8- and 12-week-old infants tended either to refuse to look or to check back and forth at the termini of the screen. Does their behavior indicate that they can only follow movement and become disrupted if another movement is introduced, as the authors argue, or does it indicate that they had learned to expect the object to reappear instantaneously and the failure of the object to appear disrupted their conduct? For comparable reasons, one cannot know what role object features play for the infants they studied.

Fortunately, Gardner (1971) carried out a line of study which is very comparable to the study of Bower, Broughton, and Moore (1971) and which supplies some of the information they do not. In one study, 3- to 21-week-old infants tracked an object that moved behind a screen. Gardner varied the size of the screens, and found, like Piaget and the previous authors, that infants looked beyond ever wider screens with increasing age. To determine whether they were looking for an object or were just tracking, she presented a trial series in which half the time the same object reappeared and half the time a different object reappeared. The screen was constant in size and kept the object out of view for 1 sec. When the different object appeared, 18- and 21-week-old infants looked back at the screen, as if to find the other object. Infants 12 and 15 weeks old showed a variety of reactions indicative of disruption, e.g., looking around the room, staring intensely at the new object. On the other hand, 6- and 9-week-olds simply tracked the object, irrespective of whether it was the same one or not.

Gardner's study suggests that by 20 weeks of age infants are tracking objects, are aware of specific objects while they are absent. Her results suggest both that object permanence appears far earlier than Piaget suspects and that it can develop in the absence of operative activity, the overt patterns of sensorimotor activity such as visually guided reaching which Piaget insists are necessary to construct such a notion. But there are several reasons for holding this conclusion in abeyance. Gardner reports her procedures and results in a sketchy manner. For example, it is unclear whether the older babies looked back at the screen early in the trial series or only after many trials. Further, she did not look for such events as whether the infants were surprised when the new object appeared, events that would make her case stronger. Finally, there is the discrepancy between the performance of 5-month-old infants in the tracking task and the widely observed failure of 6-month-olds to remove the cover from an object hidden in a single place. Is the discrepancy only a matter of procedure or does it point to the complexities of coming to a notion of an object as a substantial, permanent, constant three-dimensional form? We will return to these issues in Section IV-D.

B. Spatial Localization of Hidden Objects by Infants Six or More Months of Age

While 5-month-old infants may know that a moving object still exists when it moves out of sight, they and older infants do not appear to know this when the object stays in place and is covered. In both cross-sectional (1966) and longitudinal studies (1969), Uzgiris and her associates found that the infants can reliably retrieve a partially hidden object about a month before they retrieve a completely covered object (about 6 and 7 months, respectively). Gratch and Landers (1971) and Gratch (1972), in their longitudinal and cross-sectional studies, found comparable trends. Gratch also confirmed Piaget's observation of an intermediate step, finding when the infant is reaching before the toy is hidden (see Section II-B-1). Gratch discovered yet another step prior to this one, namely, the ability to gain the toy when the infant grasps the toy and then has his hand covered.

Thus, there appears to be a nontrivial difference between the tracking and hiding tasks and/or infants' sense of object permanence at 5 and 7 months. It is striking to note that 6- and 7-month-old infants can remove covers and yet fail to search for objects despite repeated opportunities at the task both within a session and over the course of two or more sessions. Through her longitudinal studies, Uzgiris has provided a number of interesting observations that should lead to a clarification of the discrepancy. Before infants find a toy covered in their view, they are able to release and recapture a toy in hand, repeatedly do this, engage in varied examination of toys, and are able to locate an object dropped from overhead if it falls within their view. They are able to locate it when it falls out of their view at the same age as they are able to find the toy covered in their view (Schofield & Uzgiris, 1969; Uzgiris, 1969, 1973). Uzgiris (1969) also notes that she did not confirm Piaget's observation (Section II-B-1) that search for the partially hidden object is a function of the familiarity of the visible fraction of the object.

Perhaps even more interesting were the observations Schofield and she made on how infants behaved before they retrieved the partially and totally covered objects. In both cases, the infants tended to show the following course of behavior over time. In the early sessions, they would look away when the toy was covered. In later sessions they would become distressed when the toy was covered. Still later, they would dwell on the cover, visually and tactually, but they would not remove it. Then, they would uncover in a slow, hesitant manner, and finally, they would quickly uncover the object. M. K. Moore (personal communication) has suggested that the sequence indicates that the infant gradually comes to identify a place. Through repeatedly observing the toy appear in the examiner's hand, disappear at the cover, and reappear at the cover, the infant learns first about the hand as a place, as an invariant moment of the object's presence in view, and subsequently learns that the cover is a special place. Moore contends that the infant is not aware so much of the object's presence while it is out of view as that the cover is a place where the object can be seen, a place that unites the several trajectories of the object. In Piaget's terms, the cover comes to be an index of the toy.

Moore's interpretation is consistent with Piaget's frequent observations that infants will first look to the examiner's hand after the toy is either dropped or placed under the cover. Moore, Uzgiris, and I also have made this observation. Moore's claim also is consistent with the observation that sound cues emanating from the covered object do not lead young infants to search (Fraiberg, Siegel, & Gibson, 1966; Freedman, Fox-Kolenda, Margileth, & Miller, 1969; Piaget, 1954). Moore makes an interesting prediction, based on Michotte's and Bower's views, about how ways of covering will facilitate or impede cover removal. He notes that most investigators move the cover over the object from front to back, thus rapidly occluding the object. He predicts that if the cover were slowly moved over the object from back to front then the infants would be more likely to uncover the object. J. J. Gibson has made a comparable observation (personal communication), and it would be interesting to evaluate the claim empirically.

Thus, both Moore and Piaget suggest that the infant who uncovers the hidden object is seeking at a place as opposed to seeking an object. Piaget comes to this conclusion in terms of an analysis that emphasizes the infant's sensorimotor activity whereas Moore's analysis leans more upon an analysis of the stimulus array that the infant attends to, an approach favored by both Bower and the Gibsons (J. J. Gibson, 1966; E. J. Gibson, 1969). Both lines of reasoning point to the importance of Piaget's Stage IV error, namely, that when infants first find a toy at one place, they will search at that place when they observe that the toy is hidden in a second place (A$\overline{\text{B}}$ error). As was indicated earlier, Piaget attaches great significance to this concordance of events. They indicate to him that the infant still does not properly perceive objects but rather still sees them egocentrically, in terms of his own actions.

Gratch and Landers (1971) confirmed Piaget's observation of the A$\overline{\text{B}}$ error in their longitudinal study. They observed that when infants found, for the first time, the toy at place A on two successive trials, then the infants searched at A when the toy was hidden at B.

The infants continued to do this over many B trials. Moreover, in the first sessions in which this occurred, the infants looked to A during the 3-sec delay period and did not attempt to correct their errors by searching at B. It was as if they were only aware of one place at a time, as if they failed to register the new hiding place. This interpretation is supported by the behavior of the infants in later sessions. When they finally found the toy on two successive trials at B, the object then was hidden at A. The infants tended to search at B, thus committing a B$\overline{\text{A}}$ error. Such search indicates that they had learned a new special place as opposed to having learned to search where the toy was hidden. Following the early sessions where the infants tended to orient early to A, the infants manifested conflict over the two positions. During the delay period, they looked at both A and B, and when they searched, they touched either the A or the B cloth and then removed the other. There was some evidence that, in still later sessions, they repeatedly looked back and forth between the two sides, as if they were coming to a decision. Finally, they came to orient only to the side where the object was hidden. The longitudinal pattern found in this study fits nicely with the equilibration model Piaget has proposed to account for the movement from one stage of development to another (e.g., 1967). Moreover, Webb, Massar, and Nadolny (1972) found that 14- and 16-month-old infants made a comparable error in a three-choice delayed reaction problem.

While the observations of Gratch and Landers suggest that there is a Stage IV point of view, both the observations and Piaget's account of them have been called into question. Schofield and Uzgiris (1969) report that they did not find many subjects making the A$\overline{\text{B}}$ error in their longitudinal study, and the error does not seem to occur very often in the experience of investigators developing and using Piaget-based object concept scales (Bell, 1970; Corman & Escalona, 1969; Uzgiris & Hunt, 1966).

Harris (1973) suggests that failure to find the error may be due to the amount of time that the object is out of view. He notes that Schofield and Uzgiris allowed the infants to reach for the cover as soon as it was placed over the object. Moreover, he suggests that the occurrence of the error is due to forgetting rather than, as Piaget argues, the infants' inability to register the new place of hiding. He develops his argument through a number of well-designed studies with 10-month-old infants.

In the first, Harris asked whether the error was a matter of response repetition or place repetition. To unconfound the two alternatives, he hid the toy initially in the left well of a tray with two wells. The left well was immediately in front of the infants. Then he moved the whole tray to the infant's left and either placed the toy in the original well, now on the infant's left, or in a new well, now directly in front of the infant. While very few errors occurred, those that occurred involved searching at the original well, a search that involved a new response.

In a second experiment, Harris varied the delay intervals (the tray was not moved). The toy was hidden at one well, found by the infant, and then was hidden in the other well. When the infants had to wait 5 sec before they could search, they would commit the $\overline{AB}$ error, but they did not err when they could search as soon as the toy was covered.

To specify the nature of the error, the manner in which the toy was covered was varied in a third study. The infants could search as soon as the toy was covered. There were four variations, formed from the combination of the following two factors: (1) toy hidden in the same or the other well, and (2) empty well covered before or after covering the well containing the toy. When the toy was placed in the other well and that well was covered first, the infants erred, but they did not err under the other three conditions. Harris concluded that the $\overline{AB}$ error occurred because the infants were distracted from the place where the toy was hidden by the covering of the empty well, the well where they previously had searched successfully.

While it seems clear that Harris demonstrates that 10-month-olds err because they register and then forget the new hiding place, it is not clear that he calls Piaget's Stage IV argument into question. There are several reasons for concluding that his study does not do so. One reason is that 10-month-olds are less likely to make the error than are 9-month-olds (Landers, 1968). Second, Gratch and his associates have consistently found that 9-month-olds make the $\overline{AB}$ error when the hiding procedure that did *not* lead to error in Harris's study is used, i.e., the empty well is covered first and then the toy is placed in the other well and covered. Finally, Gratch, Appel, Evans, LeCompte, and Wright (1974) conducted a study in which the delay interval was varied. The infants waited either 0, 1, 3, or 7 sec before the experimenter moved the tray within their reach following the covering of the toy. The toy was hidden five times on one side and then was hidden on the other side. The great majority of the infants in the 1-, 3-, and 7-sec conditions erred. These results suggest that Piaget is correct, that infants err because they fail to register the new place of hiding as opposed to forgetting it. However, almost none of the O-sec infants erred. The infants tended to reach toward the toy as it was being hidden, and it was hypothesized that the O-sec infants' failure to err was a result of their being "frozen" into position by the moving tray. Therefore, a number of infants were studied in a situation where the tray was not moved. Rather, the infants were restrained until the object was covered. Almost none of the infants erred when this variation on the O-sec condition was employed. Thus, the O-sec infants appear to register the new place of hiding.

I think the infants' behavior under the O-sec condition only qualifies, rather than refutes, Piaget's argument. I offer three reasons. First, Piaget and I and my associates have often noted that infants reach toward the prior side even while the toy is in view and is being moved toward the new side. Second, we conducted a study in which the toy was placed in full view. The infants took the toy five times at A, and then the toy was placed at B five times, again in full view. While none of the infants ever reached at A during the B trials, they often would take a long look at A before taking the toy at B.

Third, we reexamined the 1-, 3-, and 7-sec data for the first B trial. We classified the infants' delay behavior in two ways, attentiveness and direction of gaze. Infants who leaned toward and looked at the hiding wells through the whole period when the toy was out of view were called highly attentive. All others were called less attentive, this category including infants who looked away from the well for only a brief time and infants who essentially left the field. The direction of gaze measure referred to those gazes that were directed to the A and B wells and it was coded in three ways: (1) looking to the A side either while the toy was in view or as soon as it was covered and holding this point throughout the time the tray was out of reach; (2) looking only at the side of hiding, B; or (3) showing some pattern that involved looking at both sides. The less attentive infants were likely to err irrespective of whether their orientation was primarily to the A well or was primarily to the B well or was oriented to both wells. Thus, the error sometimes occurs because of forgetting. However, the attentive infants were likely to err only when they pointed to A. Moreover, the infants who adopted such an orientation to A when the toy was hidden at B were younger than the other infants. These latter results suggest that Piaget is correct. Early in development, the infants make the error because they interpret the hiding of the toy at B as a hiding of the toy at A; later, they make the error because they register, but forget, the new hiding place. Moreover, these results provide a possible basis for understanding, in Piaget's terms, why the O-sec condition did not lead to erroneous search. Piaget seems to argue that the infants in Stage IV do not find the toy at A because they register that an object independent of them is hidden at A. Rather, their awareness of the object is confounded with their activity. In other words, the sight of the toy's disappearance at A leads them to point to A, and the cover serves as an index that supports the continuation of their act of reaching toward A. When the toy is hidden at B, a comparable place-orienting process is initiated, and if "no delay" ensues, the child will be likely to continue to act at B and will find the toy. However, if some delay does occur, then this orientation to place will be assimilated to the infant's action-based scheme of locating objects, and that scheme will lead him to search where he has found objects before. In other words, the $\overline{AB}$ error indicates an infant who does not yet get information about disappearing objects as such; rather, the infant's orientation to the disappearance of objects is confounded with his action orientations to them.

C. The Role of Action and the Problem of Stages

In Piaget's theory, action plays the central role in the construction of the concept of the object. A number of investigations have been addressed to this issue, but, as we shall indicate, they represent preliminary considerations of the problem.

One line of investigation seems to bear on the relation between object investigation and object search, and Schofield and Uzgiris (1969) and Harris (1971) have conducted relevant studies. Schofield and Uzgiris addressed themselves to Piaget's claim that intersensory coordination is a precursor and supporter of object concept development. Through intersensory coordination, particularly vision and grasping, the infant comes to objectify his experience with objects through recognizing that there is an invariant something that his varied actions bear upon. To investigate the claim, Schofield and Uzgiris examined the way in which infants handled five toys and related such behavior to the infants' performance in a hiding game. They studied 5-month-old infants weekly until they were able to find a toy hidden behind a single screen. The children, as their ages increased, shifted from stereotyped handling of the toys to coordinated visual and manual inspection of them and increased the length of time they played with them. The most notable increase in inspectional activity came at the time when the infants were able to remove a partially covered object. These results are interesting. They are compatible with the idea that the infant makes plain to himself through his actions those object characteristics which support his various actions on them. On the other hand, their observations do not clearly point out that such activity is crucial to coming to see the object for what it is. Further, as the authors point out, the relation between such activity and object search is still open.

Harris (1971) approached the relation between action on objects and search in a more direct fashion by varying how infants handle objects and how long they handle them before they disappear. Infants 12 and $8\frac{1}{2}$ months old saw an object emerge from behind a screen and move within their reach. The object was mounted on a stick. For half of the infants, the object moved into a transparent box that permitted the infants to look at but not handle the object. For half of the infants, the front portion of the box was not covered, and these infants handled as well as looked at the object. Three objects were presented to each infant, one for 5 sec, one for 20 sec, and one for 80 sec. After that time, the object was pulled behind the screen, and the length of time the infant searched behind the screen was recorded. Older infants searched longer than younger infants, and infants who handled the object searched longer than infants who only looked at the object. There was an interaction between the two conditions such that old and young did not differ in the handling condition but older infants searched longer than the younger infants in the visual condition. The amount of time spent with the toy was not related to search. Harris's study is interesting but inconclusive. It may indicate that handling somehow promotes search. On the other hand, it may only indicate that handling promotes interest. There are several reasons for advancing the latter interpretation. We already have cited a variety of studies which indicate that 6-month-olds may search only in the sense of extending their reaching movements, and the little ones in the visual condition had little reason to reach (Section IV-B). Second, inspection of Harris's table of means suggests that many of the younger infants may not have reached at all. Finally, in the visual condition, only the older infants may have been able to appreciate that they were looking at a "handleable" disappearing. In this regard, it is interesting to note that the older infants in the 80-sec visual condition appeared to search longer than the older infants who had a chance to handle the toy for 80 sec.

The role of activity also has been considered within the framework of infants' ability to search at varying places. Landers (1971) raised this question in attempting to assess the role of active search in leading 9-month-old infants to commit the $A\overline{B}$ error. In one condition, infants searched at A twice in succession before the toy was hidden at B. A second group of infants searched 8 or 10 times in succession at A. A third group observed the toy covered and uncovered at A 6 or 8 times and then found it twice in succession at A. (On observational trials, they were handed the toy after it was uncovered.) On the first B trial, the great majority of the infants in all three conditions searched at A. On the other hand, the second group made a longer run of such searches than did the other two groups, who behaved comparably. Landers concluded that searching activity, as opposed to observational activity, is crucial in leading the infants to err. On the other hand, one may question this conclusion on three grounds. First, it should be noted that a comparable number of infants in all three groups tended to err on the first trial. Second, the longer run of errors of the infants who searched many times at A may only indicate that they became more "set" in their ways. When the infants in any group erred, they still were given the toy. This procedure may simply have reinforced an already well-established habit of going to A. Finally, it should be noted that in all three conditions, the toy was not hidden at B until the toy had been found through active search on at least two trials.

Evans and Gratch (1972) commented on the last point, and Evans (1973) subsequently initiated a study in which 9-month-old infants either search at A or observe the toy covered and uncovered at A (in which case the infant is given the toy after uncovering). Within each condition, half the infants have two trials at A and half have five before the toy is hidden at B. Preliminary results indicate that comparable numbers of infants in all four conditions tend to search at A on the first B trial, and their runs of errors on subsequent B trials also are of comparable length. The latter finding casts doubt on Landers' results, particularly in the light of the fact that infants in Evans's study were not given the toy after they erred. This study does not demonstrate that activity is unimportant in determining search because it is plausible to assume that 9-month-old infants are reasonably practiced searchers and can profit from observing the experimenter hide toys in a place. On the other hand, the study is interesting in two ways. For one, given the studies of the $A\overline{B}$ error already discussed and those to be discussed in Section IV-D, it provides rather striking evidence that infants at this age do not follow the disappearance of objects but rather interpret such disappearances as place specifications. Second, it points up the ambiguity in the notion of sensorimotor activity.

Décarie's (1969) study of the development of searching in thalidomide babies makes the latter point even more dramatically. The infants studied varied considerably in the degree to which their limbs were deformed. While all were retarded in their performance on her object concept scale, even those infants who essentially had neither arms nor legs were able to twist their bodies to the covers and to somehow remove them. Clearly for the latter, "where there was a will, there was a way." The coordination of looking, reaching, and grasping played no role in the development of their achievements because they had neither arms nor hands nor fingers to bring to bear on events. On the one hand, her findings do not discomfit Piaget because his notion of activity emphasizes central rather than peripheral events. On the other hand, her findings dramatize the need for a clarification of just how sensorimotor experiences achieve "equipotentiality" and what, if any, are the limitations on awareness of things achieved through restricted sensorimotor modalities. Is it that such children can come to learn such abstract properties of objects as their permanence and substantiality despite the fact that they may not come to know particular properties such as their graspableness? Studies of blind infants, such as those begun by Fraiberg *et al.* (1966) and Freedman *et al.* (1969), may be instructive in this regard.

While present research does not provide an answer to the issues raised by Décarie's study, Uzgiris has taken an important step toward clarifying the relation between activity and the development of the object concept and the bearing of this achievement on the development of symbolically guided activity. She has administered the six scales of the Uzgiris and Hunt (1966) infancy schedule to 12 infants on a regular basis, beginning at 1 month and continuing through 24 months of age. She has reported on this study in a number of papers (Uzgiris, 1969, 1971, 1972, 1973).

Uzgiris's work brings into focus both the value and the limitations of an attempt to capture Piaget's sense of the course of infantile development in terms of psychometric scales. She and Hunt devised six Piaget-based scales, i.e., visual pursuit and permanence of objects, development of means for achieving desired environmental events, development of schemas in relation to objects, the development of causality, the construction of the object in space, and the development of imitation. The scales are in large part an attempt both to capture the Janus-faced nature of Piaget's view of the relationship between *The Origins of Intelligence* (1952) and *The Construction of Reality in the Child* (1954), i.e., patterns of action that result in awareness of external events and the actor's participation in them, and to capture the diverse ways in which Piaget characterizes both action and awareness. Through the use of the scales, Uzgiris sought to evaluate the merit of Piaget's stage hypothesis. She rightly reasoned that if intellectual development occurs in stages, then the infants, at certain ages, ought to behave in a comparable fashion in a variety of tasks. She expected to find intercorrelations among the six scales at certain age points in the course of longitudinal study. Her thoughtful search for such correlations has not been rewarded. While she has found some clusters of correlations, the patterns hold only among some of the scales, alter from age to age, and vary in their compellingness.

To a great extent, the difficulty lies in the scales rather than in Piaget's theory (though this does not imply that the theory is correct). As Broughton (1970) has pointed out, the difficulties embedded in Piaget's distinctions between schemes of action and concepts of object and space are exacerbated by Piaget's willingness to focus on the same behaviors from the perspective of the development of intelligence in *The Origins* . . . and from the perspective of awareness in *The Construction.* . . . But Uzgiris and Hunt have compounded the difficulty by specifying that the scales are distinct, by classifying some items in ways Piaget did not, and by focusing on item ordinality rather than the stage implications of items. The last issue becomes particularly important in assessing evidence of stages from the scales because the scales have different numbers of items, and therefore the concordances, or lack thereof, among scales may only speciously confirm or disconfirm the stage assertions of Piaget.

Uzgiris is aware of these problems but is understandably loathe to give up talking about relations among scales of development. However, when she explores the relations among items, and not scales, then interesting patterns of association among items appear, further observations are suggested and sometimes made, and important conjectures are put forth. I shall report some of the suggestive patterns here, and the reader is referred to her papers for the details of her results and her arguments.

During the period when infants can only search out toys when they see them hidden in view (Stages IV and V), she finds that infants not only come to locate objects that fall out of view when others drop them, but the infants also initiate the process of dropping and retrieving on their own. The infants engage in many empirically reversible actions at this time. Objects are crumpled and straightened, taken apart and put together, put in and taken out, etc. Moreover, familiar vocal and movement patterns are imitated, and the infants attentively vary their efforts to match the model. Thus in accord with Piaget's view, while the infant still does not appear to be able to innovate on a representational level, he is aware of many things and he appears to attentively study their nature.

During the time when the infants come to be able to find invisibly hidden objects (Stage VI), the infants also reveal a variety of other seemingly representationally based activities. The infants' activity appears foresightful, e.g., they do not try to put long necklaces into narrow containers. The infants begin to be able to imitate novel gestures that involve portions of their faces invisible to them, and they begin to imitate many new words and verbally recognize many objects. Uzgiris's observations do not yet permit one to decide whether Piaget is correct in his view of the role of operative activity in the formation of the object concept and the role of the object concept in symbolic development. However, a study by Roberts and Black (1972) provides support for the intuition that the achievement of the object concept is an important precondition of the use of language in a referential manner.

In sum, Uzgiris provides rich support for the series of activities and achievements that Piaget described in his three infants, and one looks forward to her reporting on the whole possible matrix of item-by-item comparisons that her data permit. These comparisons may provide important leads about the relation between operative activity and object knowledge.

D. The Role of Figural Awareness in the Search for Hidden Objects

Up until this point, the primary focus of the studies reviewed has been on whether infants search and not on what they are searching for. While this also has been Piaget's primary focus, it will be recalled that he did not entirely neglect the figurative aspect of knowing in his observations and theory (Sections II-A and II-B-2). Piaget argues that in Stage IV infants become aware of the three-dimensional nature of objects and establish shape constancy and a measure of size constancy. Further, he views the Stage IV infant as having some sense of the particular object that disappeared. As such, he interprets the Stage IV error as more than a place-going mistake. He speaks of the Stage IV infant seeking the thing-of-that-place. He suggests that the infant is seeking a specific object and yet is unaware that it is a single, a unitary, object. Piaget believes that at this stage the infant's view of objects involves no distinction between same and similar. The selfsame object may be both here and there at the same time.

Evans and Gratch (1972) have questioned this interpretation. They reasoned that if infants found a toy at A and then saw a different toy hidden at B, the infants should not err because that would not be the toy-of-the-A-place. It was found that infants were as likely to commit the $A\overline{B}$ error when a different toy was hidden as when the same toy was hidden at B. The investigators concluded that the infants were making a place error, were perhaps treating A as a "toy box" rather than the place of a particular toy. However, one can argue that the infants who saw a new toy placed at B went to A because they were seeking the other toy. While there is no direct evidence for this interpretation, it is not entirely speculative. We have fairly often noted that an infant who has found a toy at A and then found it when it was hidden at B will, with the toy in hand, search at A.

What then is the evidence with respect to what infants have in mind when they remove covers? Charlesworth (1966) has studied what happens when infants between 4 and 12 months of age see a toy hidden, search, and then either find it or discover there is no toy. By 8 months of age, he found that almost all infants consistently show some or all of the following reactions to finding no toy: change in affect, puzzlement, active visual search, and active manual search. This pattern of distress was not shown when the infants found the toy. He concluded that infants have achieved a significant measure of the object concept by the age of 8 months.

Charlesworth's study nicely points out that 8-month-old infants are expecting something to be present. But his study does not indicate what they are expecting (will any object do?), nor does it indicate whether the sight of the toy's disappearance is the reason for their search. Appel and Gratch (1969) faced the latter question. Infants presumably have long histories of pulling off covers and discovering something of interest at times. Perhaps search is a misnomer in these studies, perhaps infants only engage in operant cover-pulling, the object's disappearance only being a diffuse signal to search? Appel and Gratch studied 9- and 12-month-old infants. Half of the infants in each group saw a toy hidden and half of the infants saw "no toy" hidden. The investigators did not know how to cue the infants and so used two strategies. For half of the "no toy" infants, they simulated the hiding sequence with an empty hand. They waved an empty hand, put it in the well, covered it, withdrew it, and showed it to the infants, and then pushed the covered tray toward them. For the other infants, they simply rapped on the front of the covered tray to call their attention to it. There were five trials. The infants who saw a toy hidden searched on all five trials, and the "no toy" infants pushed the box back at the examiner on all five trials. Thus, it is clear that the sight of the toy disappearing is the cue for search.

However, the study introduces a complexity. After the five trials, the conditions were reversed for the next five trials. The results for the 12-month-olds were both straightforward and impressive. The infants who formerly saw "no toy" hidden, now searched on each trial. The infants who formerly saw a toy hidden now refused to take off the cover on all five trials when they saw "no toy" hidden. Thus, the 12-month-olds' search clearly was oriented only to the toy's disappearance. The 9-month-olds who formerly saw "no toy" hidden searched on all five trials when they saw a toy hidden. But the 9-month-olds who now saw "no toy" hidden tended to search for it, and many searched on a second and some on a third trial. Moreover, they were highly attentive while this was going on. Their behavior nicely supports Piaget's notion that Stage IV infants have a very diffuse idea of object disappearances and reappearances, one in which they confuse their actions with the events. However, the result also calls into question the meaning of the Stage IV error. These infants also find a toy at A one or more times. Do they return to A when the toy is hidden at B because the toy is hidden at B or because they are engaged in "operant cover-pulling" at A? Will they recur to A irrespective of whether a toy is hidden at B or not?

Appel compared 9- and 12-month-olds in this regard (1971). Half the infants saw and found a toy hidden at A on five trials and then saw the toy hidden at B. Half the infants had the same experience at A but "no toy" was hidden at B, "no toy" being a rap on the front of the covered B well. In the toy condition, the great majority of the 9-month-olds made the $A\overline{B}$ error whereas, the 12-month-olds did not tend to err. However, in the "no toy" condition, a significantly smaller number of 9-month-olds searched at A. Thus, hiding the toy at B is a cue for the $A\overline{B}$ search of the 9-month-olds.

However, neither the Appel nor the Charlesworth studies specify what the infants are searching for. LeCompte and Gratch (1972) directly addressed this question by having 9-, 12-, and 18-month-old infants find a toy three times in succession in one place. On the fourth trial, the toy was hidden in that place, but the infants found a toy that was grossly different from the first. The second toy was then hidden and found for three trials, and then the trick again was played, the first object now reappearing. In recreating the situation that Tinklepaugh (1928, 1932) used with chimpanzees, the authors were guided by a framework comparable to one developed by Charlesworth (1969) in his analysis of the relationship between level of understanding of a situation and emotional reaction to changes in the situation.

Charlesworth, like Piaget, assumes that one can understand the coming and going of a toy at several levels. The infant can view it as an exemplification of a rule, the entire sequence being a single event covered by the rule "what goes in must come out in the same form" (Piaget's Stage VI). Alternatively, the infant can see the event as an empirical chain, the elements being more or less articulated and more or less probabilistically related. Thus, the infant may note such successive moments as the object in view, the object being covered, the cover, the object being uncovered, and the object in view. In the case of the infant who observes a single event occurring, the trick should elicit surprise, a sudden, intense reaction to the fact that the total event did not develop as expected. In the case of the infant who has a probablistic sense of the relation between the sub-events, the trick may elicit a slowly developing puzzlement, deep (Stage V) or fleeting (Stage IV), as the infant senses that his diffuse expectations have not been confirmed. In other words, such an infant senses that the toy in hand is somehow not the toy that disappeared and the two toys somehow belong together. Finally, the infant may react to the new toy as a novel event, staring widely at the new toy but not being distressed that the old one is not there (Stage III).

LeCompte and Gratch looked to see whether the infants' initial reactions to the appearance of a new object would involve surprise, puzzlement, or novelty. Second, they looked to see what the infants would then do about the event. In keeping with Piaget's analysis of the object concept into stages, they reasoned that a Stage VI infant would set about looking for the missing toy and might seek a cause for the trick in the box or in the experimenter. They expected Stage V and Stage IV infants to be unable to represent the missing object in its absence but to have a strong or somewhat weaker sense that the toy in hand should not be there, e.g., neither to be able to accept it and play with it nor to be able to reject it, to handle it as if it were an "eerie" thing. They expected that Stage III infants would simply take the toy and systematically inspect it and then play with it.

The infants generally supported these hypotheses. The 18-month-olds tended to react initially with surprise or deep puzzlement and then would either combine searching for the missing toy with a systematic looking at the examiner in a questioning manner or would simply search for the missing toy. The 9-month-olds tended to react with mild puzzlement and then would handle the toy in a disoriented manner or they would stare with interest at the toy and then would begin to examine it systematically. The 12-month-olds' reactions tended to fall between those of the 18-month-olds.

The study by LeCompte and Gratch, in conjunction with the studies reviewed in this section, suggest that object-featural information is involved in infants' orientation to disappearing objects by 9 months of age, but it is not until about 18 months that infants can be said to be aware of disappearing objects as opposed to vanishing "pictures" and special places. Moreover, the study opens up a large number of issues that we will now touch upon.

One has to do with whether the 18-month-olds were indeed acting on the basis of such a rule as "what goes in must come out in the same form?" LeCompte and Gratch, and Piaget by implication, want to argue that children who show surprise and seek for the absent toy in fact assimilate the sight of objects into a scheme that has such a notion embedded in it. Further, they want to argue that the infants who fail to act in this way fail because they lack such a scheme. But is their reasoning warranted? Would not the younger infants of their study behave like the older if they simply had observed many more occasions of the particular toy's disappearance and reappearance? In other words, is it not possible to explain the age differences in terms of situation-specific amount of opportunity to experience the disappearance–reappearance contingency? Moreover, would infants manifest comparable reactions if a different type of disappearance–reappearance sequence were used?

The first question can be answered by a relatively straightforward study in which age and number of trials would be varied. The second question, pertaining to type of disappearance, is less straightforward. In raising it, I have two issues in mind. One issue has to do with whether the infants were distressed because the object that disappeared did not reappear or whether they were distressed because the same object that had been "emanating" from the box did not "reemanate?" In other words, implicit in the LeCompte and Gratch argument is the idea that the older children of their study were somehow aware that a rule of nature was violated, not just a rule of a particular experimental situation. But the infants might have been responding to the latter type of rule. The latter alternative can be highlighted by considering the following artificial situation, one that has strong analogies with the situations used in many studies of discrimination learning and infant schema formation, e.g., the work of Cohen and Kagan reviewed elsewhere in this volume. If the infant simply is shown a series of identical covered boxes and is invited to search and if he repeatedly finds a replica of the initial object in each box, how will he react when he ultimately finds a different object? Will he be as distressed as the infants in the LeCompte and Gratch study? Will he seek for the other "toy"? The basis on which the experimenter places toys in the boxes is hidden from the child. If his reactions to this "artificial" situation and the "natural" one employed in the LeCompte and Gratch study are comparable, then doubt will be cast upon Piaget's argument. On the other hand, if the infant shows far less concern in the artificial situation, then there would seem to be reason to believe that the reactions that LeCompte and Gratch found tap something generic about infant object concept development.

The second type of variation on how things disappear and reappear that I have in mind has to do with the Gardner study (1971; see Section IV-B). It will be recalled that Gardner employed a tracking task. Infants simply followed an object moving behind a screen, and at 5 months of age, infants were distressed when a different object appeared from behind the screen. Is it possible that the discrepancy between her results and the findings for 6-month-olds, and those of LeCompte and Gratch, lies in the nature of the two stimulus situations? In both situations, the object follows a trajectory. But the trajectory seems simpler in the Gardner case. The object appears, moves, goes behind a screen, and reappears at the other end of the screen, moves on, and stops. In the case of an object being covered by a cloth, the trajectory is far more complicated. The experimenter takes the object in hand, shows it, moves it to a place, covers the place, the infant must reach for the cover, take it off, look at the object, grasp it, play with it, surrender it to the examiner, etc. Perhaps the discrepancy between the results of the two types of studies can be accounted for in terms of task difficulty? On the other hand, a good deal of evidence has been marshaled in this review that suggests that within each task there should be levels of object awareness. In other words, the suggestion is being made that infants of different ages should be studied in the two tasks in terms of the type of observational system employed by LeCompte and Gratch. Both the perceptual differentiation theory of the Gibsons and Piaget's theory would lead to the prediction that older infants would respond comparably in the two situations because they either have their "eye" on or know the invariant hiding sequence and perceive objects rather than features of objects. On the other hand, younger children should manifest interesting patterns of differential reaction to the two situations, pointing either to a lack of object conception at younger ages or to reasons why possession of such a concept may or may not be deployed in different situations.

Finally, the general approach of LeCompte and Gratch suggests two other ways of exploring the role of featural information in infants' search for objects. In one, proposed by Saal (1973), the focus is upon whether infants primarily use featural information to guide their search or whether such information is used only tacitly? Do infants focus on the particular thing that disappears, note it well, and keep it in mind, or do they primarily focus on the fact of disappearance? If the former hypothesis is correct, then even small, but clearly detectable changes in the object should lead to strong reactions when a trick is played. In fact, some information-processing explanations of object recognition might even predict that the reaction would be stronger when the featural change is small because the infant's initial scan would confirm the object, and the subsequent recognition of the change would be experienced as highly incongruous (e.g., Kagan, 1972). On the other hand, Gibson (1966), Moore (1973), and Piaget would support the second hypothesis. They would expect that the infants would not react as strongly to small changes as to large ones. Such an approach could also be used to evaluate which features of objects become salient as a result of their use. Thus, would color changes in blocks have the same impact for older infants, who have some sense of "blockedness," as for younger infants who do not?

The second has to do with how infants, and children, become aware of the uniqueness of objects. Do they use featural information or do they employ such canons as "a thing cannot be in two places at the same time" and "two things cannot occupy the same place at the same time"? Moore (1973) has argued that infants develop their notion of the permanence and identity of objects through shifting their focus from trajectories to places to abstract rules such as those cited. He argues that object featural information does not play the central role in this course of development. Piaget (1970) has explored the role of logical rules in specifying object identity. In particular, he has employed Michotte's stroboscopic situation, where a red square light source is alternated with a green circular light source. While adults see the red square transformed into a green circle, i.e., "it" changes, children see two distinct events. The trajectural information tells the adults that a single event is occurring, whereas the children apparently rely more on the featural information. The transformation used by LeCompte and Gratch permits the study of comparable issues. Thus, the infants who searched for the missing toy in the presence of the new toy seem to have seen an object exchange rather than an object transformation. On the other hand, were the younger infants, who treated the new toy as an "eerie" thing, experiencing a transformation? What would older children do? DeVries (1969) has explored preschooler's reactions to such changes of objects from a different perspective. In raising these speculations, I strive to highlight the fact that Piaget's approach to the problem of object knowing in infancy raises numbers of issues that are highly relevant to what we mean by knowing an object, issues that have not been the focus of recent research on object perception.

V. CONCLUSION

In this chapter, I have sketched out Piaget's approach to the study of object knowing in infancy, and I have pointed out that current research addressed to his theory is taking five general directions. First, there is a strong psychometric tradition. A number of object concept scales have been developed. The intent is to index the development of representational ability, and these scales have been used to study the effect of such environmental variations as social class upon intellectual development and to study the development of social attachments. A second focus of the literature is on the question of whether very young infants perceive object permanence, whether infants come into the world programmed to be aware of the persistence of occluded objects and/or develop such an awareness on a perceptual rather than a sensorimotor basis. A third focus has been on Piaget's Stage IV error, on how infants come to be able to find an object hidden in one place and whether such an achievement indicates an awareness of object permanence or whether the infant at this point still does not unconfound the nature of the object from his actions on it. A fourth direction, rather more loosely focused than the other lines, has been an attempt to evaluate the role of sensorimotor activity in object search. The fifth focus in the literature has been upon the role of object features, figural perception, in object search.

In evaluating these research directions, I have emphasized the importance of looking at object search as a developmentally complex event. There appear to be developmental shifts in what the infant seeks for and the sense in which he seeks, the mechanisms which underlie his search. Within that framework, I have stressed the need for caution in working with object concept scales because they tend to lead investigators to ignore the complexities involved in drawing inferences about object conception from object search.

Is there a way to neatly characterize the upshot of the work reviewed? I have more or less explicitly suggested that there is not. Smillie (1972), however, has offered such a clarification, one that is both interesting and an alternative to Piaget's view. Citing Bower's evidence on early size–distance constancy and object permanence, he proposes that infants enter the world with object knowledge, and he suggests that the development that Piaget traces is a result of the infants' difficulties in deploying such knowledge. The basic competence is in the infant, the problem of development lies in the identification of such knowledge in practical contexts. This is a line of reasoning that has been applied to the learning of language, and it is an intriguing idea, one that Bower also has espoused. However, the present evidence does not support it. First, we have pointed out that the studies of object permanence by Bower and his associates are inconclusive. Second, an excellent study by McKenzie and Day (1972) seriously calls into question the evidence on size constancy in very young infants that Bower has presented. On the other hand, Gardner's (1971) study of object tracking in infants less than 6 months of age provides more support for the position of Bower and Smillie than it does for that of Piaget.

While Smillie's argument does not appear adequate, it does call attention to a contrast in perspectives and traditions which, I believe, contains the seeds of a better understanding of the issues that Piaget has raised. The traditions are the study of infant object awareness through the delayed response paradigm and through more traditional perceptual paradigms. The perspectives are those of constructivism and radical realism, of Dewey, Mead, and Piaget on the one hand and of J. J. Gibson on the other. The radical realism of Gibson both contrasts with and complements Piaget's perspective, and comparison of these theories can provide the basis for interrelating the disparate traditions of research on intellectual and perceptual processes. Both men, as opposed to psychologists of an empiricist persuasion, find it congenial to talk of knowing the solidity and permanence of objects, the intentions of men, and the causes of events. Both men view Heider's (1958) stress on the "affordableness" of objects as a central problem of object knowing. But where Piaget believes such knowledge derives from the construction of schemes through action on objects, Gibson believes such knowledge is immanent in the events and is detected rather than imposed by the viewer. While Piaget believes the infant in Stage VI directly perceives the continuing existence of an object that disappears, such a perception is possible only because the limited stimulus information is assimilated to a scheme of knowing which adds the necessary information. For Gibson, on the other hand, the stimulus information is complete, the problem of the viewer is to attend to it. For Gibson, the activity of the viewer plays a secondary role. Certain patterns of action may make it more or less likely that the viewer will be in a position to attend to and keep his "eye" on the relevant information, but the activity does not play a constitutive role in object knowing. "The acts of picking up, and reaching with, *reveal* certain facts about objects; they do not create them [J. J. Gibson, 1966, p. 274]."

A virtue of Gibson's position is the support it provides the investigator for making thorough analyses of the ecology of the situations in which they observe the actor. If one is convinced that men can make complex judgments immediately, perceptually, then there must be a stimulus to be discovered which supports the act. The possibilities that are provided by such an approach can be seen in the ingenious analysis that Bower has presented of the various ways in which objects disappear and in Ball's (1973) work on the perception of causality in infancy. Moore's (1969, 1973) analyses of the stimulus conditions that prevail when objects are hidden in Piaget's Stage III and Stage IV tasks open up many possibilities that Piaget's analysis has not suggested. The levels of awareness that LeCompte and Gratch diagnosed in their trick study need to be complemented by a comparable analysis of the stimuli the infants attended to.

However, I believe Gibson is incomplete in a way that reveals the strength of Piaget's approach. Gibson uses the metaphor of the tuner in characterizing how the perceiver detects what is out there. But his account of how the tuner works and how it changes with development so that different levels of reality are detected is not well explained. In emphasizing action, Piaget provides a way of orienting to this process. Piaget describes not so much acts as an actor. His analyses tend to be so compelling because he provides such good descriptions of the actor zeroing in on a problem. His focus is on diagnosing the schemes that underlie and direct the acts and on identifying characteristic styles of acting at different times of life. His theory leads the investigator to focus on the active, questioning child.

Thus, I am arguing that at present the virtue of both Piaget's and Gibson's views lies in the direction they give to studying the infant. We have as yet too little in the way of systematically ordered data about the development of knowing over the course of infancy to decide which of these two, or of other, points of view is the correct one. I have already indicated a number of possible directions for study, and I shall close this chapter by listing some general directions. One is naturalistic description. While Piaget and Uzgiris have made important starts in this direction, there is a dearth of information on such an event as the disappearance and reappearance of objects in home settings, e.g., the types of objects, their routes, their incidence, the ways in which infants orient and cope. Second, attention should be paid to what infants perceive about the "functional" as well as the "figural" nature of objects and of space. For example, Piaget's speculations on the development of size–distance constancy in near as opposed to far space still appear not to have been investigated. Finally, the relation of object search to symbolic play and language warrants more study. Uzgiris has made an important step in this direction within the framework of her observations on imitation. Sigel, Secrist, and Forman (1972) and Slobin (1972) have pointed out some general directions for study in the areas of play and language, Bloom (in preparation) has provided some interesting observations on the relation of infants' object conceptions to when and how they talk about events, and Flavell (1971) has set the stage for examining how the "objective" infant comes to take the perspective of the other on things.

ACKNOWLEDGMENTS

I wish to thank Eric Brown, Güney LeCompte, M. Keith Moore, and Edwin Willems for their helpful comments on the manuscript.

REFERENCES

Appel, K. J. Three studies in object conceptualization: Piaget's sensorimotor stages four and five. Unpublished dissertation, Univ. of Houston, 1971.

Appel, K. J., & Gratch, G. The cue value of objects. Paper presented at the meeting of the Society for Research in Child Development, Santa Monica, California, March, 1969.

Ball, W. A. The perception of causality in the infant. Paper presented at the meeting of the Society for Research in Child Development, Philadelphia, Pennsylvania, 1973.

Bayley, N. Comparison of mental and motor test scores for ages 1–15 months by sex, birth order, race, geographical location, and education of parents. *Child Development*, 1965, *36*, 379–411.

Bell, S. M. The development of the concept of object as related to infant-attachment, *Child Development*, 1970, *41*, 291–311.

Bell, S. M. Early cognitive development and its relationship to infant-mother attachment: A study of disadvantaged Negro infants. Final report, Project No. 508, U.S. Office of Education, 1971.

Birns, B., & Golden, M. Prediction of intellectual performance at three years from infant tests and personality measures. *Merrill-Palmer Quarterly*, 1972, *18*, 53–58.

Birns, B., & Golden, M. The implications of Piaget's theories for contemporary infancy research and education. In M. Schwebel & J. Raph (Eds.), *Application of Piaget theory to education: An inquiry beyond the theory.* New York: Basic, in press.

Bloom, L. Language development review. Draft of a chapter for the *Review of child development research*, Vol. 4, Society for Research in Child Development, in preparation.

Bower, T. G. R. The visual world of infants. *Scientific American*, December 1966, *215*, 80–92.

Bower, T. G. R. The development of object-permanence: Some studies of existence constancy. *Perception and Psychophysics*, 1967, *2*, 411–418.

Bower, T. G. R., Broughton, J. M., & Moore, M. K. Demonstration of intention in the reaching behavior of neonate humans. *Nature*, 1970, *228*, 679–680. (a)

Bower, T. G. R., Broughton, J. M., & Moore, M. K. The coordination of visual and tactual input in infants. *Perception and Psychophysics*, 1970, *8*, 51–53. (b)

Bower, T. G. R., Broughton, J. M., & Moore, M. K. Infant responses to approaching objects: An indicator of response to distal variables. *Perception and Psychophysics*, 1970, *9*, 193–196. (c)

Bower, T. G. R., Broughton, J. M., & Moore, M. K. Development of the object concept as manifested in the tracking behavior of infants between 7 and 20 weeks of age. *Journal of Experimental Child Psychology*, 1971, *11*, 182–193.

Bowlby, J. *Attachment.* New York: Basic, 1969.

Broughton, J. M. The application of Piaget's infant studies to psychometric testing. Unpublished manuscript, Harvard University, 1970.

Charlesworth, W. R. Development of the object concept: A methodological study. Paper presented at the meetings of the American Psychological Association, New York, 1966.

Charlesworth, W. R. The role of surprise in cognitive development. In D. Elkind & J. H. Flavell (Eds.), *Studies in cognitive development.* New York: Oxford, 1969.

Corman, H. H., & Escalona, S. K. Stages of sensorimotor development: A replication study. *Merrill-Palmer Quarterly*, 1969, *15*, 351–361.

Décarie, T. G. *Intelligence and affectivity in early childhood.* New York: International Univ. Press, 1965.

Décarie, T. G. A study of the mental and emotional development of the thalidomide child. In B. M. Foss (Ed.), *Determinants of infant behavior*, Vol. IV. London: Methuen, 1969.

Dennis, W., & Najarian, P. Infant development under environmental handicap. *Psychological Monographs*, 1957, *71*, 1–13.

DeVries, R. Constancy of generic identity in the years three to six. *Monographs of the Society for Research in Child Development*, 1969, Serial No. 127.

Dewey, J. *The quest for certainty.* New York: Capricorn, 1960.

Evans, W. F. The Stage IV error in Piaget's theory of object concept development: An investigation of the role of activity. Unpublished dissertation proposal, Univ. of Houston, 1973.

Evans, W. F., & Gratch, G. The Stage IV error in Piaget's theory of object concept development: Difficulties in object conceptualization or spatial localization? *Child Development*, 1972, *43*, 682–688.

Flavell, J. H. The development of inferences about others. Draft of a paper presented at the Interdisciplinary Conference on Our Knowledge of Persons. State Univ. of New York, Binghamton, New York, 1971.

Fletcher, H. J. The delayed response problem. In A. M. Schrier, H. F. Harlow, & F. Stollnitz (Eds.), *Behavior of nonhuman primates*, Vol. 1. New York: Academic Press, 1965.

Fraiberg, S., Siegel, B. L., & Gibson, R. The role of sound in the search behavior of a blind infant. *Psychoanalytic Study of the Child*, 1966, *21*, 327–357.

Freedman, D. A., Fox-Kolenda, B. J., Margileth, D. A., & Miller, D. H. The development of the use of sound as a guide to affective and cognitive behavior: A two phase process. *Child Development*, 1969, *40*, 1099–1105.

Furth, H. G. *Piaget and knowledge.* Englewood Cliffs, New Jersey: Prentice-Hall, 1969.

Gardner, J. K. The development of object identity in the first six months of human infancy. Paper presented at the meeting of the Society for Research in Child Development, Minneapolis, Minnesota, 1971.

Gibson, E. J. *Principles of perceptual learning and development.* New York: Appleton, 1969.

Gibson, J. J. *The senses considered as perceptual systems.* Boston: Houghton-Mifflin, 1966.

Golden, M., & Birns, B. Social class and cognitive development in infancy. *Merrill-Palmer Quarterly*, 1968, *14*, 139–149.

Golden, M., & Birns, B. Social class, intelligence, and cognitive style in infancy. *Child Development*, 1971, *42*, 2114–2116.

Gratch, G. A study of the relative dominance of vision and touch in six-month old infants. *Child Development*, 1972, *43*, 615–623.

Gratch, G., Appel, K. J., Evans, W. F., LeCompte, G. K., & Wright, N. A. Piaget's

Stage IV object concept error: Evidence of forgetting or object conception? *Child Development,* 1974, *45,* 71–77.

Gratch, G., & Landers, W. F. Stage IV of Piaget's theory of infants' object concepts: A longitudinal study. *Child Development,* 1971, *42,* 359–372.

Harris, P. L. Examination and search in infants. *British Journal of Psychology,* 1971, *62,* 469–473.

Harris, P. L. Perseverative errors in search by young infants. *Child Development,* 1973, *44,* 28–33.

Heider, F. *The psychology of interpersonal relations.* New York: Wiley, 1958.

Hochberg, J. Perception. In J. W. Kling & L. A. Riggs (Eds.), *Woodworth and Schlosberg's experimental psychology* (3rd ed.). New York: Holt, 1971.

Hunter, W. S. The delayed reaction in animals and children. *Behavioral Monographs,* 1913, *2,* No. 1 (Serial No. 6).

Kagan, J. Do infants think? *Scientific American,* March, 1972, *226,* 74–82.

Kuhn, T. S. *The structure of scientific revolutions* (2nd ed.). Chicago: Univ. of Chicago Press, 1970.

Landers, W. F. The effects of different amounts and types of experience on infants' object concepts. Unpublished dissertation, Univ. of Houston, 1968.

Landers, W. F. The effect of differential experience on infants' performance in a Piagetian Stage IV object-concept task. *Developmental Psychology,* 1971, *5,* 48–54.

LeCompte, G. K., & Gratch, G. Violation of a rule as a method of diagnosing infants' level of object concept. *Child Development,* 1972, *43,* 385–396.

Lewis, M., & McGurk, H. Evaluation of infant intelligence. *Science,* 1972, *178,* 1174–1177.

McKenzie, B. E., & Day, R. H. Object distance as a determinant of visual fixation in early infancy. *Science,* 1972, *178,* 1108–1110.

Mead, G. H. *Mind, self & society.* Chicago: Univ. of Chicago Press, 1934.

Miller, D. G., Cohen, L., & Hill, K. A. A methodological investigation of Piaget's theory of object concept development in the sensory motor period. *Journal of Experimental Child Psychology,* 1970, *9,* 59–85.

Moore, M. K. A revision of Piaget's theory of the development of object permanence: A study of infant search for absent objects. Unpublished paper, Harvard Univ. 1969.

Moore, M. K. The genesis of object perception. Unpublished dissertation, Harvard Univ., 1973.

Munn, N. L. *The evolution and growth of behavior.* Boston: Houghton-Mifflin, 1955.

Paraskevopoulos, J., & Hunt, J. McV. Object construction and imitation under different conditions of rearing. *Journal of Genetic Psychology,* 1971, *119,* 301–321.

Piaget, J. *The psychology of intelligence.* New York: Harcourt, Brace, 1950.

Piaget, J. *The origins of intelligence in children.* New York: Norton, 1952.

Piaget, J. *The construction of reality in the child.* New York: Basic, 1954.

Piaget, J. *Six psychological studies.* New York: Random House, 1967.

Piaget, J. *The mechanisms of perception.* New York: Basic, 1969.

Piaget, J. *Psychology and epistemology.* New York: Viking, 1970.

Polanyi, M. *Personal knowledge.* New York: Harper Torchback, 1964.

Roberts, G., & Black, K. N. The effect of naming and object permanence on toy preferences. *Child Development,* 1972, *43,* 858–868.

Saal, D. A comparison of the effects of small and large transformations upon infants' reaction to the violation of object permanence. Unpublished dissertation proposal, Univ. of Houston, 1973.

Schofield, L., & Uzgiris, I. C. Examining behavior and the development of the concept of the object. Paper presented at the meetings of the Society for Research in Child Development, Santa Monica, California, March, 1969.

Serafica, F. C., & Uzgiris, I. C. Infant-mother relationship and object concept. Paper presented at the annual meeting of the American Psychological Association, Washington, D.C., 1971.

Sigel, I. E., Secrist, A., & Forman, G. Psycho-educational intervention beginning at age two: Reflections and outcomes. Paper presented at the second annual Blumberg Symposium on Compensatory Education, Johns Hopkins Univ., 1972.

Slobin, D. I. Seven questions about language development. In P. C. Dodwell (Ed.), *New horizons in psychology*, Vol. 2. Baltimore: Penguin, 1972.

Smillie, D. Piaget's constructionist theory. *Human Development*, 1972, *15*, 171–186.

Tinklepaugh, O. L. An experimental study of representative factors in monkeys. *Journal of Comparative Psychology*, 1928, *8*, 197–236.

Tinklepaugh, O. L. Multiple delayed reaction with chimpanzees and monkeys. *Journal of Comparative Psychology*, 1932, *13*, 207–272.

Uzgiris, I. C. Some antecedents of the object concept. Paper presented at the symposium "the development of the concept of the object" held at the meetings of the Eastern Psychological Association, Philadelphia, Pennsylvania, 1969.

Uzgiris, I. C. Patterns of vocal and gestural imitation in infants. Paper presented at the first symposium of the International Society for the Study of Behavioral Development, Univ. of Nijmegen, Netherlands, 1971.

Uzgiris, I. C. Some observations on early cognitive development. Paper read at the Second Annual Symposium of the Jean Piaget Society, Temple Univ., Philadelphia, Pennsylvania, 1972.

Uzgiris, I. C. Patterns of cognitive development in infancy. *Merrill-Palmer Quarterly*, 1973, *19*, 181–204.

Uzgiris, I. C., & Hunt, J. McV. An instrument for assessing infant psychological development. Mimeographed paper, Psychological Development Laboratory, Univ. of Illinois, 1966.

Wachs, T. D., Uzgiris, I. C., & Hunt, J. McV. Cognitive development in infants of different age levels and from different environmental backgrounds: An explanatory investigation. *Merrill-Palmer Quarterly*, 1971, *17*, 283–317.

Webb, R. A., Massar, B., & Nadolny, T. Information and strategy in the young child's search for hidden objects. *Child Development*, 1972, *43*, 91–104.

chapter 4: Infants' Social Perception: A Constructivist View[1]

MICHAEL LEWIS
Educational Testing Service

JEANNE BROOKS
Educational Testing Service

The study of perception, like any study, is prescribed by one's particular model of the nature of man. Historically two views of human nature have prevailed. In the former, man is viewed as rather passive, an organism being acted upon. Under this model man's perception is controlled by the stimulus, its structure, or its compelling nature. In addition, there is assumed to be a one-to-one correspondence between the stimulus event and man's percepts. Historically this view of man has its roots in the philosophic position that there exists a real world and the function of man's perception is to uncover that world.

There are, of course, alternative views of human nature. These assume a nonpassive organism, one who models his world and who by his action affects his environment. In this position the world of experience is an interaction between something out there—the external world—and man himself. In fact, it is quite difficult to define the external world since it exists only in relationship to man.

[1] This research was supported in part by a National Institute of Mental Health grant 1 RO1 MH24849-01.

Under this view perception is a function of the external world and man's cognitive plans, strategies, and needs.

We shall hold to the latter view of man while recognizing that these two views cannot be easily refuted. Rather than refutation we will accept as given the constructivistic view and seek to account for the empirical data using this particular model. In the present chapter we shall use a constructivistic model—namely that of the self—to argue that social perception in particular is a function of the interaction between the infant's cognitions and its social world.

After presenting the stimulus-oriented, traditional constructivistic, and ethological positions, we will present a theory and data toward a model of the development of the self in infancy. This model will then be used to explain a variety of data on social perception in infancy.

I. ALTERNATIVE PERSPECTIVES

A. Mechanistic Position

One view of perception is that the information within the stimulus is more important than the act of reconstructing the information according to the organism's plans, strategies, and needs. The structure is thought to be in the stimulus, not in the organism. Although the organism may possess structures for uncovering the stimulus properties, these properties reside in the stimulus itself. This view is exemplified by the Gibsons and by ethologists such as Lorenz.

The Gibsons's (E. J. Gibson, 1969; J. J. Gibson, 1963, 1966) view of perception is essentially that of a passive organism absorbing information which is already structured. Although the organism actively seeks and attends to information, he does not structure it himself. "I assume with J. J. Gibson (1966) that there is a structure in the world and structure in the stimulus, and that it is the structure in the stimulus . . . that constitutes information about the world [E. J. Gibson, 1969, pp. 13–14]." Therefore this theory is stimulus-oriented. The organism must discover the invariances present in the environment, even though the environment itself changes. Learning does not occur through a constructivist process, but through the infant's increasing ability to extract information from the environment by learning to differentiate among properties, to distinguish patterns, and to recognize distinctive features. Representations of these distinctive features are stored although the information is not actively reconstructed before processing occurs.

This lack of central activity in organizing and reorganizing sensory input has been criticized. Gyr (1972) summarizes physiological evidence for the self-regulating nature of cognition, stating that both central and peripheral inputs affect one another and cannot be considered separately. The stimulus-oriented nature of the Gibsons's theory is considered inadequate by cognitive theorists such as Neisser (1967). Information not only is extracted from the stimulus but is actively reconstructed. The Gibsons's theory does not define how an internal representation is stored and altered or why a representation (schema) may differ from the original encoded stimulus. The theory is appealing even though simplistic, since it explains the development of perception of the human face, for example, through a differentiation procedure. Facial features are first distinguished, separated, and then combined to differentiate among persons. For Gibson (1969), differentiation precedes the development of a schema instead of following it. The infant has little direct input into the process of constructing a schema for face.

While the Gibson position argues chiefly for the exploration of structural aspects of stimuli which are compelling and which force the organism to attend, there are alternative views which also concentrate on the compelling power of the stimulus.

The innate releasing mechanism (IRM) of the ethological position (see Lorenz, 1965) provides the mechanism wherein a stimulus compels the organism to act. In this case the IRM, through some as yet undisclosed neural system, predisposes the organism to act. Action could be either approach behavior, as in imprinting, or flight behavior to avoid some predator. These actions are necessary for the survival of the species. The neural structures and the fixed action patterns triggered by certain stimulus patterns may be evoked to account for certain infant behavior.

Infants may be predisposed to enjoy and seek out human interaction, as specific human behaviors are most salient and act as IRMs. IRMs may exist both for adult behaviors elicited by the sight or actions of the very young (Hess, 1970) and for infant behaviors elicited by the response patterns of adults (Bowlby, 1969). The circularity of the behavior patterns between an adult and infant might result in rapid discrimination of social and nonsocial events.

In fact, infants are more likely to respond to a moving object than a static one, to a human voice than a nonhuman sound, and to a humanoid pattern or contour than a nonhumanoid one (Bowlby, 1969; McGraw, 1943; Wolff, 1963). If these are predispositions they would obviously be of value for species survival.

Evoking innate releasing mechanisms as an important determiner of social perception provides us with another noncognitive mechanism for describing the infant's behavior. However, these mechanisms do not seem to be supported by the data. While Fantz (1963) originally claimed this function for humanoid patterns—specifically faces—the data indicate that complexity rather than any innate pattern explains early fixation preferences (Gibson, 1969; Hershenson, 1965; Wilcox, 1969).

B. Constructivist Position

The constructivist position holds to the view that perception does not involve an organism passively receiving sensory stimulation. Rather this position holds to a view of man actively seeking stimulation and utilizing it as a function of his individual plans, personality, and cognitive organization. In fact this view states that it is not possible to consider the stimulus event as something defined and existing in and of itself nor behavior as fixed by the nature of the stimulus event. It is an interactive position and as such rejects the notion of a pure sensory event independent of the perceiver, and action independent of the plans, strategies, and motives.

Bartlett (1932) was one of the first proponents of constructivism. He defined a schema as an organized internal structure which is formed by the active process of reconstructing stimulus information. The structures themselves are reorganized because of the interpretation of the incoming information. Structure is defined as originating within the organism, not within the stimulus. Many cognitive theorists have adopted Bartlett's position. Neisser (1967) has elucidated the various processes which occur in perception. Two general processes, the primary and the secondary, are outlined. In the former, stimulus properties are crudely and multiply processed as an object is defined by the incoming stimuli. However, the organism then reorders, directs, and develops the percept. This action is deliberate, as the object is reconstructed on the bases of past experiences, preferences, and expectations (Neisser, 1967).

The information is reconstructed for storage and there is no one-to-one correspondence between the stored material and the stimulus properties.

Piaget also has rejected the notion of a passive copy theory. He espouses growth through the interaction of the organism's internal structures and the external world. Through the processes of assimilation and accommodation, cognitive structures for organizing the world are formed and, by the dual nature of the process, are constantly being reconstructed. With age and experience the structures are altered; the orderly progression of structural change is the focus of genetic epistemology (Piaget, 1952).

The nature of the internal structures is never clearly outlined by Piaget and has been subject to much debate. In infancy research, schema and structure are often used synonymously, even though definitions of schema vary (Lewis & Lee-Painter, 1972). For the purposes of this discussion, schema will be defined as "a relatively persistent organized classification of information, a model which the organism uses in arranging information [Lewis, 1969, p. 84]."

Piaget, although a constructivist, limits the effects of specific environmental experience. He cites four factors that interact to facilitate cognitive development: maturation, equilibrium, the experience of the physical environment, and the action of the social environment (Piaget, 1970). Congruent with his theory, the social and physical characteristics of the environment are only salient when the infant's schema is capable of assimilating them, and therefore are restricted in their influence. However, the theory limits the effects of experience in terms of the existing schema; social experience cannot contribute much to development as the progression of structures is invariant across cultures, social class, situation. Relatively general experience, available to all organisms, provides the material required for knowing. Therefore, experience is necessary even though the structures resulting from organism–environment interaction are invariant. This viewpoint has been considered preformationist by Beilin (1971).

Even though the concept of invariance in structure acquisition may be correct for logical-mathematical knowledge, it may not be for social knowledge. "Piaget has chosen to observe phenomena which are invariant, both with respect to time, place, culture, or specific individual characteristics. Space, time, volume as content and the associated cognitive structures may well be invariant but the structures for logical mathematical phenomena may be different than for those in the social emotional realm [Lewis & Lee-Painter,

1972, pp. 2–3]." If this is so, the concept of invariant structures resulting from social interaction may be questioned. We take the view that the cognitive structure *is* influenced by social interaction; therefore the notion of invariance in structure is called into question even though the invariance in processes (assimilation and accommodation) is not.

We realize that theorists such as Kohlberg (1969) have argued for invariance in social as well as cognitive development and therefore have emphasized the role of general rather than specific experience. In infancy, we have little evidence for the existence of invariant structures for dealing with the social world. Person permanence (Bell, 1970; Décarie, 1965) is the only social concept that has been examined in terms of invariant development, and the results are mixed. The development of person permanence is similar to that of object permanence, although the invariant acquisition of knowledge is not as stable for the former (Bell, 1970). An example of the role of specific experiences in determining schema development might be appropriate. An infant acquires knowledge of his mother through her actions toward him. Since there are consistent differences in mothers' modes of responding (Lewis, 1972; Lewis & Freedle, 1973), the structure for schema of "mother" may be affected. Does the nature of the social experience influence the nature of the schema or is the schema for "mother" similar for all infants? Although the question cannot be answered at the present time, we believe that the environment of the infant plays a greater role in schema development than do those who argue strongly for invariance in structure as well as process. The infant's schema not only interacts with stimulus input, but his resulting structures are affected by the specific social environment encountered.

II. SOCIAL PERCEPTION

In this chapter our attention will be directed toward our interest in social or person perception. Social perception has been defined as "the processes by which man comes to know and to think about other persons, their characteristics, qualities and inner states [Tagiuri, 1969, p. 395]."

Numerous issues are raised in the study of adult social perception. Attention has classically been given to the recognition of various emotions exhibited by others and to the ability of persons to judge others' emotional states (Bruner & Tagiuri, 1954; Darwin, 1965; Tagiuri, 1969). Also the specific cues and categories which are utilized in judging emotion or personality are often analyzed. However, in infancy research the emphasis is somewhat different. Rather than being interested in how a person perceives his own personality or emotions (an epistemologically difficult task), emphasis has been placed on the origins of recognition and differentiation. Recognition involves responding to familiar persons, such as the mother. Differentiation involves responding discriminately between familiar and unfamiliar, such as between mother and stranger.

How does the development of person or social perception differ from that of form or depth perception? Tagiuri (1969) states that social or person perception involves a similarity between the perceived and the perceiver, since both are human. The notion of similarity implies that the organism must know that he is human for social perception to occur. Therefore, the infant must perceive the similarity between himself and others; such a comparison probably involves the developing notion of self, a concept which will be discussed shortly. This position and its elaboration has been developed by Hamlyn (1974). Hamlyn argues that only in *interaction* with other social objects (persons) can we come to understand them: "a . . . condition of our being said to know X is that we understand what kinds of relations can exist between X and ourselves [p. 86]." Indeed, it is in the interaction with adults that the infant first comes to consider itself a social object and at the same time learns the nature of other social objects.

When considering perception, especially social perception, two questions must be asked. First, what unique human characteristics might be important for the development of social perception? This question implies attributes of the perceiver and assumes that the perceiver may not be a passive recipient of stimulation. Very few nonsocial objects in the environment provide consistent and responsive feedback and even objects which *do* provide contingent feedback usually require the organism either to initiate the interaction or to respond in an appropriate or highly stylized manner. Only the self and other persons (sometimes animals, but people, especially children, often think of animals as people) are able to emit a multitude of responses contingent on the situational cues.

Likewise one might ask what are the dimensions of social events as distinguished from nonsocial events? The answer to this must be humanness (form) and responsivity.

A. Dimensionality in Social Perception

Social perception may also differ from other types of perception in terms of stimulus dimensions. Nonsocial perception usually involves the study of the static stimulus properties of the object. The structure of the stimulus event is more likely to be invariant or at least predictable in its changes. Therefore, the infant may be able to extract information from the environment by differentiating properties and recognizing distinctive features. In addition, an experimenter may easily vary or hold constant certain stimulus properties in order to discover their salience and discriminability. Color, shape, size, configuration, and a number of elements may all be varied easily and have been studied extensively. However, the stimulus properties which must be analyzed in social perception are much more complex. To form a schema of "person" from an analysis of single stimulus properties would take much longer than if some underlying organizational property was involved. Infants by 4 weeks appear to have a face–voice schema, hardly likely if the infant has to build element by element (Aronson & Rosenbloom, 1971; Lewis, Townes-Rosenwein, & McGurk, 1974). Properties such as color and shape may be included in larger social categories. At least three social categories involving the stimulus event (in this case, another person) are hypothesized to explain the development of differentiation: familiarity, age, and gender. Obviously, these dimensions often overlap and include more than one salient characteristic. Also, we realize that defining different dimensions does not simplify the process of developing differentiation. Even if these dimensions were easily operationalized, the interaction between the organism and the stimulus event makes it difficult to specify the nature of the stimulus. The perceived event is not merely the stimulus, but involves the situation or context in which the observed person is encountered. For example, weariness may be observed when a stranger approaches, but not when a stranger passes on the street. However, since little work has been done on recognition and differentiation of social objects, we feel these three distinctions provide a beginning point for investigation.

The first social dimension that has been studied extensively involves, first, recognition of the primary caregiver and, second, differentiation between the caregiver and strange social objects. Both indices of familiarity are related to attachment. Usually differentiation is thought to occur after the infant has an internal representation of the mother which serves as a comparison point.

A second characteristic of social objects which may lead to differentiation is age, a factor which has been neglected in infancy research. Few studies have considered infants' reactions to strangers other than adults even though infants' responses to strangers varying in age is much different (Lenssen, 1973; Lewis & Brooks, 1974; Lewis, Young, Brooks, & Michalson, in press). Age subsumes various visual physical characteristics which may be involved in differentiation. Height, facial characteristics, and vocalizations may all provide cues for distinguishing between persons of different ages.

Gender is the third dimension that is hypothesized to provide cues for the infant. Since infants may be socialized differentially as a function of their sex (Brooks & Lewis, 1974; Goldberg & Lewis, 1969; Lewis, 1972; Moss, 1967; Robson, Pederson, & Moss, 1969), the gender category may become salient in differentiating among other social objects. Thus, infants may respond to others as a function of sex. Obviously, some of the characteristics which identify gender are biological, while others are environmental (length of hair, dress).

Dimensions such as age, gender, and familiarity have been postulated to be salient cues for early differentiation since young children seem to describe social objects in terms of features, not emotions. Lévy-Schoen (1964) found that, even though children under 8 years could recognize facial expressions, they did not utilize these cues to form impressions about social objects. Instead, external, physical features are used to categorize (Lévy-Schoen, 1964) and to describe (Watts, 1944) social events by younger children. Since it has been shown that 6- to 8-year-old children use external, physical cues, that infants use familiarity cues to differentiate and describe social events, and that 3-year-olds can correctly identify gender (Kohlberg, 1966), we have hypothesized that age and gender, as well as familiarity, may be relevant dimensions used by the infant to structure his percepts.

B. Dimensions of Social Perception: An Overview

Most research on social perception has studied features of humanoid stimuli (these we shall call social stimuli). Two major theories have generated the research: Cognitive theorists have been interested in schema development while perceptual theorists have concentrated on stimulus dimensions. These two interests often result in similar studies and it would be arbitrary to separate them.

1. SOCIAL VERSUS NONSOCIAL STIMULI

The first question to be raised in the study of social perception deals with the differentiation of social and nonsocial stimuli. At what age do infants first exhibit this differentiation? That human infants prefer social stimuli to nonsocial stimuli is not disputed, although when and how this preference develops is open to study. Evidence regarding the preference for social stimuli in the first month of life is conflicting. Fantz (1963), Fitzgerald (1968), and Stechler and Latz (1966) report that infants younger than 1 month prefer social to nonsocial stimuli, while Fantz (1966), Hershenson (1965), Salzen (1963), Thomas (1965), and Wilcox (1969) report that neonates do not look longer at faces than at other objects, and Spitz and Wolf (1946) found that infants under 20 days of age did not smile at a real face. Thus, the data are unclear as to whether there is a preference for social stimuli in the first month of life. By 2 months of age, it seems clear that infants can differentiate between social and nonsocial objects (Carpenter, 1973; Fantz, 1966; Gibson, 1969). An immobile, unsmiling, and silent real face will elicit a smile from infants by the age of 6 weeks (Ambrose, 1961).

Koopman and Ames (1968) outline three general theories which may be evoked to account for the discrimination of social objects. First, the organism may be innately predisposed to respond to human features (Bowlby, 1969; Spitz & Wolf, 1946). The human face would act as an innate releasing mechanism for increased attention or positive affect. Second, social preference may result from progressive learned differentiations of the physical characteristics of the face (Gibson, 1969). A third theory, which incorporates both ethology and learned differentiation, states that preferences for social stimuli are determined by the physical properties of the face. In fact, movement and contrast seem to be the characteristics which first hold the neonate's attention (Bond, 1972; Fantz, 1966; Haith, 1966; Kagan, 1970; Salapatek & Kessen, 1966) and, of course, the human face amply provides this type of stimulation.

2. DIMENSIONS OF FACES

Having established that infants at very early ages can differentiate between social and nonsocial events, investigators have turned their attention to the dimension of humanoid forms. We have just suggested that movement of stimuli per se and contrast may be important dimensions. There are other social dimensions which have been explored using both attentional and affective responses. When a live face is presented, smiles are most easily elicited by a nodding motion and a voice (Polak, Emde, & Spitz, 1964; Salzen, 1963; Wolff, 1963). It is interesting to note that a high-pitched voice is more effective than a low-pitched one, a characteristic that often differentiates between males and females. The facial characteristic which is most preferred and most easily elicits smiling is the eyes. Eye-to-eye contact elicits smiles by 5 weeks of age (Wolff, 1963). Bergman, Haith, and Mann (1971) have studied scanning patterns of infants viewing a live face. Infants younger than 7 weeks examine high-contrast borders while attention is shifted to the eye section of the face in older infants. The eye scan increases if a human voice is presented with the face. The same eye preference is reported by Donnee (1973) for photographic faces. Ahrens (1954) reports that infants smile more at the eye than at the mouth–nose section, while Wilcox (1969) found no fixation differences for the same comparison. However, Fantz (1963) and Ahrens (1954) found that a dot pattern approximating the eye configuration elicits greater attention than other patterns. Caron, Caron, Caldwell, and Weiss (1973) have attempted to further delineate the salience of various structural features of the face. Using a habituation paradigm, 4- and 5-month-olds were presented with one of 16 distortions of schematic faces. At 4 months of age, the eyes are more salient than the mouth area and facial contour is more salient than inner facial elements. By 5 months, these differences are no longer apparent.

Another question which is studied, although the dimensionality is not specified, is whether infants can discriminate between photographs, line drawings, and live faces. One of the first studies to report differences between representations was made by Polak, Emde, and Spitz (1964); they found that infants between 6 and 8 weeks of age are able to differentiate between a real face and a photograph, so that the real face was smiled at earlier and longer. Ahrens (1954) also found that the 3-month-old prefers a real face to a photograph or line drawing. The 2-month-old prefers a solid over a flat cutout representation of the human face (Fantz, 1965). The 3- and 4-month-old prefers a photograph to a line drawing, in terms of fixation and smiling (Kagan, Henker, Hen-Tov, Levine & Lewis, 1966; Lewis, 1969; Lewis, Kagan, & Kalafat, 1966; Wilcox, 1969). Therefore, it seems that the 3- and 4-month-old infant discriminates among representations in terms of similarity to a real face since the more realistic faces elicit the most smiling and fixation.

Distortion of humanoid form is another area of study. Usually a regular and a scrambled representation of a face or a face with various features missing is presented. In general the data indicate that two- and three-dimensional nondistorted representations of faces are looked at longer than are distorted faces in the 2- to 6-month-old (Fantz, 1965, 1966; Haaf & Bell, 1967; Kagan *et al.*, 1966; Lewis, 1969). This preference for regular representations may be related to congruity and symmetry. Koopman and Ames (1968) presented a schematic, scrambled, and symmetrically scrambled face to 2½-month-old infants and found no fixation differences. In a similar study with older infants, no preference between a regular and symmetrically scrambled face were reported (Wilcox, 1969). Other investigators have found that infants prefer facelike to more complex stimuli (Haaf & Bell, 1967; Kagan & Lewis, 1965). With the exception of Koopman and Ames (1968) and Wilcox (1969), investigators have found that infants under 6 months of age overwhelmingly prefer a regular to a scrambled face. However, this preference seems to diminish in the second 6 months of life (Kagan, 1970; Lewis, 1969). Lewis has explained the shifts in attentional preference in terms of the discrepancy hypothesis, as the older infant, with a highly developed schema of face, becomes interested in moderately discrepant events such as facial distortions.

The research on the perception of faces has shown that the human infant is able to differentiate social from nonsocial objects in the early months, to distinguish between different representations of faces by 2 to 4 months of age, and to differentiate between regular and scrambled faces by 4 months of age. There is little research on more complex discriminations, such as facial expression, sex of stimuli, or familiar versus unfamiliar persons involving representations rather than live people. Only two investigators have compared infants' responses to photographs of a male and female face (Fagan, 1972; Kagan & Lewis, 1965). In a series of studies, Fagan presented 4-, 5-, and 6-month-old infants representations of adult females, adult males, and infants. In general, the 4-month-olds did not discriminate among conditions while the older female infants were able to differentiate between pictures of adults and infants and between male and female adults. When masks rather than pictures were presented, the older male infants were able to discriminate between male and female adults. In the Kagan and Lewis study, 6-month-olds differentiated the male from the female photograph when vocalizations were examined. Of course, differential responding to males and females has consistently been shown in the fear of stranger literature (Benjamin, 1961; Lewis & Brooks, 1974; Morgan & Ricciuti, 1969; Shaffran & Décarie, 1973) To our knowledge, differentiation of familiar from unfamiliar persons in representational form has only been studied by Fitzgerald (1968), who presented pictures of mother and an adult female stranger to 1-, 2-, and 4-month-old infants and measured the autonomic pupillary response. The 4-month-olds discriminated between mother and stranger while the younger infants did not.

Discrimination of facial expressions has been studied by Ahrens (1954), Buhler and Hetzer (1928), Charlesworth and Kreutzer (1973), and Wilcox and Clayton (1968). In the earliest study reported, Buhler and Hetzer (1928) observed 3- to 11-month-old infants' reactions to a positive and a negative face and a positive and a negative voice. By 5 months, infants both discriminate between the positive and negative conditions and respond appropriately. Ahrens (1954) also found that by 5 months infants discriminate between facial expressions presented in schematized form. And, in a recent study by Kreutzer and Charlesworth (1973), angry, sad, happy, and neutral facial expressions (accompanied by the appropriate vocalizations) were acted out by an adult for 4-, 6-, 8-, and 10-month-old infants. The 4-month-olds were the only infants who did not discriminate between the expressions. The older infants not only discriminated but responded with the appropriate affect; for example, the infants expressed more negative affect in the angry and sad conditions. In contrast, two studies did not find discrimination of facial expressions. Spitz and Wolf (1946) only tested 2- to 6-month-olds; presumably the use of an older sample would have yielded results consistent with those reported earlier. Wilcox and Clayton (1968), who measured fixation rather than affect, found that 5-month-old infants could not discriminate between moving and nonmoving pictures of facial expressions. The studies reported earlier measured affect rather than fixation, which may explain the conflicting results.

This brief overview makes clear that only a few dimensions—those relatively molecular—have been studied. No attempt at integration has been made except by E. J. Gibson (1969). However, in any discussion of social perception it is necessary to include a much wider array of social dimensions and situations, for example, studies with live persons rather than representations and the observation of such stimulus dimensions as sex and age. From very early ages the infant appears to have the perceptual capability to differentiate its social world. The task before us is to explore both how and why this differentiation occurs. Without a broader view our conclusions will have to be limited. In the following section we will present three theories to account for differential social perception.

III. THREE THEORIES OF SOCIAL PERCEPTION

Both ethological and cognitive theories have attempted to explain the development of recognition of the familiar and differentiation between familiar and strange. However, no theory adequately accounts for what we now know about infants' social behavior.

A. Ethological

The ethological position uses the mechanisms of biological adaptation and evaluation to explain fear of the strange and attachment to a caregiver. Differentiation of familiar and unfamiliar is necessary for attachment and fear and is thus necessary for survival. Fear, which is the outcome of differentiation, is seen as the homologue of flight in other primates and mammals (Bowlby, 1969; Freedman, 1961). Such fear is adaptive since it strengthens the attachment bond and protects the infant from harmful situations. Therefore, strangeness per se accounts for fear. However, differentiation of familiar and unfamiliar can occur *without* the expression of fear. Infants do not exhibit negative affect to infant or child strangers (Lewis & Brooks, 1974; Lewis *et al.*, in press). Infants are more negative to male than to female adult strangers (Benjamin, 1961; Morgan & Ricciuti, 1969; Shaffran & Décarie, 1973). Therefore, it seems first, that infants do not perceive all strange persons as harmful or frightening and second, that infants are able to distinguish among unfamiliar persons. Other dimensions besides familiarity must be evoked to explain fear of the strange.

The ethological explanation for fear and differentiation also does not account for exploration and curiosity. Infants do not always withdraw from novel stimuli but often explore them. Ainsworth has attempted to reconcile the conflict between exploration and fear, since infants tend to use the mother (familiar) as a secure base for exploration. As long as the infant is able to return to the secure and familiar, the novel will not be perceived as threatening. From a survival viewpoint, a mother who is present is able to control the exploration by avoiding harmful situations.

The ethological viewpoint by itself is too simple an explanation of differentiation. Cognitive processes, which are needed to represent the familiar and unfamiliar, and past experiences with situational context, which are needed to explain specific responses, are not included. Fear is not exhibited toward all strange humans and differentiation among strangers occurs.

B. Incongruity Hypothesis

As the ethological perspective, the incongruity viewpoint deals specifically with the dimension of familiarity–unfamiliarity. An organism is believed to need an internal representation of the familiar in order to perceive a discrepancy. The incongruity hypothesis presupposes differentiation, since differential responses will only occur when a schema of familiar referents exists. The incongruity hypothesis has been used to explain both negative affect to strangers and attention to novel events.

Hebb (1946, 1949) was the first to relate incongruity to affect. Events which are highly discrepant from past experiences tend to evoke negative affect. Three assumptions follow from this statement. First, an internal representation of the familiar is necessary for discrepancy to occur. There will be no negative responses to a stranger unless a central patterning or schema defines the familiar. Second, the familiar schema is used as a comparison figure; the event being perceived is compared to the familiar referent. The familiar comparison figure is usually thought to be the mother (Schaffer, 1966). Therefore there is no differentiation until an attachment to a caregiver is formed (Schaffer, 1966). The attachment leads to recognition and to the formation of a familiar referent. Third, the theory attempts to specify the amount of discrepancy needed for fear to occur. The relationship between affect and discrepancy is thought to be curvilinear. If the incoming event is too similar to the referent, boredom occurs and no affect is exhibited; if the event is too discrepant, no information is processed, distress occurs, and the infant withdraws. However, a moderate degree of mismatch evokes pleasure, as the infant attempts to assimilate the information. However, the amount of incongruity necessary for pleasure is never specified.

The incongruity hypothesis has also been related to attention. Experience with the environment leads to the formation of internal representations which are defined in terms of the distinctive elements of the event (Kagan, 1970). The schema is not constant and changes as more information is processed. Organisms attend to events which are moderately discrepant from the existing schema and ignore familiar events which do not elicit interest and highly discrepant events which cannot be processed. Kagan (1970) presents evidence for the discrepancy hypothesis from observing infants' fixation times to pictures of regular and scrambled faces. The 1-week-old infant looks at the faces and meaningless stimuli for equal amounts of time, while the 4-month-old looks longest at the regular human face. Kagan hypothesizes that the schema for face is just emerging and therefore the picture of the regular face is preferred over the scrambled face. When the schema for face has been established, the scrambled faces elicit the most attention.

However, it is difficult to integrate the affect and attention incongruity hypotheses. Moderately discrepant stimuli could elicit both positive affect and high attention. But how could highly discrepant events elicit fear and little attention? Does fear or inability to assimilate the new information cause the infant not to attend? In order to make the judgment of incongruity, the infant must initially attend to the event. Also, low levels of attending do not always occur when a stranger approaches. We found, as did Morgan and Ricciuti (1969), that infants observe a stranger's approach intently. And only 13% of Schaffer's (1966) infants avoided the gaze of an approaching stranger. In terms of survival, it does not seem prudent to take one's eyes off a threatening (and approaching) social event.

Another problem with the incongruity hypothesis is that it is difficult to predict on an *ad hoc* basis whether an event is similar to or discrepant from a referent. In a naturalistic observation, how can discrepancy be defined? Incongruity has been defined experimentally in studies of nonsocial objects. McCall and Kagan (1967) have presented a standard mobile and then presented variants of the mobile to infants. Presumably, the standard mobile became encoded as familiar and the variations were perceived as discrepant. However, schemas that are developed naturally, such as that of mother, cannot be experimentally manipulated.

It is also difficult to know which referent is being used by an infant in a similar–dissimilar judgment situation. Since infants have many different internal representations, how are we to predict which will be used? Different comparison figures may be used in different situations. For example, I may order my mother, my nephew, and a strange adult female differently. If familial relationship is the comparison, mother and nephew would be judged similar; whereas, if sex is the comparison, mother and strange female would be judged similar. Therefore, the comparison figure and the infant's strategy must be taken into account.

The incongruity hypothesis predicts that the observation of a familiar event will result in withdrawal or in low levels of attending. However, infants enjoy and respond positively to familiar social events, such as mother's approach (Lewis & Brooks, 1974). Thus, familiarity is not the only cognitive dimension, since pleasant associations due to past experience may be evoked by specific persons. In addition, aversions to familiar persons may develop due to distressing experiences. Mothers report that their infants exhibit fear toward certain individuals (Bronson, 1972). For example, a familiar baby-sitter may evoke fear since she is associated with the mother's absence. Therefore familiar persons may evoke positive *or* negative affect contingent on past experience.

The incongruity hypothesis, although appealing, does not adequately explain many differentiations. Discrepancy is not operationalized, past experience is not taken into account, and multiple referents are not considered. However, incongruity does have an import and function, as violation of expectancy results in general arousal (Lewis & Brooks, 1974; Lewis & Goldberg, 1969). Its function is to alert the organism to discrepancies in the environment but not to specify the specific affectual and attentional responses. Whether the infant responds positively or negatively, looks or turns away, depends on the context of the violation and the nature of the infant's cognitive strategy. We still need a dynamic theory to predict the nature of the infant's response. Therefore, we have introduced the concept of self.

C. The Concept of Self

The concept of self has been a major theme in Western thought as evidenced by early Homeric writings (Diggory, 1966). Although Aristotle's questions concerning the soul have given way to speculation on the nature of the ego and the self-concept, the same issues remain. While psychology has continued the theoretical investigation of self, experimentation has received little attention, especially in the area of the early development of self.

The following comments are intended to explore the origins of the self both theoretically and experimentally, since we believe that the notion of self in infancy has been neglected and should be investigated. It is not clear why the study of the infant's schema development has explored highly sophisticated knowledge while at the same time neglecting the infant's schema of self. Indeed, it is difficult logically to conceive of a schema of other without at the same time discussing a schema of self. From our critique of the ethological and incongruity positions, it is obvious that many phenomena in social perception have not been adequately explained by existing theories.

Two aspects of self seem to develop in the first 2 years. The first is the categorical self (I am female, I am big or small, I am capable). The second, and by far the more primitive, is the existential self, I as distinct from other.

1. EXISTENTIAL SELF

The basic notion of existence separate from other (both animate and inanimate) develops as the infant differentiates *self* from other persons. The first social distinction probably involves the mother or caregiver, a position advocated by psychoanalytic theorists (Erikson, 1937; Spitz & Wolf, 1946). This primitive self develops from birth and therefore exists in some form in the early months. In fact, 3- and 4-month-old infants are able to differentiate between mother and female stranger as measured by a variety of infant responses (cardiac deceleration—Banks & Wolfson, 1967; vocalization—Turnure, 1971 and Rebelsky, 1971; wariness—Bronson, 1972; differential reinforcing properties—Wahler, 1967). It is not unreasonable to assume that the self–other differentiation also occurs by this time. In fact, differentiation of self from other may be a precondition for differentiation of other persons.

This nonevaluative, existential self is developed from the consistency, regularity, and contingency of the infant's action and outcome in the world. The mechanism of reafferent feedback provides the first contingency information for the child; therefore the kinesthetic feedback produced by the infant's *own* actions forms the basis for the development of self. For example, each time a certain set of muscles operates (eyes close), it becomes black (cannot see). The action of touching the hot stove and the immediacy of the pain tells me it is my hand that is on the stove. This self is further reinforced if, when I remove my hand, the pain ceases. These kinesthetic systems provide *immediate* and *regular* action–outcome pairings.

Such contingent feedback is also provided by the environment. Infants' interactions with objects provide consistent information (a round object always rolls while a square object does not). In addition, social stimuli (especially the caregiver) provide extensive feedback and are potent reinforcers. First, social reinforcement may be the most effective behavior-shaping mechanism in infancy. Wolff (1963), in his intensive study of infant behavior in the first weeks of life, has found that social stimuli (such as vocalizations and facial movement) elicit smiling responses more readily than do nonsocial stimuli. Social reinforcers (an adult smiling, talking, patting an infant) can also be used to condition smiling (Brackbill, 1958) and vocalizing (Rheingold, Gewirtz, & Ross, 1959) by the age of 3 months. Since social stimuli are such potent reinforcers, it is not surprising that differentiation between familiar and unfamiliar occurs early. The caregiver is the person who provides the bulk of social reinforcement in the first year of life.

Second, the contingency feedback given by the primary caregiver probably provides for generalized expectancies about the infant's control of his world. Such expectancies would also help differentiate the infant's actions from others' actions. The generalized expectancy model (Lewis, 1967; Lewis & Goldberg, 1969) proposes that a mother's responsiveness to her infant's cues determines the infant's expectations. The consistency, timing, and quality of the mother's responses create expectancies about control and competence. If the infant's demands (defined as his behavioral repertoire) are reinforced, he is, in a sense, controlling his environment. Thus, his actions may produce outcomes in the social as well as the kinesthetic realm. Such contingencies should relate to the development of self–other differentiation. Moreover, since self–other interaction always involves the other's relating to a specific locus in space, the interactive nature of self–other should facilitate a schema for self. For example, action by the other directed toward self is always space specific. Thus, not only is there interactive reciprocity in time but reciprocity in space as well.

The development of self may also be related to the general issue of permanence. Permanence deals with the recognition that objects and people exist even when perceptually absent. Self-permanence may exist when the infant is aware that the existence of other objects is not contingent on his presence. That the self is distinct from other environmental events is a necessary condition for later development of self-identity (Guardo & Bohan, 1971)—the concept of self as identity is elucidated by Guardo (1968), who defines self "from the point of view of the experiencer as a phenomenological feeling or sense of self-identity [Guardo, 1968, p. 139]."

The rudiments of object and person permanence have been studied in infancy (Bell, 1970; Piaget, 1952), although self-permanence has not. Object permanence, at least the ability to recover a hidden object, is present by 8 months (Charlesworth, 1968); person permanence follows a similar, often accelerated, pattern of development (Bell, 1970). Person permanence should be more rapid, since persons are more responsive and therefore more compelling than inanimate objects. In fact, person permanence is only more rapid in infants who are securely attached to their mothers (Bell, 1970). If the mother–infant relationship can affect the development of person permanence, it may also be relevant for self-permanence.

If object and person permanence exists by 8 months, it may not be unreasonable to suppose that self-permanence may also exist. In fact we hypothesize that these processes probably occur simultaneously. Thus the early differentiation of self and other should take place at the same time the child is differentiating its mother from others and is acquiring object permanence.

2. CATEGORICAL SELF

The categorical self, which refers to the categories by which the infant defines itself vis-à-vis the external world, is somewhat different. First the categorical self is subject to many changes. Ontogenetically it should change as a function of the child's other cognitive capacities as well as with changing social relationships. The categorical self, then, undergoes a lifelong change. Some categories, like gender, remain fixed; others, like size, strength, and competence, change either by being added to or altered entirely. Historically and socially this categorical self should be expected to change. If this conceptualization is at all valid, it becomes necessary to consider what categories may be available to the infant and how they are altered.

The question of the existential self is not open to confirmation or refutation and is, as such, metascientific. The categorical self, however, is open to refutation and confirmation. Therefore, we have turned our attention to the categories which may be experimentally verified. This is not to ignore the importance of the existential self and its etiology.

One important category which is established early and remains invariant over life is that of gender. Sex may be a salient cue for both recognizing oneself and differentiating others. Therefore, gender identity and gender differentiation are considered complementary processes which develop concurrently.

3. Self-Recognition as a Measure of Self

Self-recognition is only one part of the self-construct, but it is easy to define and to observe. The kinesthetic feedback produced by our actions is continuous and such action–outcome contingencies must theoretically form the basis for self-recognition. However, observing self-recognition experimentally may be more difficult than defining it theoretically. For example, facial recognition should be universal in our society as a result of repeated exposure to mirrors and pictures. The only adults who would have difficulty recognizing their faces visually are psychotic patients and patients suffering from certain central nervous system (CNS) dysfunctions (Cornielson & Arsenian, 1960; Frenkel, 1964). Therefore there is usually a high degree of correspondence between the general concept of self and facial recognition, although we recognize that these two constructs are not synonymous. However, the demonstration of self-recognition may give us insights on the general concept of self. It is to be noted that visual self-recognition is only one aspect of self-recognition, one which in fact may be the last to develop. For example, proprioceptive recognition of self may occur much earlier. This being so, visual self-recognition may not be demonstrable in infants who do in fact already have some self-recognition and concept of self.

The development of self-recognition has not been studied extensively in primates and human infants. The most comprehensive work has been done by Gallup (1970), who observed chimpanzees and rhesus monkeys in front of mirrors. First, Gallup distinguishes between self-directed and other-directed behaviors: "self . . . is the referent through the reflection, where in cases of social behavior the reflection is the referent [1970, p. 86]." Chimpanzees with as little as 10 hr of mirror play are able to groom visually inaccessible parts of their bodies with the use of the mirror. In order to experimentally demonstrate his belief that primates engage in self-recognition, Gallup devised a situation in which he experimentally tests self

versus mirror-directed responses. Red dye was painted on chimpanzees' and rhesus monkeys' ears while they were anesthetized. A
control group also anesthetized received no red dye. When the
primates awoke their mirror behavior was observed. Specifically
observed was whether they reached for the dye by touching the
"mirror ear" or whether they reached for their "own ears." The
experimental chimpanzees reached for their "own ears" while
looking in the mirror. Neither the control nor the rhesus monkeys
showed the reaching for their own ears. This experiment shows that
chimpanzees did not reach for the chimp-in-the-mirror-with-a-
strange-color but instead reached for their own ears. That is, they
recognized the image in the mirror as *their own* and reached for the
strange dye there. By this demonstration Gallup argues that there is
an evolutionary history since primates lower than chimpanzees do
not have the capability to recognize themselves visually, even after
repeated exposures to a mirror. Since chimpanzees are able to
recognize themselves after limited experience with a mirror, it
would not be unreasonable for human infants to also demonstrate
this ability. Infants are not only cognitively sophisticated, but they
spend much time engaging in mirror play. Mothers often report that
their infants enjoy mirror play and that they sometimes use a
mirror to soothe a fussy infant.

Therefore we believe that the study of infants' responses to
mirrors will indicate that visual self-recognition is present from an
early age. Observation of the literature lends strong support to this
belief.

Amsterdam (1969) and Dixon (1957) report that 3- and 4-month-
olds seem to enjoy observing their own movements in a mirror, and
Rheingold (1971) has found that a mirror elicits more smiling than
other social stimuli do.

Gesell (Gesell & Thompson, 1938) gathered normative data on the
development of social responses to the mirror in infants 40–56
weeks of age. By 40 weeks, 61% of Gesell's infants smile and bring
their hands to the mirror although few approach or bring their faces
to the mirror. By 56 weeks, almost three-fourths smile at their
images and over half vocalize, bring hands and face to the mirror,
pat it, and play peek-a-boo with it. Sixty-four percent are also
approaching the image socially, as if it were another infant.
Unfortunately, Gesell does not give us a behavioral definition of
"approaching socially." Dixon (1957), in observing five infants
longitudinally, relates a different sequence of events: At 4–5 months
of age, the infant acts as if the image were another baby. By 6

months, much repetitive activity and staring is observed. At 1 year, there seems to be self-recognition, since the behaviors are directed to the self rather than to the image. Rheingold (1971) also examined the potency of the mirror situation for eliciting smiling. Her 4-month-old infants exhibit more smiling to a mirror image than to a moving picture or a picture of an infant. However, there were no differences in amount of smiling to nonsocial stimuli and to the two social stimuli. She postulates that it is not the *social* nature of the mirror condition which produces the smiling, but it is the contingent feedback of movement producing an observable change.

In the most comprehensive developmental study of responses to a mirror, four infants were observed at each month of age from 3 to 24 months (Amsterdam, 1969). Her sequence of mirror behavior is somewhat different from that of Dixon. From 3 to 6 months, Amsterdam's infants smile at, vocalize to, and touch their images. In the second 6 months, friendly approach was coupled with repetitive activity and deliberate movements, a finding that parallels that of Dixon. However, instead of self-recognition occurring at 1 year, Amsterdam reports that the infants begin to withdraw from the image and actually may attempt to avoid the mirror. By 18 months, self-recognition is evident, as measured by responses directed to the self rather than to the image.

One might infer from the Dixon and Amsterdam data that there are three or four developmental behavioral sequences exhibited by the infant to the mirror. The young infant (3–6 months) responds positively because of the contingency feedback the mirror provides. By the second half of the first year, viewing bodily actions may still provide enjoyable contingency feedback, but the behavior is similar to that exhibited toward another infant. In fact, the infants will sometimes look behind the mirror, presumably searching for the infant (Amsterdam, 1969). Goodall's chimpanzees have also been observed looking behind mirrors. At some point after the first year, Amsterdam reports avoidance and withdrawal, which she hypothesizes is the beginning of self-consciousness. By 18 months, responses are directed to the self rather than to the image (Amsterdam, 1969).

In order to experimentally distinguish between self- and mirror-directed behaviors and to discover the developmental timetable for self-recognition, we have adapted Gallup's situation to human infants. We have observed 96 infants with rouge on their noses in front of a mirror. The rouge was applied by the infants' mothers under the guise of wiping their faces. After the application the infants were brought to a floor-length mirror. None of the 9- and 12-month-olds ($N = 32$), 25% of the 15- and 18-month-olds ($N = 32$), and 75% of the 21- and 24-month-olds ($N = 32$) touched their noses. Amsterdam (1972) reports that mark-directed behaviors first occur at 18 months and are common by 20 months. Thus, the development of self-recognition as measured by self-directed behavior is consistent across two studies and indicates that facial self-recognition exists in many infants by 18 months.

Self-recognition may also be determined by examining infants' responses to photographs and videotape recordings of themselves. We are currently investigating visual recognition by both methods. However, recognition may occur later when the contingency feedback provided by a mirror image is absent. Static and noncontingent representations provided fewer cues and are experienced less often than mirrors.

The mirror data support our hypothesis that by 18 months the infant is capable of recognizing himself. A concept of self exists in the preverbal child and should be studied more extensively in infancy.

IV. FEAR, RESPONSE TO PEOPLE, AND GENDER—HOW THE CONSTRUCT OF SELF EXPLAINS THESE PHENOMENA

Is our understanding of social differentiation and recognition helped by evoking the concept of self? We would argue, yes. We will present data on infants' reactions to self, mother, and strangers which are, in our view, best explained by evoking the concept of self. In addition, studies which support the notion of gender identity will be reviewed in light of construct of self.

A. Infants' Reactions to People

Surprisingly, most of the research on the infants' reactions to people has been chiefly concerned with the phenomena of attachment and fear. Thus, in order to discuss social perception it is necessary to discuss fear.

In general, the social dimensions most studied in fear are familiarity–novelty and gender. It has been well established that the more familiar the social event the less fear or wariness the infant will exhibit. However, most studies only look at mother or father (both familiar) as compared to an unfamiliar social event, a complete stranger. The data for these studies are clear; fear or wariness is elicited by the unfamiliar (for example, Bronson, 1972; Schaffer, 1966). Unfortunately, there have been almost no studies where social familiarity has been varied, for example, between a friend of the family (someone the infant has seen on occasion), the parents, and a complete stranger. Gender differences have been observed as well, male strangers eliciting more fear than female ones (Morgan & Ricciuti, 1969; Shaffran & Décarie, 1973).

Lewis and Brooks (1974) have recently studied infants' responses to a wide variety of social events. Specifically, they were interested in observing the response to five social events: The infant itself (mirror image), the infant's mother, an adult female stranger, an adult male stranger, and a 4-year-old female stranger. Twenty-four subjects, 7 to 19 months old, were seen. The mother, child, female, and male strangers each walked slowly across a room toward the infant smiling and without talking. When they reached the infant they touched its cheek. In the fifth condition the mother rolled the infant, who had been sitting in a movable "Baby Tenda," toward a mirror on the other side of the room. The infant was unable to see the mother in the mirror.

Behind a one-way mirror the infants' facial and motoric expressions were being coded (see Lewis & Brooks, 1974, for full details). Figure 4.1 presents the affect data for each of these five social events. It is clear that the mother and self elicit positive affect. The strange child also elicits positive affect although the strange adults both elicit negative affect. These same results are obtained for infants under 1 year (see Figure 4.2). All of these differences were quite significant. These data are hard to explain. Ethological theory accounts for fear as a function of strangeness per se. This being so, all three strangers should have elicited negative affect.

Incongruity theory might be able to explain these findings on a *post hoc* basis arguing that the strange child was more like the mother than the strange adult female or male. This seems hardly reasonable.

We suggest that the concept of self may explain the results and argue that the strange child was not frightening because the infant evoked the cognition "like me." Therefore, the infant showed positive affect to the strange child as well as to its mother and its own mirror image.

The referent for the social comparison may not always be the infant's mother. There could be multiple referents, one of them

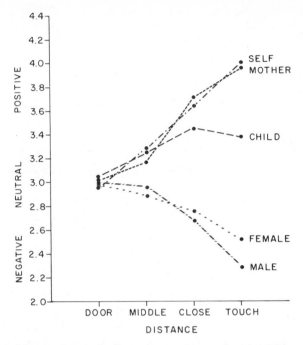

Figure 4.1.   Mean amount of affect expressed toward each of five social events.
[From Lewis & Brooks, 1974.]

being the mother, another being the self. Exactly what category of
self the infant uses to compare the child stranger and itself is not
clear. In this case it may have to do with size or facial configuration.[2]

[2] To see whether size or facial configuration accounted for the child–adult
differentiation, these two physical characteristics were systematically varied by the
use of different sized strangers. We have recently completed a study comparing
infants' reactions to children, adults, and a small adult (midget). Six different persons
including a male and female child, a male and female adult, and a small female adult
who was the same height as the children, each approached 40 infants. The results
indicate that the infants responded as if there were three classes of strangers—children, adults, and small adults. The infants were most likely to exhibit fearful
behaviors (e.g., crying, frowning, and gaze averting) in the presence of the strange
adults and less likely to do so in the presence of the small adult. Negative affect was
never evidenced during the approach of the children. Instead, infants smiled and
reached toward the children but not toward the adults. The most characteristic
response to the small adult was prolonged and concentrated staring with little
movement or affect exhibited. These findings suggest that both size and facial
configuration are used by the infant to categorize his social world.

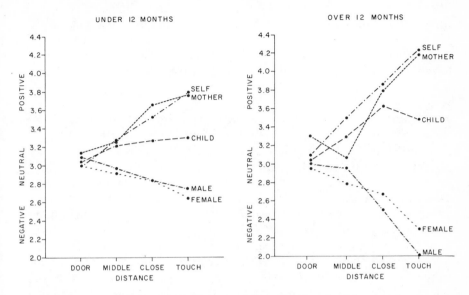

Figure 4.2. Mean amount of affect expressed toward each of five social events as a function of age. [From Lewis & Brooks, 1974.]

B. Infants' Reactions to Pictures of People

We also attempted to study visual self-recognition and person differentiation through pictorial representation. The use of pictures allows us to compare infants' responses to representations of humans and to control for such characteristics as size.

1. SUBJECTS

Twenty-eight male and 25 female Caucasian infants were seen. Infants were divided into four age groups; the mean age, age range, and number of subjects in each group are presented in Table 4.1. The four groups will be referred to as the 10-, 12-, 16-, and 18-month-old groups. Social class composition of the sample was primarily middle and upper middle class, since the majority of the infants had fathers who were professionals or graduate students. Birth announcements in the paper were used to contact subjects; of the mothers asked to participate, only four declined.

2. STIMULUS CONDITIONS

Pictures of 10 persons were presented to each infant. The 10 social stimuli were: (*1*) the mother of the infant, (*2*) the infant himself, (3) a female infant the same age as the subject, (4) a male infant the same age as the subject, (5) a female 5-year-old, (6) a male 5-year-old, (7) a female 10-year-old, (8) a male 10-year-old, (9) a female adult, and (10) a male adult. A week before the experimental sessions 35 mm colored slides of each mother and infant were taken by the experimenters in the infants' homes. Only the head was photographed, and head length of each stimulus person was approximately 6 to 7 inches when projected on a screen in front of the infant. Since, in an earlier study (Lewis & Brooks, 1974), infants responded negatively to adult and positively to child strangers, size or facial configuration differences between adults and children may have been salient distinguishing characteristics for the infants. Therefore, we held head length constant in order to minimize the effect of the size variable. Characteristics such as hair length, hair color, and eye color were not held constant, and the females had longer hair than the males in the pictures of children and adults.

Two different sets of 10 pictures were shown to each infant. The same slides of mother and self were used in both sets. The order of set presentation was counterbalanced, with half the subjects in each age group receiving one set first, the other half the other set first. Six different presentation orders for the 10 slides were used so that eight infants received order 1, eight infants received order 2, and so on.

The slides were projected on a screen approximately 2 feet in front of the infant for 15 sec with a 15-sec intertrial interval between pictures. Viewing time for each set of 10 pictures was approximately 5 min.

TABLE 4.1   AGE AND SEX OF SUBJECTS IN EACH GROUP

Mean age in months	Age range in months	Number of subjects
9.96	9.00–10.77	8 males
		6 females
12.18	11.07–13.07	6 males
		8 females
15.99	14.20–16.96	8 males
		5 females
18.69	17.96–19.43	6 males
		6 females

3. MEASURES

Three experimenters observed each infant and the entire session was videotaped. The observers did not know which order was presented and did not know which stimulus was on the screen (when observing the infant, the observers could not see the screen or the projected picture). One observer recorded eye fixation on the screen, another recorded smile and fret/cry on an event recorder. The third used a checklist similar to the one developed by Lewis and Brooks (1974). The checklist contains three behavioral scales—facial expression, vocalization, and motor activity. Since no negative responses to the pictures were observed, only the positive end of the scale is relevant. For each stimulus condition the infant was given a score for each of the behavioral scales: score of 1 (no response), 2 (slight positive: slight smile, pleasant vocalization, move forward toward the slide), or 3 (very positive: broad smile, laugh, wave, or point at the slide). Since the infant was rated twice for each stimulus condition, the affect scores ranged from 2 (no response) to 6 (very positive response).

4. RELIABILITY

Reliability on the checklist was obtained by comparing the "live" ratings with ratings made from the videotape by another observer. Reliabilities for all 53 subjects were computed by dividing the number of agreements by the number of agreements and disagreements. Reliabilities for the four age groups ranged from .92 to .98.

Although the videotapes were originally to be used only as a reliability check, we felt, as did Ricciuti and Poresky (1972), that an examination of the videotapes would provide more accurate data than the live ratings would. Therefore, two of the three observers viewed the tapes, made judgments independently, and then discussed their ratings to reach a consensus. The affect scores reported here are a result of the consensus ratings.

5. PROCEDURE

A short home visit was made in order to take the pictures of the mother and infant. After the pictures were developed, the infant was scheduled for one visit to the laboratory.

The mother and infant were greeted by one of the experimenters.

The infant was given approximately 5 min to adjust to the unfamiliar setting while the experimenter and the mother discussed the procedure. The following instructions were given:

> You will be sitting a few feet from your infant who will be in a high chair in front of the screen. We would like you to remain quiet during the session unless your infant does not look at a picture. Then, please point to the stimulus and say "look" once. If he does not look, do *not* insist or repeat the instructions. Do not, under any circumstances, indicate recognition of the picture. Do not say "look, there is mommy," etc. If your baby becomes restless or wants to get out of the chair, you may give him a toy (the mother had a choice of two toys, which were relatively uninteresting). After the first ten pictures are shown, we will return to the playroom for five minutes. Then we will go back to view the second ten pictures. Each set of pictures takes approximately five minutes to show, since each picture is projected for 15 seconds and there is a 15-second blank period between pictures. Three observers will be in the room with you. We will be watching your baby through three wire mesh holes. Any questions?

The baby was then taken into the projector room and seated in a high chair directly in front of the screen. Lights were dimmed and the procedure began. After both sets of pictures were shown, the mother was given a short interview.

Three types of responses to the pictures were analyzed: (a) total affect (a combination of the three behavioral ratings), (b) total fixation, and (c) spontaneous verbalizations to each stimulus.

Since there were many comparisons which could be made among the 10 stimulus conditions, we decided *a priori* which we wished to make. Three comparisons, based on our original questions, were examined. (1) Self versus other baby: Responses to the self were compared only to the baby condition, since physical characteristics associated with age (e.g., facial configuration, hair style) are held constant. (2) Mother versus adult stranger: Again, only the age-appropriate comparison was made. (3) Children versus adult strangers: The infants' ability to differentiate between different-aged strangers on the basis of facial configuration and not size cues was also tested.

6. AFFECT SCORES[3]

On the basis of our earlier findings (Lewis & Brooks, 1974), we had expected that the infants would exhibit more positive affect to

---

[3] Overall significance for the affect and fixation measures was tested by a series of repeated measured analyses of variance. Two different analyses, examining different aspects of the stimulus comparisons, were run. In the first, the stimulus condition effect tested the differences among the self, mother, infant, 5-year-old, 10-year-old,

the pictures of mother, self, and baby conditions than to the slides of child and adult strangers. In terms of our three comparisons: (1) The infants did not discriminate between self and other infants in terms of affect. (2) They tended to be more positive toward the pictures of mother than toward the pictures of the adult strangers (although these differences were not significant). (3) They were more positive toward the pictures of the babies than toward the pictures of the older children and the adults. Specifically, the older infants (16- and 18-month-olds) responded more positively to the baby strangers than to the 5-year-olds ($t_{(22)} = 2.51$, $p < .02$), 10-year-olds ($t_{(22)} = 2.76$, $p < .02$), and adults ($t_{(22)} = 2.12$, $p < .05$).

The affect scores are interesting in that no wariness or fear was exhibited by our infants toward the slides of strangers, even though the presence of adult strangers has been shown to elicit negative affect in at least some infants (Bronson, 1972; Lewis & Brooks, 1974; Morgan & Ricciuti, 1969; Scarr & Salapatek, 1970). There are several possible explanations. First, we know that by 3 months of age, infants are able to differentiate a representation of a face from a real face (Polak, Emde, & Spitz, 1964). But differentiation can occur without negative affect. Earlier studies of fixation preferences for nonsocial as well as social representations do not report incidences of negative affect (Kagan & Lewis, 1965; Lewis, 1969). A person is responsive to the infant, while a representation of a person is not. Contingent feedback may be necessary for the elicitation of negative affect. A static representation of a stranger is not threatening since the infant does not expect specific contingent responses. Alternatively, the lack of negative affect may also be related to the absence of movement or approach.

Without a negative end to our affect scale, the discriminative power of the affect measure was reduced. However, it is interesting that static representations of familiar persons, in this case the self and the infant's mother, did not elicit more positive affect than pictures of unfamiliar persons. This was true even though the infants responded differentially to the different-aged strangers,

---

and adult conditions. In the second, the stimulus effect was divided into age of stimulus (baby, 5-year-old, 10-year-old, and adult stranger) and sex of stimulus effects.

When the sample is divided into two age groups (10- to 12- and 16- to 18-month-olds), the main effect of age of subject was significant ($F_{(1, 45)} = 8.71$, $p < .005$). The main effect of stimulus condition was also significant ($F_{(5, 235)} = 2.50$, $p < .03$) as was the age of stimulus effect ($F_{(3, 141)} = 3.34$, $p < .02$). The sex of stimulus effect did not reach significance.

since they were more likely to smile at, vocalize to, and reach toward the pictures of babies than the pictures of the older children and adults.

7. FIXATION SCORES[4]

a. *Age.*   Differences appear when the amount of looking to the 10 conditions is examined (see Table 4.2 and Figure 4.3). Amount of fixation and positive affect increases with age irrespective of stimulus condition.

In general the subjects were divided into a younger group (ages 10 and 12 months) and an older group (ages 16 and 18 months) in that *t* tests failed to distinguish within these groups.

b. *Differential responses to self and other.*   In order to examine the emergence of self-recognition, responses to the self-condition were compared to the baby condition. This comparison was limited to the self-condition–baby condition in that there were no distinctive features which distinguished the two sets of slides other than

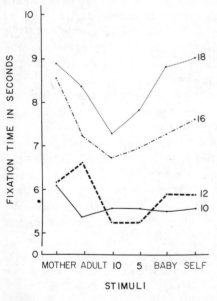

Figure 4.3.   Mean amount of looking time in seconds by age to each of the five classes of stimuli. For adult and 5- and 10-year-old stimuli, male and female slides are combined.

[4] For the total fixation measure, the main effect of age of subject was significant when the sample was divided into two age groups ($F_{(1, 48)} = 15.36$, $p < .001$). All three main stimulus effects were also significant: stimulus ($F_{(5, 250)} = 2.71$, $p < .02$); age of stimulus ($F_{(3, 150)} = 2.50$, $p < .06$); and sex of stimulus ($F_{(1, 50)} = 4.12$, $p < .05$).

TABLE 4.2 MEAN AMOUNT OF FIXATION BY AGE AND BY SEX

Groups by age and sex	Self	Social stimuli												Mother
		Baby females	Baby males	Baby total	5-year females	5-year males	5-year total	10-year females	10-year males	10-year total	Adult females	Adult males	Adult total	
10- and 12-month-old males	5.89	5.75	6.81	6.31	5.98	4.87	5.43	5.78	5.98	5.88	6.02	5.83	5.93	5.85
10- and 12-month-old females	5.57	5.56	4.80	5.07	5.78	5.08	5.40	4.29	5.75	4.89	6.85	5.74	6.14	6.28
10- and 12-month-olds, total	5.73	5.65	5.82	5.69	5.88	4.97	5.41	5.05	5.87	5.38	6.44	5.79	6.03	6.06
16- and 18-month-old males	7.09	6.65	6.63	6.64	7.07	6.37	6.74	6.92	5.96	6.32	6.54	6.41	6.39	7.50
16- and 18-month-old females	9.35	10.18	8.63	9.41	8.68	7.53	8.04	8.18	7.24	7.71	8.87	10.16	9.51	10.08
17- and 18-month-olds, total	8.14	8.21	7.51	7.86	7.80	6.91	7.33	7.48	6.54	6.94	7.57	8.11	7.77	8.64
Males	6.44	6.18	6.72	6.47	6.48	5.56	6.05	6.32	5.97	6.09	6.26	6.10	6.15	6.63
Females	7.18	7.51	6.45	6.86	6.94	6.15	6.52	5.93	6.38	6.05	7.68	7.65	7.53	7.85
Total	6.80	6.81	6.60	6.65	6.72	5.84	6.27	6.14	6.16	6.07	6.94	6.82	6.80	7.21

that one was self and the other not. A comparison of self and any of the other conditions would be unfair since differentiation could take place as a function of some distinctive age feature such as facial configuration or hair style, and would not be due to recognition that this was self or not self. Over all ages and sexes there was no significant differentiation although self was looked at longer than the same-age baby.

The self–other distinction may also be studied in terms of the sex of subject-sex of stimulus interaction. We have suggested that gender is a category of self that probably develops early. If an infant is able both to differentiate others in terms of their sex and to recognize his own gender, then differentiation and preference for same-sex social objects may occur. Preference for the same-sex person would follow the judgment of "like me." While the infants did not distinguish between the pictures of self and other baby, differences appear when the sex of the other baby is considered. Figure 4.4 presents the data for this comparison. The infants look equally long at the self and the same-sex baby but look longer at the self than at the opposite-sex baby (sign test $z = 1.68$, $p < .05$). This effect is most pronounced for the female infants ($p < .02$).

In addition, the infants prefer to look at the same-sex infant more than at the opposite-sex infant. Male infants look longer at male baby pictures while female infants look more at female baby pictures (see Figure 4.5). This interaction was tested by a second-order difference score ($t_{(49)} = 2.68$, $p < .05$). There were no age

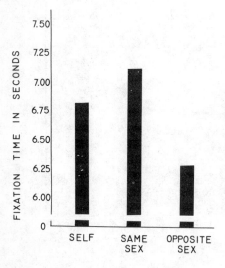

Figure 4.4.   Mean amount of looking time in seconds to self and to same-sex and opposite-sex infants for all subjects. [From Lewis & Brooks, 1974.]

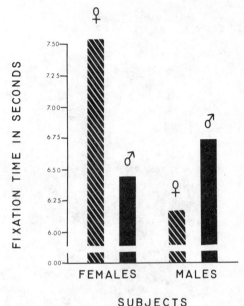

Figure 4.5. Mean amount of looking time in seconds to male and female infants by sex of infant observer. [From Lewis & Brooks, 1974.]

differences although the older group tended to show greater differentiation than the younger one. It is interesting that these sex-of-subject–sex-of-infant-picture interactions were found in all age groups. Recall that each of the four age groups saw a different set of infant pictures (shown in Figure 4.6). Therefore, the fact that the infants looked at the same-sex peers longer than at the opposite-sex ones is not due to a bias in picture selection.

c. *Differentiated responses to mother and adult strangers.* The perception of mother has been widely studied in terms of attachment, learning, and fear. The mother is the first person an infant recognizes and is considered to be a comparison figure for later discriminations (Schaffer, 1966). While there are a few experimental studies which specifically compare the infant's reaction to the mother and a strange adult (the Ainsworth paradigm being the most widely used), there are none using a pictorial form of the mother and strange adult.

As can be seen in Table 4.2, the mother is looked at longer than any other adult social event. The fixation data indicate few significant effects, neither by age nor by sex. The only significant finding is for the older group; mothers are looked at longer than the adult female ($t_{(23)} = 2.68$, $p < .05$).

AGE IN   MALE   FEMALE

MONTHS

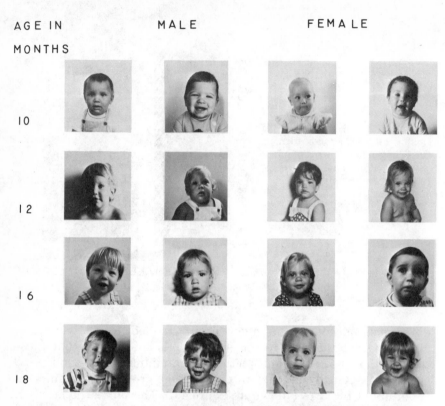

10

12

16

18

Figure 4.6.   Male and female infant strangers across the four age groups.

It is interesting to note the relative lack of differentiation between the mothers and adult strangers. It is clear from the existing literature that infants of this age have no difficulty differentiating their mothers from other adults. Why the failure to find fixation differences? We suggest that several factors play a role in the length of fixation. Fixation responses can serve several functions. We look at something because we enjoy it or we look at it to understand it. Finally we may look at it to make sure it will not harm us. Thus the equal fixation time does not tell us about its function. It seems reasonable to suppose that looking at mother was related to a positive preference strategy while looking at a stranger was related to an information strategy.

d. *Differential responses to children and adults.* In the study reported earlier (Lewis & Brooks, 1974) we found that infants responded differently to child and adult strangers. It was of interest to determine whether infants were capable of differentiating between adults and children when only the face was available. The infants spent more time looking at the adults than at the 5- or 10-year-olds ($t_{(51)}$ = 2.44, $p < .02$ and $t_{(51)}$ = 2.40, $p < .05$, respectively) while the fixation difference between the adults and babies was not significant. As with the other comparisons, the female infants were the ones who showed significant differentiation while the male infants did not.

e. *Differential responses between children.* Infants looked most at babies their own age, then at 5-year-olds, and finally at 10-year-olds. These differences tended to be significant: baby–5-year-old comparison ($t_{(50)}$ = 1.84, $p < .10$); baby–10-year-old ($t_{(23)}$ = 2.18, $p < .05$ for female infants but nonsignificant for the total sample). There were no differences between responses to the 5- and 10-year-olds. In general then there were relatively few fixation differences between the children.

8. VERBAL LABELING OF THE SOCIAL STIMULI

Spontaneous verbalizations to the pictures were noted during the experimental session. Three of the 16-month-olds and eight of the 18-month-olds labeled at least one of the pictures with utterances that could be understood by the observer; the responses are presented in Table 4.3.

Since the older infants labeled the pictures spontaneously, a direct attempt at eliciting verbal labels was part of a follow-up study involving the 12-, 16-, and 18-month-olds. Three months after the original testing, the infants were brought to the laboratory and shown six slides: (1) the mother of the infant, (2) the infant himself, (3) a 9-month-old male, (4) a baby the same age and sex as the infant, (5) an adult female, (6) an adult male. Pictures of the infant were taken a week before the experimental session, and the mother's picture was taken again only if she had changed her hair style or color. The four stranger slides were different from those used in the first session. When the infant was seated in front of the screen, the mother would point at the slide and ask her infant "Who is that?" as each picture was presented. Each slide was on the screen for 15 sec, with a 5-sec intertrial interval. There were three different presentation orders, with a third of the sample receiving each order. The infants' utterances are presented in Table 4.4. Nine

TABLE 4.3 SPONTANEOUS UTTERANCES TO THE TEN STIMULUS CONDITIONS

		Stimulus conditions								
Subjects	Self	Mother	Baby female	Baby male	5-year female	5-year male	10-year female	10-year male	Adult female	Adult male
16-month-olds										
Male	baby									
Female	baby			baby						
Female		mommy								
18-month-olds										
Male	girl		baby			baby				
Male		mommy	girl			baby	girl	mommy	girl	man
Female	Cindy	mommy	baby	baby			baby	baby		daddy
Female		mommy	Cindy	baby				boy	mommies	daddy
Female	girl	mommy		boy	girl	girl	girl	boy	lady	man
Female	baby	mommy		baby	mommy	baby	baby	daddy	mommy	daddy
Female			baby							

TABLE 4.4   ELICITED UTTERANCES TO SIX STIMULUS CONDITIONS

			Stimulus conditions			
Subjects	*Self*	*Mother*	*21-month-old same-sex baby*	*9-month-old male*	*Adult female*	*Adult male*
21-month-olds						
Male		mommy		boy	Carol (aunt)	daddy
Male	me			baby	man, mommy	man, daddy
Male			baby			daddy
Female		mommy	baby	baby		mommy
Female	Cindy	mommy	Christa (friend)	Jeff (brother)		man
Female	Martha, girl					
Female	Erika	mommy	no, not Erika	Erika	lady	a daddy, man
Female						
Female	Christa	mommy	Christa			
19-month-olds						
Male	Erin		baby			
Male			baby			
Female	mamma	mamma	babe		mamma	daddy
Female		mommy	Mary	baby	mommy	daddy
Female		daddy				
Female	Casey	mommy	babe	baby		papa

out of 12 infants 21 months old labeled at least one picture (3 males did not), 6 out of 11 infants 19 months old vocalized (4 males and 1 female did not), and only 3 out of 14 infants 15 months old verbalized (6 males and 5 females did not).

The most striking finding is that the infants who used labels tended to use them correctly, either an appropriate label was given or there was no utterance at all. "Mommy" and "baby" are the first words to be applied to the pictures. There were 14 instances of the correct use of "mommy"; only 1 infant mislabeled the picture of the mother. "Baby" was used to refer to the self-condition and the baby conditions, although 3 infants also labeled the children conditions as "baby." The responses to the self-condition vary from "baby" to "girl" to specific names. Six infants (only one male) uttered their own names when asked "who is that?"; one subject said "me." The 19- and 21-month-olds did *not* label themselves "baby"; either the proper name was uttered or no label was produced. Moreover 11 of the 12 infants who labeled self and/or the same-age baby labeled them differentially. The labeling of the self-condition provides the strongest evidence for the existence of self-recognition; 7 of the 17 infants 19 and 21 months old who verbalized in the elicited condition recognized themselves and gave a proper verbal label; they did not mislabel a same-age and same-sex infant.

Although we had expected the infants to differentiate between the 9-month-old baby and the older infant condition in the second visit, this does not seem to be the case. The adult strangers were frequently labeled, with the label "daddy" being most prevalent for the picture of the adult male. Only three infants used the word "man." Perhaps "daddy" is first used as a general category to include all adult men and is later used to refer specifically to the infant's father. The labels "lady" and "mommy" probably follow the same developmental sequence. One infant distinguished between her mother and the strange adult female by using the singular for the former and the plural for the latter ("mommies").

The verbal labels used by the older infants complement the fixation data. Not surprisingly, the picture of mother was labeled earliest and looked at longest. The "baby" label was applied to both self-pictures and other infant pictures, while the adults were referred to as lady-mommy or man-daddy. However, the labels directed to the pictures of the children were confused. It seems that the 18-month-old infant is able to differentiate between various strangers, although the category of children is most difficult (and also elicits the least visual regard). Self-recognition is also evident, since more than half of the 21-month-olds responded to the self-picture by the appropriate name.

C. Gender Identity–Differentiation

Earlier we hypothesized that one category of the self-construct and that one dimension of social perception was gender. If gender identity develops in the infant, we would expect infants to respond to males and females as a function of their own sex. Interactions between sex of infant and sex of the object are especially important since they reflect both gender identity and gender differentiation.

In attachment behavior exhibited to parents in a low-stress free-play situation, sex differences are evident. When infants are observed with their mothers, the girl infants touch, maintain proximity to, look at, and talk to their mothers more than boys do. This is true for a middle-class sample (Goldberg & Lewis, 1969; Lewis, 1972; Moss, 1967; Moss, Pederson, & Robson, 1969), a lower-class sample (Messer & Lewis, 1972), and a sample of opposite-sex twins (Brooks & Lewis, 1974).

When infants are observed with each parent, sex of parent and sex of infant interactions appear. At 1 year, boys looked more at their fathers and girls looked more at their mothers (Ban & Lewis, 1971). At 2 years of age, girls looked at their mothers more during play while boys looked at their fathers more (Lewis & Weinraub, 1974).

Differential eye regard as a function of the sex of the child and sex of the social object have been observed in two other studies. In the study reported in this chapter, male infants looked longer at pictures of male infants than at female infants, while just the reverse is true for females. And in a study of peer group interaction, where eight sets of four 1-year-old infants and their mothers were observed in a playroom, infants tended to look more at the same sex infant (Lewis *et al.*, in press). Preferences for same-sex playmates have also been observed in dyads and groups of preschoolers (Abel & Sahinkaya, 1962; Langlois, Gottfried, & Seay, 1973).

Distal regard is not the only variable which may give us clues as to the development of gender identification. Labeling behavior was observed in our 16- and 18-month-old infants 3 months after the original testing. Appropriate sex labels were used by nine out of 15 infants 19 and 21 months old in our study of infants' responses to pictures. A few subjects used "girl" and "boy" correctly and nine infants applied "mommy-lady" and "daddy-man" to the adult female and male strangers respectively.

Gender seems to be a salient characteristic in infants' perception since they spontaneously label by sex and look significantly longer at the same-sex infant than at the opposite-sex infant. Infants not only differentiate others by sex, but may also label themselves (Money, Hampson, & Hampson, 1957). In our sample, two infants used the word "girl" when they saw their pictures (self-condition). Perhaps more infants would be able to do so if they had been asked whether they were boys or girls.

V. CONCLUDING COMMENTS

We have argued for the constructivist position in perception. We believe that the organism's plans, strategies, and needs are of primary importance in determining its perceptual experience. This does not imply that we reject the external world or the dimensions of that world. Rather we see perception from a functional point of view, namely to enable the organism to act. Thus, for us, perception must involve both the external world and the constructs of the perceiver in interaction. We reject the model of man as a passive receiver, on a one-to-one basis, of the stimuli imposing on him.

This is not to state that there is no external world or properties of it. If we wish to consider stimulation we would do so from a psychophysical point of view. Using this model we recognize that although a sound may be physically twice as loud as another, subjects may not perceive it twice as loud but only $1\frac{1}{2}$ times as loud. If we are interested in defining stimuli and their dimensions, we think the psychophysical technique an ideal one for scaling the psychological dimensions to physical dimensions. Moreover we recognize that there may be no general transformational function from physical to psychological scales which exists for all subjects. There must exist individual differences based on, among other things, biological needs, plans, and skills.

We adhere to a constructivist position. Thus we have centered our attention on the organism–perceiver side of the issue. Rather than consider in detail the stimulus elements or dimensions which affect social perception we have tried to outline a theory relating to the organism, the function of which should be to guide the organism in constructing its social world. One such theory that has received wide attention is the incongruity theory. As we have pointed out, however, incongruity only has the effect of arousing the organism. The nature of the behavior following this general arousal must be based on the cognitive needs and plans of the organism at that particular time. One such cognition is the infant's concept of self. The acquisition of the self has been considered from two aspects; the first, the *existential self,* the initial differentiation of self from all other; and second, the *categorical self,* or the categories by which we consider ourselves. The first, the *existential self,* may not be open to confirmation or refutation and thus must be considered a metatheory. The *categorical self,* on the other hand, should be open to confirmation and refutation, and it is mostly this aspect of the self which we have suggested is observed when we look at self-recognition. Moreover it is our belief that the *categorical self* undergoes observable ontogenic, cultural, and social changes. It has been our intention to point out just some of these changes.

Unfortunately there are still insufficient data to confirm or refute the theory. We recognize this but at the same time feel that it is necessary to present the view of the organism constructing its perception rather than being solely dependent on the stimulus properties. What is needed is a comprehensive theory of the psychophysical scaling of physical properties and a constructivist view. No theory of social perception will be complete without both.

ACKNOWLEDGMENTS

We wish to thank Susan Lee-Painter for data analysis and Gina Rhea and Marsha Weinraub for data collection on the picture study.

REFERENCES

Abel, H., & Sahinkaya, R. Emergence of sex and race friendship preferences. *Child Development,* 1962, *33,* 939–943.

Ahrens, R. Beitrage zur entwickiung des physiognomie-und mimikericenne's. *Zeitschrift fur experimentelle und angewandte psychologie,* 1954, *2,* 412–454.

Ambrose, J. A. The development of the smiling response in early infancy. In B. M. Foss (Ed.), *Determinants of infant behavior.* New York: Wiley, 1961. Pp. 179–196.

Amsterdam, B. K. Mirror behavior in children under two years of age. Unpublished doctoral dissertation. Chapel Hill, North Carolina: Univ. of North Carolina, 1969.

Amsterdam, B. Mirror self image reactions before age two. *Developmental Psychobiology,* 1972, *5*(4), 297–305.

Aronson, E., & Rosenbloom, S. Space perception in early infancy: Perception within a common auditory–visual space. *Science,* 1971, *172,* 1161–1163.

Ban, P., & Lewis, M. Mothers and fathers, girls and boys: Attachment behavior in the one-year-old. Paper presented at the Eastern Psychological Association meetings, New York, April 1971.

Banks, J. H., & Wolfson, J. H. Differential cardiac response of infants to mother and stranger. Paper presented at the Eastern Psychological Association meetings, Boston, April 1967.

Bartlett, F. C. *Remembering.* Cambridge: Cambridge Univ. Press, 1932.

Beilin, H. The development of physical concepts. In T. Mischel (Ed.), *Cognitive development and epistemology.* New York: Academic Press, 1971. Pp. 85–119.

Bell, S. M. The development of the concept of object as related to infant-mother attachment. *Child Development,* 1970, *41,* 291–311.

Benjamin, J. D. Some developmental observations relating to the theory of anxiety. *Journal of the American Psychoanalytic Association,* 1961, *9,* 652–668.

Bergman, T., Haith, M. M., & Mann, L. Development of eye contact and facial scanning in infants. Paper presented at the Biennial meetings of the Society for Research in Child Development, Minneapolis, April 1971.

Bond, E. K. Perception of form by the human infant. *Psychological Bulletin,* 1972, *77*(4), 225–245.

Bowlby, J. *Attachment and loss,* Vol. I. *Attachment.* New York: Basic Books, 1969.

Brackbill, Y. Extinction of the smiling response in infants as a function of reinforcement schedule. *Child Development*, 1958, *29*, 115–124.

Bronson, G. W. Infants' reactions to unfamiliar persons and novel objects. *Monographs of The Society for Research in Child Development*, 1972, 47(148).

Brooks, J., & Lewis, M. Attachment behavior in thirteen-month-old, opposite sex twins. Paper presented at the Society for Research in Child Development meetings, Philadelphia, March 1973. *Child Development*, 1974, *45*, 243–247.

Bruner, J. S., & Tagiuri, R. The perception of people. In G. Lindzey (Ed.), *Handbook of social psychology*, Vol. 2. Cambridge, Massachusetts: Addison-Wesley, 1954. Pp. 601–633.

Buhler, C., & Hetzer, H. Das erste Verstandnis fur Ausdruck in ersten Lebensjalr. *Zeitschrift für Psychologie*, 1928, *107*, 50–61.

Caron, A. J., Caron, R. F., Caldwell, R. C., & Weiss, S. J. Infant perception of the structural properties of the face. *Developmental Psychology*, 1973, *9*, 385–400.

Carpenter, G. C. Mother–stranger discrimination in the early weeks of life. Paper presented at the Biennial meeting of the Society for Research in Child Development, Philadelphia, March 1973.

Charlesworth, W. R. Cognition in infancy: Where do we stand in the mid-sixties? *Merrill-Palmer Quarterly*, 1968, *14*, 25–46.

Charlesworth, W. R., & Kreutzer, M. A. Facial expressions in infants and children. In P. Ekman (Ed.), *Darwin and facial expression: A century in review.* New York: Academic Press, 1973.

Cornielson, F. S., & Arsenian, I. A study of the responses of psychotic patients to photographic self image experience. *Psychiatric Quarterly*, 1960, *34*, 1–8.

Darwin, C. *The expression of the emotions in man and animals.* Chicago: Univ. of Chicago Press, 1965.

Décarie, T. G. *Intelligence and affectivity in early childhood.* New York: International Univ. Press, 1965.

Diggory, J. C. *Self-evaluation.* New York: Wiley, 1966.

Dixon, J. C. Development of self recognition. *Journal of Genetic Psychology*, 1957, *91*, 251–256.

Donnee, L. H. Infants' developmental scanning patterns to face and nonface stimuli under various auditory conditions. Paper presented at the Biennial meeting of the Society for Research in Child Development, Philadelphia, March-April, 1973.

Erikson, E. H. *Childhood and society.* New York: Norton, 1937.

Fagan, J. F. Infants' recognition memory for faces. *Journal of Experimental Child Psychology*, 1972, *14*, 453–476.

Fantz, R. L. Pattern vision in new born infants. *Science*, 1963, *140*, 296–297.

Fantz, R. L. Visual perception from birth as shown by pattern selectivity. *Annals of the New York Academy of Science*, 1965, *118*, 793–814.

Fantz, R. L. Pattern discrimination and selective attention as determinants of perceptual development from birth. In A. H. Kidd & J. L. Rivoire (Eds.), *Perceptual development in children.* New York: International Univ. Press, 1966.

Fitzgerald, H. E. Autonomic pupillary reflex activity during early infancy and its relation to social and nonsocial visual stimuli. *Journal of Experimental Child Psychology*, 1968, *6*, 470–482.

Freedman, D. G. The infant's fear of strangers and the flight response. *Journal of Child Psychology and Psychiatry*, 1961, *2*, 242–248.

Frenkel, R. E. Psychotherapeutic reconstruction of the traumatic amnesic period by the mirror image projective technique. *Journal of Existentialism*, 1964, *17*, 77–96.

Gallup, G. G. Chimpanzees: Self recognition. *Science*, 1970, *167*, 86–87.

Gesell, A., & Thompson, H. *The psychology of early growth.* New York: Macmillan, 1938.

Gibson, E. J. *Principles of perceptual learning and development.* New York: Appleton, 1969.

Gibson, J. J. The useful dimensions of sensitivity. *American Psychologist*, 1963, *18*, 1–15.

Gibson, J. J. *The senses considered as perceptual systems.* Boston: Houghton Mifflin, 1966.

Goldberg, S., & Lewis, M. Play behavior in the year-old infant: Early sex differences. *Child Development*, 1969, *40*, 21–31.

Guardo, C. J. Self revisited: The sense of self identity. *Journal of Humanistic Psychology*, 1968, *8*, 137–142.

Guardo, C. J., & Bohan, J. B. Development of a sense of self identity in children. *Child Development*, 1971, *42*, 1909–1921.

Gyr, J. W. Is a theory of direct visual perception adequate? *Psychology Bulletin*, 1972, *77*(4), 246–261.

Haaf, R. A., & Bell, R. O. The facial dimension in visual discrimination by human infants. *Child Development*, 1967, *38*, 893–899.

Haith, M. M. The response of the human newborn to visual movement. *Journal of Experimental Child Psychology*, 1966, *3*, 235–243.

Hamlyn, D. W. Person-perception and our understanding of others. In T. Mischel (Ed.), *Understanding other persons.* Totowa, New Jersey: Rowman and Littlefield, 1974. Pp. 1–36.

Hebb, D. O. On the nature of fear. *Psychological Review*, 1946, *53*, 259–276.

Hebb, D. O. *The organization of behavior.* New York: Wiley, 1949.

Hershenson, M. Form perception in the human newborn. Paper presented at the Second Annual Symposium, Center for Visual Science, Univ. of Rochester, June 1965.

Hess, E. H. Ethology and development psychology. In P. Mussen (Ed.), *Carmichael's manual of child psychology*, Vol. I. New York: Wiley, 1970. Pp. 1–38.

Kagan, J. Attention and psychological change in the young child. *Science*, 1970, *170*, 826–832.

Kagan, J., Henker, B., Hen-Tov, A., Levine, J., & Lewis, M. Infants' differential reactions to familiar and distorted faces. *Child Development*, 1966, *37*, 519–532.

Kagan, J., & Lewis, M. Studies of attention in the human infant. *Merrill-Palmer Quarterly*, 1965, *11*, 95–127.

Kohlberg, L. A cognitive-developmental analysis of children's sex-role concepts and attitudes. In E. E. Maccoby (Ed.), *The development of sex differences.* Stanford, California: Stanford Univ. Press, 1966. Pp. 82–173.

Kohlberg, L. Stage and sequence: The cognitive developmental approach to socialization. In D. Goslin (Ed.), *Handbook of socialization theory and research.* Chicago: Rand McNally, 1969. Pp. 347–380.

Koopman, P. R., & Ames, E. W. Infants' preferences for facial arrangements: a failure to replicate. *Child Development*, 1968, *39*, 481–495.

Kreutzer, M. A., & Charlesworth, W. R. Infants' reactions to different expressions of emotions. Paper presented at the meetings of the Society for Research in Child Development, Philadelphia, March 1973.

Langlois, J. H., Gottfried, N. W., & Seay, B. The influence of sex of peer on the social behavior of preschool children. *Developmental Psychology*, 1973, *8*, 93–98.

Lenssen, B. G. Infant's reactions to peer strangers. Unpublished Ph.D. dissertation, Stanford University, 1973.

Lévy-Schoen, A. *L'image d'autrui chez l'enfant*. Paris: Presses Universitaire de France, 1964.

Lewis, M. Mother–infant interaction and cognitive development: A motivational construct. Paper presented at the National Institute of Child Health and Human Development, Symposium on Issues in Human Development, Philadelphia, November 1967. [Also in Victor C. Vaughan (Ed.), *Issues in human development*, pp. 32–38.]

Lewis, M. Infants' responses to facial stimuli during the first year of life. *Developmental Psychology*, 1969, *1* , 75–86.

Lewis, M. Parents and children: Sex-role development. *School Review*, 1972, *80*(2), 229–240.

Lewis, M., & Weinraub, M. Sex of parent × sex of child: Socioemotional development. In R. C. Friedman, R. M. Richard, & R. L. Vande Wiele (Eds.), *Sex differences in behavior*. New York: Wiley, 1974. Pp. 165–189.

Lewis, M., & Brooks, J. Self, other, and fear: Infants' reactions to people. In M. Lewis & L. Rosenblum (Eds.), *Fear: The origins of behavior*, Vol. II. New York: Wiley, 1974.

Lewis, M., & Freedle, R. Mother–infant dyad: The cradle of meaning. In P. Pliner, L. Krames, & T. Alloway (Eds.), *Communication and affect: Language and thought*. New York: Academic Press, 1973.

Lewis, M., & Goldberg, S. Perceptual–cognitive development in infancy: A generalized expectancy model as a function of the mother–infant interaction. *Merrill-Palmer Quarterly*, 1969, *15*(1), 81–100.

Lewis, M., Kagan, J., & Kalafat, J. Patterns of fixation in infants. *Child Development*, 1966, *37*, 331–341.

Lewis, M., & Lee-Painter, S. An infant's interaction with its social world: The origin of meaning. Paper presented at the Canadian Psychological Association meetings, Symposium on parent-child observation studies and their problems, Montreal, June 1972.

Lewis, M., Townes-Rosenwein, L., & McGurk, H. Normal and discrepant face-voice integration in early infancy. Research Bulletin 74-4. Princeton, New Jersey: Educational Testing Service, 1974.

Lewis, M., Young, G., Brooks, J., & Michalson, L. The beginning of friendship. In M. Lewis & L. Rosenblum (Eds.), *Friendship and peer relations: The origins of behavior*, Volume III. New York: Wiley, in press.

Lorenz, K. Z. *Evaluation and the modification of behavior*. Chicago: Univ. of Chicago Press, 1965.

McCall, R. B., & Kagan, J. Attention in the infant: Effects of complexity, contour, perimeter, and familiarity. *Child Development*, 1967, *38*, 939–952.

McGraw, M. B. *The neuromuscular maturation of the human infant*. New York: Columbia Univ. Press, 1943.

Messer, S. B., & Lewis, M. Social class and sex differences in the attachment and play behavior of the one-year-old infant. *Merrill-Palmer Quarterly*, 1972, *18*(4), 295–306.

Money, J., Hampson, J. G., & Hampson, J. L. Imprinting and the establishment of gender role. A. M. A., *Archives of Neurology and Psychology*, 1957, *77*, 333–336.

Morgan, G. A., & Ricciuti, H. N. Infants' responses to strangers during the first year. In B. M. Foss (Ed.), *Determinants of infant behavior*, Vol. IV. London: Methuen Press, 1969.

Moss, H. A. Sex, age, and state as determinants of mother-infant interaction. *Merrill-Palmer Quarterly*, 1967, *13*, 19–36.

Moss, H. A., Pederson, F., & Robson, K. S. Determinants of maternal stimulation of infants and consequences of treatment for later reactions to strangers. *Developmental Psychology*, 1969, *1*, 239–246.

Neisser, U. *Cognitive psychology*. New York: Appleton, 1967.

Piaget, J. *The origins of intelligence in children*. New York: International Univ. Press, 1952.

Piaget, J. Piaget's theory. In P. H. Mussen (Ed.), *Carmichael's manual of child psychology*. New York: Wiley, 1970. Pp. 703–732.

Polak, P. R., Emde, R. N., & Spitz, R. A. The smiling response to human face. II. Visual discrimination and the onset of depth perception. *Journal of Nervous and Mental Disorders*, 1964, *139*, 407–415.

Rebelsky, F. Infants' communication attempts with mother and stranger. Paper presented at the Eastern Psychological Association meetings, New York, April 1971.

Rheingold, H. L. Some visual determinants of smiling in infants. Unpublished Ph.D. dissertation, University of North Carolina, Chapel Hill, 1971.

Rheingold, H. L., Gewirtz, J. L., & Ross, H. W. Social conditioning of vocalizations in the infant. *Journal of Comparative Physiological Psychology*, 1959, *52*, 68–72.

Ricciuti, H. N., & Poresky, R. H. Emotional behavior and development in the first year of life: An analysis of arousal, approach-withdrawal, and affective responses. In A. D. Pick (Ed.), *Minnesota symposia on child psychology*, Vol. 6. Minneapolis, Minnesota: Univ. of Minnesota Press, 1972. Pp. 69–96.

Robson, K. S., Pederson, F. A., & Moss, H. A. Developmental observations of diadic gazing in relation to the fear of strangers and social approach behavior. *Child Development*, 1969, *40*, 619–627.

Salapatek, P., & Kessen, W. Visual scanning of triangles by the newborn. *Journal of Experimental Child Psychology*, 1966, *3*, 113–122.

Salzen, E. A. Visual stimuli eliciting the smiling response in the human infant. *Journal of Genetic Psychology*, 1963, *102*, 51–54.

Scarr, S., & Salapatek, P. Patterns of fear development during infancy. *Merrill-Palmer Quarterly*, 1970, *16*, 53–90.

Schaffer, H. R. The onset of fear of strangers and the incongruity hypothesis. *Journal of Child Psychology and Psychiatry*, 1966, *7*, 95–106.

Shaffran, R., & Décarie, T. G. Short-term stability of infants' responses to strangers. Paper presented at the Society for Research in Child Development meetings, Philadelphia, March–April 1973.

Spitz, R. A., & Wolf, K. M. The smiling response: A contribution to the ontogenesis of social relations. *Genetic Psychology Monographs*, 1946, *34*, 57–125.

Stechler, G., & Latz, E. Some observations on attention and arousal in the human infant. *Journal of the American Academy of Child Psychiatry*, 1966, *5(3)*, 517–525.

Tagiuri, R. Person perception. In G. Lindzen & E. Aronson (Eds.), *The handbook of social psychology*. Reading, Massachusetts: Addison-Wesley, 1969. Pp. 395–449.

Thomas, H. Visual-fixation responses of infants to stimuli of varying complexity. *Child Development*, 1965, *36*, 629–638.

Turnure, C. Response to voice of mother and stranger by babies in the first year. *Developmental Psychology,* 1971, *4,* 182–190.

Wahler, R. Infant social attachments, a reinforcement theory: Interpretation and investigation. *Child Development,* 1967, *38,* 1079–1088.

Watts, A. F. *The language-mental development of children: An essay in educational psychology.* Boston, Massachusetts: Heath, 1944.

Wilcox, B. M. Visual preferences of human infants for representations of the human face. *Journal of Experimental Child Psychology,* 1969, *7,* 10–20.

Wilcox, B. M., & Clayton, F. L. Infant visual fixation on motion pictures of the human face. *Journal of Experimental Child Psychology,* 1968, *6,* 22–32.

Wolff, P. H. Observations on the early development of smiling. In B. M. Foss (Ed.), *Determinants of infant behavior,* Vol. II. New York: Wiley, 1963.

part B: THE DISCRIMINATION
OF SPEECH AND SOUND

chapter 5: Electrophysiological
Correlates of Human
Auditory Development[1]

KURT HECOX[2]
University of California, San Diego

I. INTRODUCTION

Since the early investigations of Preyer (1880), Demetriades (1923), and Aldrich (1928), demonstrating the reduced responsivity[3] of the human infant to auditory signals, little progress has been made in defining the nature of this impairment. One of the newest of the many response measures available to developmentalists is the auditory evoked potential. This chapter will provide a summary of the developmental auditory evoked response literature, with special emphasis on the brainstem evoked response (Jewett & Williston, 1971). A brief review of the developmental anatomy of the auditory pathway has also been included, with the goal of providing a

[1] Preparation of this manuscript was supported by the National Aeronautics and Space Administration grant NGR 05-009-198 and the Sloan Foundation.

[2] Present address: Department of Pediatrics, University of Texas, Southwestern Medical School, Dallas, Texas.

[3] The term *sensitivity* will not be used in this chapter since it implies a psychological measurement based on psychophysical procedures. Instead, the broader term, *responsivity,* will be used, recognizing that any electrophysiological measurement may or may not be directly related to the psychological property of "sensitivity."

framework around which the available physiological and psychological "facts" may be organized.

The chapter begins with a definition of the problem of diminished auditory responsivity, followed by a consideration of those anatomical and physiological factors relevant to the determination of auditory development. The final section describes a set of experiments designed to further refine our understanding of the nature of the human infant's auditory impairment. The unifying theme behind this chapter is that the nature of auditory development cannot be understood apart from the unfolding of those anatomical structures responsible for its occurrence.

II. STATEMENT OF THE PROBLEM

An infant's ability to respond to auditory signals is limited in comparison to adults. For example, startle (Suzuki, Kamijo, and Kiuchi, 1964; Stubbs, 1934), respiration rate changes (Barnet & Goodwin, 1965), auropalpebral reflexes (Wedenberg, 1956), and heart rate measures (Steinschneider, Lipton, and Richmond, 1966) all show that infants exhibit elevated auditory thresholds. A comparison of the studies cited shows that the amount by which thresholds are elevated is a function of both the response measure and the type of stimulus employed. Any such comparisons are of only limited value, however, because of the general lack of concern for stimulus control and complete reporting procedures. The interaction of response and sensory variables in the determination of behavioral performance is a familiar issue in adult psychophysics. Special mathematical and experimental techniques have been devised to separate the relative contributions of sensory and nonsensory factors (Green & Swets, 1966; Swets, 1964). However, nowhere is the interaction of response and sensory factors better illustrated than in developmental psychoacoustics. Both motor and integrative functions of the infant are undergoing rapid changes, at the same time as the limits of his sensory capacities are expanding. Methodologies, at least as sophisticated as signal detection procedures (Green & Swets, 1966), will be required before the role played by "purely" sensory variables in determining auditory development can be evaluated behaviorally.

An alternative means of obtaining "pure" sensory measures is to directly record electrophysiological responses originating from afferent structures. The availability of such techniques (Jewett,

Romano, and Williston, 1970; Picton and Hillyard, 1974; Sohmer and Feinmesser, 1973; Yoshie, 1968) circumvents the need for special mathematical procedures to separate afferent from efferent contributions. The use of these physiological measures translates the behavioral problem into a search for the anatomical locus of and physiological mechanisms responsible for the infants' diminished auditory capabilities. These are the problems to be considered in the following sections.

III. DEVELOPMENTAL ANATOMY OF THE AUDITORY PATHWAY

This section deals with certain anatomical and physiological facts that relate to the auditory responsivity of the human infant. The aim is to cite those structural aspects of the development of the auditory pathway that may contribute to age-related changes in responsivity. Where possible, human data will be used, although evidence from animal studies is cited when it illustrates a general property of mammalian auditory development. The description proceeds, in order, from the external conductive apparatus through the inner ear into the brainstem neural structures that lead to the cortex.

A. External and Middle Ear

The external auditory apparatus serves to conduct sound waves from the external atmosphere to the fluid medium of the inner ear (Figure 5.1). To avoid the considerable energy loss as a consequence of the impedance mismatch between the inner ear fluid and the surrounding atmosphere the middle ear serves as an impedance matching device. The two middle ear mechanisms operating to overcome the energy loss are the lever properties of the ossicular chain and the ratio of the area of the tympanic membrane to that of the stapes footplate. The ratio of tympanic membrane area to that of the footplate of the stapes accounts for most of the 30-dB gain provided by middle ear mechanisms (Wever & Lawrence, 1950).

Any alteration in the transfer efficiency of the ossicular chain, whether due to residual mesenchymal tissue in the middle ear cavity or relative changes in the areas of the tympanic membrane or stapes footplate, could serve to elevate electrophysiological or behavioral thresholds.

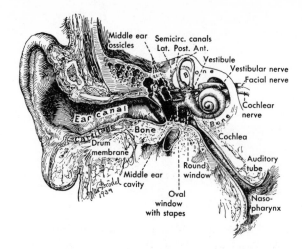

Figure 5.1.   The external, middle, and internal ear. [From Brödel, 1946.]

An additional factor in considering structural effects of the external auditory apparatus is the introduction of resonant frequencies in both the middle and external ear cavities. The dominant frequency in the latter is about 3000 Hz while the middle ear has two resonant peaks, at 1200 Hz and 800 Hz (Littler, 1965). The effect of dimensional changes in the external cavities as a function of age would be to alter these resonance characteristics. A shorter external auditory meatus, for example, would produce higher resonance frequencies, thus producing a shift from the sensitivity–frequency relationship exhibited by adults.

Thus the transfer characteristics of the external auditory apparatus are intimately related to the anatomical maturation of its constituent structures. It is to these maturational variables that we now turn our attention.

The embryological origins of the external and middle ear structures are extremely complex, and will be treated only briefly. A more detailed account of their formation can be found in Streeter (1906, 1918) and Bast and Anson (1949).

Briefly, the external auditory meatus originates from the first pharyngeal cleft by an invagination that reaches the primitive tympanic cavity (future middle ear cavity) at the fetal age of 5 weeks. Its invagination begins by the third week and continues postnatally through puberty (Ballenger, 1969), at which time it reaches the adult dimensions of 2.4 to 2.7 cm (Bezold, 1882). While the tympanic membrane does not attain its adult position and size until about 12 months postpartum (Ballenger, 1969), the stapedial footplate reaches adult dimensions by birth (Bast & Anson, 1949). The auricle, or pinna, appears during the sixth week, grows rapidly through infancy with continued growth into adolescence. The middle ear cavity and associated eustachian tube are of endodermal origin. They begin as outpouchings of the primitive pharynx (4 weeks) and continue to elongate throughout intrauterine life and early childhood (Bast & Anson, 1949).

The middle ear ossicles appear at approximately 7 weeks as a thickening in the mesenchymal tissue rostral to the primitive tympanic cavity (Figure 5.2, parts a–d). All three bones reach terminal size by 6 to 8 months, while their rigidity and transmission properties attain maturity by birth (Kirikae, 1960).

To summarize, the adult dimensions of the external auditory canal, the tympanic membrane, and middle ear cavity are not reached until at least 1 year postpartum. By contrast, the ossicular chain and stapedial footplate area have reached adult proportions by 6 to 8 months after gestation, and the transfer efficiency of the ossicles appears to be mature by birth (Kirikae, 1960). There is insufficient information on the relative areas of the tympanic membrane and stapes footplate as a function of age to evaluate its contribution to developmental changes in the middle ear transfer function. The development of "impedance audiometry" (Lilly, 1972) has provided direct measures of some of the impedance properties of the middle ear. Impedance audiometry (Keith, 1973) shows that the compliance of the tympanic membrane in newborns is high compared to that of adults. Any change in the compliance of the tympanic membrane will affect the transfer efficiency of the middle ear by selectively attenuating some frequencies. The amount of attenuation and the frequency dependency associated with these values of compliance are not known. A second dependent variable used in impedance audiometry is the impedance change accompanying the elicitation of the acoustic reflex. In a series of newborns, Robertson, Peterson, and Lamb (1968) found a 5- to 10-dB threshold elevation of the acoustic reflex threshold, as a function of frequency. These results argue against the existence of a conductive impairment greater than the observed 5 to 10 dB, but do not rule out the possibility of a greater sensorineural impairment (Metz, 1952). Robertson's results do not support the commonly held notion that there is a 30- to 40-dB conductive impairment due to the persistence of mesenchymal tissue in the middle ear cavity of the newborn.

Thus we conclude that developmental changes in the dimensional

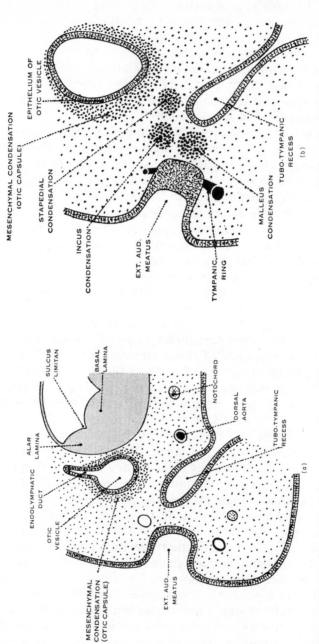

Figure 5.2 (a)–(d). Four stages in the development of the infant middle ear. [From Hamilton, W. J., Boyd, J. D., & Mossman, H. W. *Human embryology*, 3rd ed. Baltimore, Maryland: Williams & Wilkins, 1962.]

(b)

MESENCHYMAL CONDENSATION (OTIC CAPSULE)

EPITHELIUM OF OTIC VESICLE

STAPEDIAL CONDENSATION

INCUS CONDENSATION

EXT. AUD. MEATUS

TYMPANIC RING

MALLEUS CONDENSATION

TUBO-TYMPANIC RECESS

(a)

SULCUS LIMITAN

BASAL LAMINA

ALAR LAMINA

ENDOLYMPHATIC DUCT

OTIC VESICLE

MESENCHYMAL CONDENSATION (OTIC CAPSULE)

EXT. AUD. MEATUS

NOTOCHORD

DORSAL AORTA

TUBO-TYMPANIC RECESS

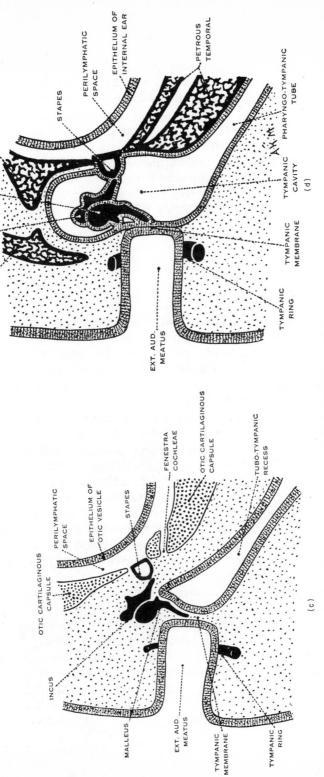

Figure 5.2 (continued)

characteristics of the external and middle ear cavities must produce shifts in resonance characteristics and consequently alter the frequency dependency of the middle ear transfer function; the impedance matching properties of the middle ear must also be altered to some extent by the changing ratio of the tympanic membrane and stapedial footplate areas and the elevated compliance of the tympanic membrane. Direct measurements suggest, however, that these anatomical considerations may account for no more than a 10-dB conductive loss in sensitivity. The possibility of a greater sensorineural recruiting type of loss remains unevaluated.

B. Inner Ear

1. Cochlear Function

The function of the inner ear is to faithfully transform stapedial footplate movements into auditory nerve discharges. The sensory receptor cells of the ear are called hair cells, so named for the cilia-like structures protruding from their superior surface. Attached to the base of the four to six rows of hair cells are the afferent and efferent fibers of the auditory nerve. The precise mechanism by which the nerve is activated is not known, although it appears that shearing forces developed by the differential movement of tectorial and basilar membranes produce mechanical displacements of hair cell structures. This mechanical disturbance is then somehow transmitted to the afferent ending at the inferior surface of the hair cell. The vibration pattern of the basilar membrane and its dependence on signal characteristics, hydrodynamics of inner ear fluid, and the stiffness of cochlear partition were the subject of the elegant experiments by von Bekesy. The reader is referred to von Bekesy (1960) or Tonndorf (1970) for more detailed expositions of cochlear mechanics.

The importance of the structural specialization within the organ of Corti, illustrated by the differences in innervation patterns of inner and outer hair cells, is undetermined. One current hypothesis is that outer hair cells provide high-sensitivity, low-threshold information, while inner hair cells mediate suprathreshold phenomena (Portmann & Aran, 1971; Davis, 1973). However, general theories on the encoding of frequency, intensity, and localization are absent. Perhaps by the careful documentation of developmental changes in inner ear morphology and its relationship to the onset of auditory function, we may obtain additional insight into the structure–function relationships of the auditory periphery.

2. COCHLEAR DEVELOPMENT

The inner ear is composed of several morphologically and functionally distinguishable elements (Figure 5.3). In this section we will review the development of only those elements whose principal function relates to the transduction of acoustical signals. More exhaustive descriptions of human inner ear development can be found in Streeter (1906, 1918), Retzius (1884), and Bast and Anson (1949).

The inner ear begins as a thickening of the surface ectoderm in the region of the primitive hindbrain. These thickenings—auditory placodes—invaginate to form successively the otic pit and then the otic vesicle, which loses contact with the external surroundings at the end of the fourth week (Figure 5.4). The otic vesicle, or otocyst, then divides into a dorsal portion from which the utricle, semicircular canals, and endolymphatic duct develop, and a ventral portion

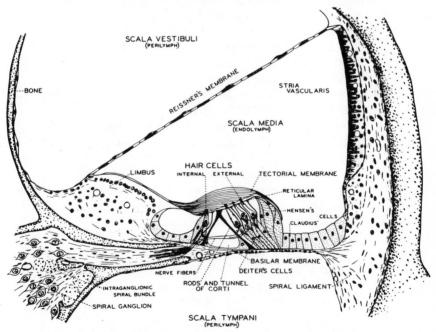

Figure 5.3. Cross section of the cochlear canal of a guinea pig. [From Davis *et al.* Acoustic trauma in the guinea pig. *Journal of the Acoustical Society of America,* 1953, *25.*]

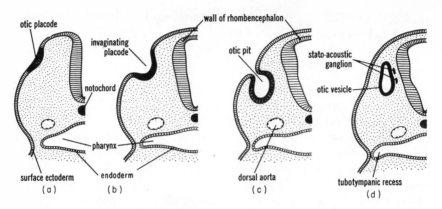

Figure 5.4. Transverse section through the rhinencephalic region showing the gradual formation of the otic vesicle: (a) at 22 days; (b) at 24 days; (c) at 27 days; (d) at 4½ weeks. [From Langman, J. *Medical embryology.* Baltimore, Maryland: Williams & Wilkins, 1963.]

from which the saccule and cochlear duct are derived. The cochlear duct is formed as an outpouching of the lower pole of the saccule during the sixth week, its first spiral forming within a few days and the full two and one-half turns being completed by the tenth week. The size of the cochlea continues to increase beyond this time, reaching adult dimensions by the fifth month. The mesenchymal tissue surrounding the membranous labyrinth condenses to form the scala tympani and scala vestibuli, during the tenth week, in a base-to-apex direction. The perilymphatic spaces (Figure 5.5) attain adult dimensions during intrauterine life (Bast & Anson, 1949).

The transduction of the fluid pressure waves of the inner ear into neural activity requires the presence of shearing forces generated by the differential movement of the tectorial and basilar membranes. The size of these shearing forces will certainly depend upon the mobility of both the basilar and tectorial membranes, their respective mechanical response properties, and the geometric relationship between them and the mediating hair cells. The little information available on the mobility and geometry of these structures suggests that no major changes occur postnatally, but existing descriptions are insufficiently detailed to make definitive statements on the matter. The possibility that changes in the mechanical response characteristics of either the basilar or the tectorial membrane may be responsible for shifts in sensitivity or changes in frequency–sensitivity functions remains unevaluated, despite the availability of techniques for its determination (von Bekesy, 1960; Johnstone & Boyle, 1967).

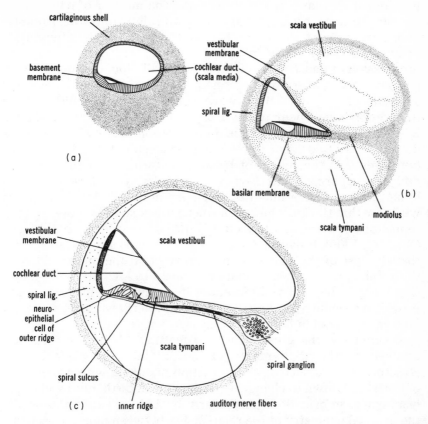

Figure 5.5   Schematic representation of the development of the scala tympani and scala vestibuli. (a) The cochlear duct is surrounded by a fibrous basement membrane and a cartilaginous shell. (b) During the tenth week, large perilymphatic spaces appear in the cartilaginous shell. (c) The cochlear duct (scala media) is separated from the scale tympani and scala vestibuli by the basilar and vestibular membranes respectively. On its lateral aspect it is connected to the bony cochlea by the spiral ligament. Note the auditory nerve fibers and spiral ganglion. [From Langman, J. *Medical embryology*. Baltimore, Maryland: Williams & Wilkins, 1963.]

The sensory receptor cells (hair cells) develop from the outer ridge of neuroepithelial cells lining the cochlear duct. First apparent by the twenty-second week as distinguishable inner and outer hair cells, their differentiation proceeds from base to apex, although their final mitoses are in the opposite direction (Ruben, 1967).

Most of the available information on the timetable of human hair cell maturation can be found in a 1968 monograph by Bredberg, in which he makes the following observations: (*1*) Inner hair cells mature earlier than outer hair cells. (2) The number of hair cells in the newborn nearly equals those of an adult, only the irregular outermost row of the outer hair cells continues to differentiate postnatally, particularly in apical regions. (3) The base to apex progression of hair cell development typically found in mammalian cochleas was generally confirmed, although there was a small segment of the most basalward region of the cochlea whose maturation lagged behind that of adjacent regions of the basal turn. Bredberg indicates that this final observation is at odds with other descriptions of cochlear development (Streeter, 1906; Sher, 1971), but notes that the region of basal immaturity is technically very difficult to approach and therefore has probably not been examined in most cases. Concerning the development of intracochlear spaces we know that the internal spiral sulcus, the spaces of Nuel, and the tunnel of Corti are well formed by birth, at least in the basal turns (Streeter, 1906). It has also been noted in several subhuman species that the last of the hair cells to mature lie in the outermost row, those cells presumed to mediate responses to low intensity signals (Bredberg, 1968). This observation, if extended to humans might provide a specific hypothesis to account for a threshold elevation, if any, encountered in human infants.

In summary, the gross structural features of the inner ear are attained by the sixth month of intrauterine life. While certain structural details such as the formation of spaces within the organ of Corti are known to change up to the time of birth, until additional histological information, particularly on hair cell maturation and the detailed geometry of the relationship between hair cell tectorial membrane and basilar membrane becomes available, and the mechanical response properties of the basilar and tectorial membrane have been determined, the role played by cochlear structural immaturity in determining the reduced responsivity exhibited by infants will remain undetermined. The only gross features which could account for postnatal changes in responsivity are the development of the outermost row of hair cells and the maturation of the most basalward portion of the cochlea.

C.   The Eighth Nerve

1.   AUDITORY NERVE FUNCTION

The human auditory nerve consists of nearly 30,000 fibers whose peripheral extensions reach the lower surface of the hair cells and whose central terminations distribute throughout the various divisions of the cochlear nucleus. The function of the eighth nerve is to transmit information on the time–space pattern of basilar membrane motion to the central nervous system. This information must be sufficiently precise to permit accurate auditory discriminations of signal direction, loudness, and pitch, yet operate over a wide dynamic range. Much of our knowledge concerning the age at which the auditory nerve attains structural maturity depends upon physiological criteria. That is, structural maturity is inferred from functional maturity. To appreciate the limitations of this logic we must keep in mind the structural elements involved in the generation of the criterion responses.

Measures of auditory nerve activity may be divided into two types—single fiber and whole nerve responses. Since there are no human developmental studies of single unit functioning, and few from any other mammals, we will focus on the properties of the whole nerve action potential. In 1962, Teas, Eldredge, and Davis demonstrated that basal turn fibers are responsible for the generation of the compound action potential. This is due to the superior synchronization of firings arising from the basal region, where the traveling wave velocity and innervation density are greatest. Thus, whole nerve responses give us only a partial view of auditory nerve fiber activity, that of the high frequency basal region. In the same study, Teas *et al.* showed that the more intense a stimulus the more basal were the fibers producing the response. Thus latency shifts, as a function of intensity, reflect differences in traveling wave delays in addition to decreased neural delays. The developmentalist must keep clear the distinction between these sources of latency change —mechanical and neural—if he is to properly interpret the decreasing latency known to occur with maturation. The neural structural changes that may account for latency shifts are multiple—growth in fiber diameter, progressive myelination, and increased dendritic arborization are all candidates. At the subcellular level changes in the time required to reach spike-initiating levels could also produce latency shifts. Thus, latency values, which have been used so effectively to estimate the sensation level of a stimulus for adults, may bear a complex relationship to signal intensity as a function of age. Likewise response amplitude shows such considerable individual differences, in addition to being influenced by all of the previously mentioned factors, that it may be an ever poorer correlate of sensitivity.

Any morphological description of the auditory nerve must include its distribution within the cochlea. Nearly 90% of the afferent fibers terminate on the single row of inner hair cells, while the outer three or four rows receive only 10% of the afferent innervation. The efferent system shows the reverse pattern, its fibers ending primarily on outer hair cells. The functional significance of this dual innervation pattern remains unknown (Spoendlin, 1966).

The relationship between the degree of myelination, nerve fiber diameter, dendritic arborization, or innervation pattern and the processes underlying responsivity changes is obscure. Thus, we must simply catalog the structural differences distinguishing the infant auditory nerve from its adult counterpart, hoping eventually to demonstrate or eliminate the possibility that the altered responsivity exhibited by the human infant may be due to immaturity of the auditory nerve.

2. AUDITORY NERVE DEVELOPMENT

The tissue of origin of the eighth nerve ganglion (spiral ganglion) has been a matter of considerable debate. Current evidence indicates that the cochlear division of the stato-acoustic ganglia is derived from cells of the auditory vesicle (Yntema, 1937). These cells are distinguishable as the spiral ganglia by the fourth week and begin invading the cochlear duct tissue at the same time, even before the sensory receptor cells have emerged (Bredberg, 1968; Pujol & Hilding, 1973). The invasion of auditory nerve fibers proceeds from base to apex in the same sequence as does hair cell development (Streeter, 1906).

The age at which the number of fibers attains adult values, and the age dependency of the fiber diameters, has not yet been determined. Most accounts of human innervation pattern show that auditory nerve fibers can be identified even before the differentiation of hair cells (Bredberg, 1968); yet, attempts to quantify innervation density or degree of dendritic arborization, as a function of age, do not exist.

There are numerous accounts of cranial nerve myelination, some entirely qualitative, others more quantitative (Yakovlev & Lecours, 1967; Flechsig, 1920). Myelination appears to begin in the human fetus at the 30-cm stage (Bechterew, 1885) and most descriptions propose that eighth nerve myelination is completed by birth. The importance of myelination is that myelinated fibers conduct more rapidly than unmyelinated fibers; this increased conduction velocity results in decreased latencies (Bunge, 1968).

It is interesting to note that efferent fibers are the last neural elements to assume their adult configuration in several mammalian species (Pujol & Hilding, 1973). This observation has not yet been extended to human material.

The relation between the onset of auditory functioning and histological development has been the subject of investigation in several mammalian species (Pujol & Marty, 1970; Alford & Ruben, 1967). The story emerging from these descriptions is that the eighth nerve is capable of responding even before the anatomical development of the cochlea has reached the functional stage (Marty & Thomas, 1963). Peripheral transducer maturation lags behind the development of the neural elements.

Thus, we are left with a very incomplete picture of auditory nerve development. It emerges early, completes its proliferative activity rapidly, and is "well" myelinated in the human newborn; quantitative descriptions of these and other structural aspects of auditory nerve development are absent, however. This lack of information is particularly unfortunate since electrophysiological measures of eighth nerve functioning have become relatively simple to obtain, which affords an excellent opportunity to make morphological–physiological correlations.

D. Brainstem

1. BRAINSTEM FUNCTION

The brainstem auditory pathway consists of a series of relay nuclei and tracts from the cochlear nucleus at the pontomedullary junction to the medial geniculate body of the thalamus (Figure 5.6). The neuroanatomy of this region is complex with its ipsilateral and contralateral afferent inputs, internuncial neurons, descending efferent system, and fibers decussating at nearly every level of the brainstem.

It is probably not reasonable to speak of a unitary function of the brainstem, nor for any of its constituent nuclei. There is extraordinary heterogeneity of response patterns within each of the nuclei, as determined by single unit studies in subhuman species (Boudreau & Tsuchitani, 1973; Whitfield, 1967). One of the few commonalities between nuclei is the tonotopic arrangement of fibers (Galambos, 1954; Whitfield, 1967).

The functional distinctiveness of the brainstem auditory centers can be inferred from the selective impairment of auditory behavior

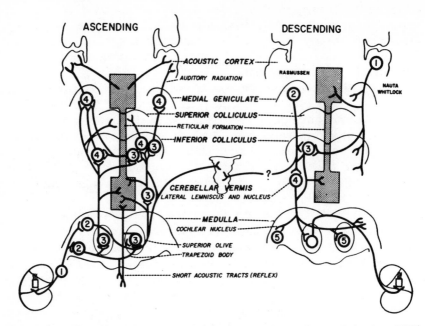

Figure 5.6.   Ascending and descending auditory pathway. [From Galambos, 1958. By permission of *Laryngoscope*.]

as a function of the structure which is lesioned (Diamond & Neff, 1957; Raab & Ades, 1946) and from studies in which cells of a particular nucleus seem especially well suited for the analysis of restricted acoustical aspects of auditory signals (Galambos, Schwartzkopff, & Rupert, 1959; Gersuni, 1971). While it is probably safe to assume the species generality of functional specialization of subcortical centers, the assignment of specific functions to individual nuclei in humans, on the basis of results obtained from subhuman species would ignore the possibility of "encephalization" of function. Thus, we must admit virtual ignorance of the specific role played by each of the human brainstem auditory nuclei.

The effect of brainstem lesions on auditory sensitivity has been investigated in a series of experiments with cats (Meyer & Woolsey, 1952). In general, the unilateral destruction of auditory tracts at any anatomical level, results in no more than 3-dB changes in sensitivity. Human clinical data also suggest that extensive bilateral pathology must be present before appreciable changes in sensitivity become apparent (Jerger, Weikers, Sharbrough, & Jerger, 1969).

The surgical inaccessibility of brainstem auditory centers, the anatomical complexity of their interrelationships, and until recently the absence of suitable neurophysiological measures of its electrical activity in humans have resulted in only fragmentary information on auditory brainstem functioning. As newer and more sophisticated means of measuring subcortical electrical activity are developed, our understanding of the neurophysiological mechanisms of auditory signal processing will surely advance.

2. BRAINSTEM DEVELOPMENT

There is very little information on the developmental anatomy of the human brainstem auditory pathways, particularly when compared to that available on cochlear development.

The major relay nuclei emerge in an orderly sequence, the cochlear nucleus appearing first at the 13-mm stage, the superior olive emerging within the next few days, the lemniscal fibers reaching the inferior colliculus by the 37-mm stage, and the medial geniculate appearing in the 30-mm embryo (Cooper, 1948). The medial geniculate bodies originate from the thalamus, while the other nuclei and tracts are derived from the caudal extensions of the alar plates. No systematic brainstem fiber or cell count as a function of age could be located. Even if such data existed, the relationship of changes in fiber and cell counts to the development of adult responsivity is obscure at best. Adequate data do exist to demonstrate that at least the most rostral portions of the brainstem are not mature with respect to cellularity or intercellular organization until some time after birth (Rorke & Riggs, 1969).

One aspect of brainstem development which has been the subject of numerous investigations is the time course of myelination. There is near unanimity concerning the caudorostral progression of myelination and the fact that the structures of the lower brainstem are "well" myelinated before birth (Langworthy, 1933; Flechsig, 1920; Yakovlev & Lecours, 1967). A more recent report by Rorke and Riggs (1969) suggests that myelination of the inferior colliculus and medial geniculate is not completed by birth. The functional implication of incomplete myelination is that conduction velocity is slower, resulting in prolonged response latencies. We do not possess sufficiently detailed histological information on the degree of myelination to determine its role in producing age-dependent latency changes.

Since there are no models of auditory development whose confirmation requires anatomical information, the paucity of data on the development of subcortical auditory structures is understandable. This lack of theoretical motivation, coupled with the relative inaccessibility of brainstem structures, and the difficulties in obtaining human histological material, have led to the current situation in which no structural–functional correlations of auditory development can be made at the level of the brainstem.

E. Cortex

1. CORTICAL FUNCTION

The primary cortical reception area for audition is the transverse temporal gyrus, or Heschl's gyrus. This "projection" area is surrounded by the so-called auditory "association" areas, whose anatomical limits are broad and ill-defined. Since destruction of the projection area results in impairment of auditory behavior unlike that seen when lesions are confined to association areas, we conclude that these two regions do not perform identical functions (Masterton & Diamond, 1973).

While the general functions of the auditory cortex are to elaborate incoming auditory sensations, integrate those sensations with other prior or concurrent experiences, ultimately resulting in stimulus appropriate response patterns, the specific mechanisms responsible for language processing are currently attracting much attention from both psychologists and physiologists. Two physiological observations relevant to the neuroanatomy of language processing are: (1) Cells responsive exclusively to acoustically complex signals are more frequently encountered the more cephalad the structures from which recordings are obtained (Worden & Galambos, 1972). (2) Left cerebral hemisphere lesions exert more profound effects on language behavior than do similar lesions of the right hemisphere (Gazzaniga, 1970; Mountcastle, 1962). We may infer from these observations that if there are anatomical centers specifically responsible for the processing of complex signals such as language sounds, they probably reside in the cerebral cortex and, in the case of language, the left cerebral cortex.

While it is possible to seek specific anatomical information on hemispheric differences, the relation between developmental changes in cortical histology and the emergence of adult responsivity is not at all apparent. Until we have clearer notions of the neurophysiological basis of auditory responsivity, we can only catalog some of the more striking age-related differences and place the timing of cortical development in relation to the maturation of more caudally located structures.

2. CORTICAL DEVELOPMENT

The cortical reception area of audition is part of the neopallium (neocortex), so named for its late emergence in phylogenetic history. The first signs of neocortical proliferative activity and migration are seen in the 2-month embryo, continuing until the seventh month when the fetal cortex has the six-layered appearance typical of an adult. While there is no postnatal proliferative activity, differentiation and migration of young neurons continues for several years after birth. The most exhaustive accounts of the postnatal changes of the human cortex were made by J. L. Conel. A number of important facts emerge from Conel's observations: (1) The earliest temporal lobe fibers to mature are the primary projection fibers from the pars principalis of the medial geniculate. (2) The number of projection fibers (or any other fiber type) does not increase postnatally, although the axonal and dendritic lengths and diameters do increase for several years after birth. (3) The myelination of projection fibers is sparse at birth, and is virtually completed by 4 years of age, while the myelination of intracortical fibers continues into adolescence. (4) With respect to hemispheric differences, in reference to the brains of 6-year-olds, Conel states that, "No significant differences have been observed . . . between the two hemispheres of any one brain according to all of the criteria." The myelination and fiber growth descriptions of Conel agree with those of earlier investigators, but hemispheric histological differences have been demonstrated recently by Witelson and Pallie (1973). In both neonates and adults Witelson and Pallie were able to demonstrate linear and areal differences in the planum temporale of the temporal lobe.

Thus the auditory cortex presents in a very immature state at birth. Only layers V and VI appear to have reached the functional stage, although they too will undergo considerable histological changes during the early years of life. The prolonged latency and diminished amplitude of the newborn cortical evoked response provides a striking physiological correlate of this structural immaturity. However, little that is definitive can be said about the influence of cortical postnatal structural changes on the altered responsivity exhibited by the human infant.

F. Summary

There is little reason to believe that the human infant or newborn has significantly reduced auditory sensitivity of peripheral origin. Middle ear and external auditory canal changes, as a function of age can account for no more than a 10-dB reduction in responsivity while the extent to which changes in neural elements might contribute to altered responsivity is unclear. The only suggestion that developmental changes in the cochlea might account for altered responsivity is Bredberg's (1968) finding that the most basalward portion of the cochlea may not be mature at birth, and that the outermost row of hair cells is not completed by birth.

The frequently noted evoked potential latency changes as a function of age, may be due in part to changes in the effective sensation level of the stimulus secondary to the previously cited peripheral mechanisms. Additional processes that may contribute to latency changes are myelination of the fiber paths, increased fiber diameters, or purely peripheral changes in cochlear responsiveness. The evidence on developmental changes in myelination indicates that not until the level of the inferior colliculus are immature myelination patterns evident in the newborn. Perhaps the most striking fact to emerge in the comparison of neuroanatomical changes along the auditory pathway is that the more caudal the anatomical level, the greater is the histological maturity. The most cephalad structures of the cortex are the last to reach structural maturity.

IV. ELECTROPHYSIOLOGICAL DEVELOPMENT
OF THE AUDITORY PATHWAY

This section reviews current electrophysiological measures of human auditory functioning, from the cochlear microphonic response (mechanical) to the most rostrally generated cortical evoked neural response. Results of these measures will be organized around three dependent variables—response latency, amplitude, and threshold—all of which have been used to index developmental changes in the auditory system. The discussion will parallel the anatomy of the afferent auditory system, proceeding from the periphery to the most rostrally generated responses.

A. Cochlear Microphonic

There are no available data on developmental changes in the human cochlear microphonic response, although techniques do exist for its measurement (Terkildsen, Osterhammel, & Husin't Veld, 1973).

B. Auditory Nerve

Information concerning the functioning of the human eighth nerve as measured by the whole nerve action potential has been elicited using "surgical" (Portmann & Aran, 1971), "nonsurgical" (Yoshie, 1968; Coats & Dickey, 1970), and surface electrode recording techniques (Sohmer & Feinmesser, 1967). Several results are common to all of these procedures: (1) It is possible to elicit reliable recordings in most infants and newborns (Portmann & Aran, 1971; Liebermann, Sohmer, & Szabo, 1973). (2) These responses exhibit longer latencies, diminished amplitudes, and elevated thresholds when compared to responses obtained from adults. (3) Infant responses display increased latency and decreased amplitudes in responses to decreases in stimulus intensity, these functions being essentially similar to those found in adults. Basic information on fatiguability, effect of rise–fall times, frequency specificity, and masking properties as a function of age has not yet been obtained. The previously cited studies have employed click stimuli, presented from one to 10 times per sec. We were unable to locate systematic estimates of infant or newborn thresholds as a function of age for the "nonsurgical" or "surgical" techniques, although Portmann, Aran, and LaGourque (1973) do show normal threshold responses from infants as young as 10 months. Threshold estimates based upon surface electrode recordings have demonstrated 10-dB threshold differences between adults and newborns, this difference disappearing sometime during the first year of life (Liebermann, Sohmer, & Szabo, 1973). This last study is somewhat difficult to interpret since response records included eighth nerve and brainstem evoked responses, and the authors did not specify which of the response components were being used to estimate thresholds.

Thus, the meager data available indicate that infant eighth nerve action potentials exhibit prolonged latencies, diminished amplitudes, and elevated thresholds. These responses attain adult values sometime during the first year of life.

C. Brainstem Evoked Responses

The most recently described components of the auditory evoked potential are the brainstem evoked responses (Jewett & Williston, 1971). These potentials apparently reflect the activation of the auditory nerve and successive brainstem auditory nuclei and tracts. Like the eighth nerve action potential, here designated as wave I in a series of at least five waves, these responses are sensitive to a variety of acoustic parameters including rise-time, intensity, repetition rate, and frequency (Figure 5.7). These responses appear to represent "onset responses" since they are sensitive to signal rise-time, insensitive to signal fall-time, and do not exhibit temporal integration (Hecox, Squires, & Galambos, 1975). All of the studies described in this section employed click, noise burst, or tone burst stimuli. Also, like the action potential, these responses are generated primarily in the high and middle frequency regions of the cochlea (Hecox, 1975).

Most of the acoustic dependencies detailed in the preceding discussion have only been elicited from adults. The latency–intensity function exhibited by wave V, the most reliable of the response components, did not differ significantly between adults and infants aged from 3 weeks to 2 years (Hecox & Galambos, 1974a).

Until the time of writing of this chapter, only one report of

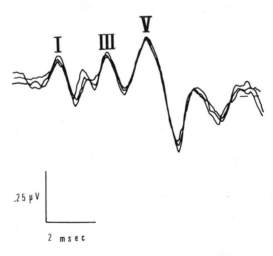

Figure 5.7.   Human auditory evoked potential in response to a monaural 60-dB click presented 10 times per sec. Each tracing represents the sum of 2048 presentations. Positively to the vertex is up in these recordings.

newborn responses had appeared (Liebermann, Sohmer, & Szabo, 1973). Reliable responses were obtained from 10 of the 19 newborns in that study, at an average of 45 dB HL (hearing level); only 10 dB above that required for reliable adult responses. As mentioned in the previous section, the authors did not explain which of the response components were being used as criterion components. Since the earlier waves disappear at higher intensities than does wave V, there may be a considerable disparity in threshold estimates depending upon the component or components being utilized.

Wave V of the infant response is distinguished by its prolonged latency which attains adult values by 18 months (Hecox & Galambos, 1974a) and diminished amplitude which reaches adult values sometime during the first year of life (Liebermann, Sohmer, & Szabo, 1973). Similar developmental trends have been reported for rat pups and kittens (Jewett & Romano, 1972). In this animal study, the latency of all of the response components as a function of age was described. The authors concluded that only a portion of the latency delay encountered in later components could be accounted for by delays to wave I (which corresponds to the eighth nerve action potential). Thus, both peripheral and central maturation was presumed to be involved. The notion that purely peripheral processes will be reflected in delays to wave I, while central processes such as myelination will be reflected in changes in intercomponent delays may be helpful in determining the nature of age-dependent latency and amplitude shifts.

Thus, we conclude that like the eighth nerve action potential, brainstem evoked responses exhibit prolonged latencies, diminished amplitudes, and elevated thresholds during early infancy. The nature of the observed latency shift as a function of age will be taken up again in Section V of this chapter.

D. Cortical Evoked Potentials

The components of the auditory evoked response which follow the occurrence of the brainstem components are divided into mid-latency (10–50 msec) and long latency (50–500 msec) responses (Picton, Hillyard, Krausz, & Galambos, 1974). Since there are no quantitative developmental studies involving the mid-latency components, this section will be exclusively concerned with the long latency "vertex" potential (Davis & Zerlin, 1966).

Although there remains some debate concerning the relative contributions of association and projection areas in the generation of the vertex potential, it is generally felt that the neural generators responsible for its occurrence are cortical. Many of the acoustical dependencies of this response have been determined and are reviewed in Regan (1972) and Skinner (1972). Signal rise–fall times, presentation rate, intensity, frequency, and duration have all been demonstrated to influence response properties. Because of the need for objective measures of infant auditory functioning in the diagnosis of hearing impairment, numerous infant studies have appeared (Davis, 1965; Goldstein, 1973). However, there are relatively few systematic comparisons of latency, amplitudes, or thresholds beyond the newborn period.

The intensity necessary to elicit threshold responses in adults has been variously estimated at 5.0 dB HL (McCandless & Best, 1964) to 12.5 dB ISO (International Organization for Standardization) (Davis, 1965) for tone burst stimuli. Similar results have been found for click thresholds in adults, while in infants thresholds for click stimuli have been variously set at 45 dB SL (sensation level) (Barnet & Goodwin, 1965), 50 dB SL (Barnet, 1964), and 50 to 60 dB SPL (sound pressure level) (Rapin & Graziani, 1967). Unfortunately, very little attention has been given to the precise nature of the click stimulus from the acoustical standpoint, so that comparisons across studies or laboratories may be hazardous. At least one notable exception is a study employing tone burst stimuli whose duration was 60 msec, whose rise–fall time was 30 msec, and whose amplitude was specified with respect to ISO (Taguchi, Picton, Orpin, & Goodman, 1969). Newborn thresholds were estimated to be 46 to 56 dB ISO by Taguchi *et al.*, with lower frequencies (500–2000), and deeper stages of sleep producing lower thresholds. This sleep-stage dependency of cortical responses has been well documented for both adults and infants (Weitzman & Kremen, 1965; Weitzman, Fishbein, & Graziani, 1965). The exact age at which adult thresholds are attained has not been determined, although Suzuki and Taguchi (1968) describe developmental changes up to 3 or 4 years of age.

A considerable body of evidence has accumulated demonstrating that newborn responses exhibit prolonged latencies (Barnet & Goodwin, 1965; Weitzman & Graziani, 1968; Monod & Garma, 1971; Taguchi, Picton, Orpin, & Goodman, 1969). However, systematic investigations of the maturation of latency and amplitude of the cortical evoked response beyond the newborn period are absent.

The effect of variations in acoustic parameters as a function of age has not been explored, with the exception of the previously cited threshold determinations.

E. Summary

Regardless of the level at which the responses are obtained, infant auditory evoked potentials exhibit prolonged latencies, diminished amplitudes, and elevated thresholds. The uniformity of these findings does not extend to their timetable of maturation. The more rostrally located the generator of a response, the more prolonged is its maturation cycle. Thus, the last of the auditory evoked potential components to attain maturity is the cortical evoked response.

Comparisons of threshold estimates obtained by the various electrophysiological measures demonstrate two major facts. First, threshold estimates based upon direct neurophysiological measures show that the human infant is more sensitive than previously thought on the basis of behavioral data. Second, electrophysiological estimates of threshold depend upon the anatomical structures responsible for the generation of the response. The more caudally located the structures, the lower the threshold exhibited by young infants. Thus, there is no single electrophysiological estimate of infant auditory responsivity but a series of estimates, corresponding to the anatomical dispersion of structures along the auditory pathway. The younger the infant, the greater will be the discrepancy between results obtained at the various neuroanatomical levels.

V. EXPERIMENTS: BRAINSTEM EVOKED POTENTIALS

Brainstem evoked responses offer several advantages over other components of the auditory evoked potential. First, they appear not to depend upon the physiological or psychological state of the subject (Picton & Hillyard, 1974) and second, they do not require the "nonsurgical" recording techniques employed in studying the action potential. The universality with which the responses are elicited in adults and infants who have normal hearing is an additional advantage. In this section the results of several sets of measurements will be described. The goal of these measurements was the more precise definition of the age-dependent latency shifts of brainstem evoked potentials, in hopes that a better understanding of the physiological mechanisms underlying these changes might bring us to a better understanding of human auditory development. The results described in the following section are presented in the spirit of a progress report, not a definitive statement.

A. Methods

Fifty infants, aged 1 day to 3 years, participated in this study. Thirty-five of the infants were brought to the outpatient clinic of University Hospital in San Diego and were considered by the attending pediatricians to be "well babies." Six older children, found normal by physical examination, were also included. An additional 15 infants were obtained through an auditory screening program being conducted by San Diego Speech and Hearing Center. All of the infants had responded normally in the screening program. Additionally, six newborns were obtained from Sharp's Hospital Nursery. All of the newborns weighed at least 2400 gm, and had Apgar scores of at least 8. Informed consent was obtained from the parents after the nature of the procedure was fully explained.

The stimulus generating and response recording system have been described in earlier publications (Hecox & Galambos, 1974a). Click thresholds were specified with respect to the average thresholds of adult observers run under essentially identical stimulus conditions, using the method of limits. The threshold sound pressure level was 30 dB SPL, while the ambient noise level in the room was 37 dB SPL.

B. Age Dependencies of Waves I, III, and V

The results of repeated measurements of wave V latency, as a function of age, to a 60-dB monaural click, presented 30 times per sec, is shown in Figure 5.8. Each point is the mean latency of at least three replications, while the entire range of values is included within the vertical bars. Wave V latency progressively shortens from 8 msec at birth to about 6 msec by 12 to 18 months of age. The shortening of response latency is also quite obvious from an examination of the raw responses shown in Figure 5.9.

Although the repetition rate selected for this study was not ideally

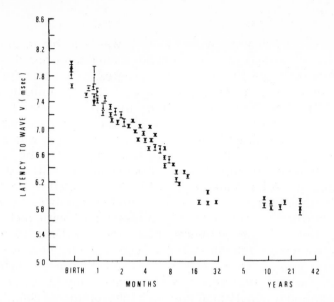

Figure 5.8. Latency of wave V as a function of age. The relationship between wave V latency and age of subject, in response to a 60-dB SL monaural click is shown. Each point represents the mean of at least three replications of the summed response to 2048 presentations. The vertical bars embrace the entire range of measurements from each individual.

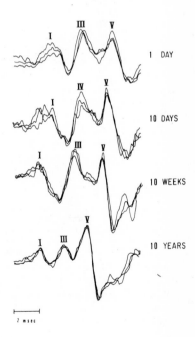

Figure 5.9. Click-evoked potentials as a function of age. Evoked responses to a 60-dB monaural click at four age levels are shown. Each tracing represents the sum of 4096 presentations at a repetition rate of 30 per sec. Note the progressive shortening of latency, as a function of age. The adult comparison tracing is written at half-scale. Wave V is designated in each of the tracings.

177

suited for clearly evoking waves I–IV, it was possible to unambiguously define the peak of wave III in 20 of the infants and five of the six newborns. Wave III latency also progressively shortens to the adult value of 4 msec, by approximately 12 to 18 months of age (Figure 5.10). For the newborn group, the average delay from the peak of wave III to the peak of wave V is 2.4 ± .12 msec, while the average for interpeak adult delay in a prior experiment was 2.0 ± .2 msec (Hecox, 1975). This suggests that there may be a slight decrease in the intercomponent delay between waves III and V with increasing age. Additional data need to be collected to verify this small difference since it is based on a limited number of subjects.

There is a great deal of ambiguity associated with picking the peak of wave I in the youngest infant records. Only 15 infants' tracings showed a reliable wave I. This may be because of its diminished amplitude, poorer synchronization of neural firings, or the particular repetition rate chosen for the study. A lower repetition rate would probably facilitate such measurements significantly.

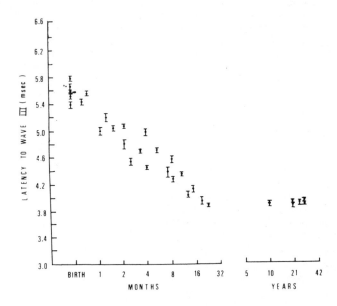

Figure 5.10.   Latency of wave III as a function of age. The relationship between wave III latency and age of subject, in response to a monaural 60-dB SL click is shown. Each point represents the mean of at least three replications of the summed response to 2048 presentations. The vertical bars embrace the entire range of values obtained from each individual.

Only three of six newborns showed reliable wave I responses and the mean of their latency was 2.88 ± .42 msec, as compared to the 1.9- to 2.1-msec latency generally elicited from adults, to the same stimulus. All of the infants aged 7 months or older (5 of them) showed wave I latencies of 2.1 msec or less. Thus it appears that the auditory nerve action potential has attained its adult latency value by 7 months, which is at least 5 months before waves III and V reach maturity.

In summary, the latency of each of the respective waves—I, III, and V—systematically shortens with age, attaining adult values by 7 months, in the case of wave I, and by 12 to 18 months, in the cases of waves III and V. These findings confirm earlier reports of age-related latency shifts, provide additional data on the age at which adult values are attained, and suggest that about 50% of the latency change exhibited by wave V can be accounted for by purely peripheral processes, occurring before wave I.

C. Rate Effects

A frequent finding among developmental electrophysiologists is that immature animals exhibit greater fatiguability than their adult counterparts (Rose & Ellingson, 1970; Myslivecek, 1970). One of the most common ways in which this "fatiguability" factor is measured is to determine the effect of varying repetition rate on response latency and amplitude. Jewett and Romano's (1972) finding that brainstem evoked responses obtained from rat pups and kittens exhibit diminished responsivity (latency and amplitude) at high rates of stimulation suggest that such a phenomenon may account for some of the age-related latency differences observed in humans. To explore this possibility 20 infants, aged 3 weeks to 16 months, from the University Hospital population, were presented 60-dB SL clicks at a rate of 10 times per sec, in addition to the standard 30 per sec rate. There were no significant differences between repetition rates and no interaction of rate with age. The infants were divided into five age groups of 4 infants each; there was, therefore, some heterogeneity of ages within groups which may have obscured any subtle effects. Nonetheless, we can conclude that the age dependency of wave V latency is not unique to the particular rate employed in this study. In fact, results of a repetition rate series are shown in Figure 5.11, for a 4-week and an 8-week-old infant. Despite interstimulus intervals as short as 15 msec, highly reliable re-

4 WEEKS   8 WEEKS

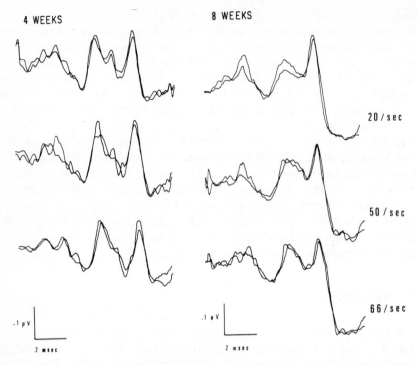

20/sec

50/sec

66/sec

.1 µV

2 msec

.1 µV

2 msec

Figure 5.11.   Infant evoked responses as a function of repetition rate. Evoked responses to a 50-dB SL monaural click, are shown from two infants at three rates of presentation. Note that reliable recordings were obtained at all rates. Each of the superimposed tracings represent the summed response to 2048 stimuli. Positivity to the vertex is upwards.

sponses may be obtained. Thus, there is little evidence for a peripheral contribution to the elevated fatiguability of the human infant, as demonstrated by heart rate and behavioral measures (Bartoshuk, 1962a, b; Lipton, Steinschneider, & Richmond, 1966).

D. Intensity Effects

In the initial series of 35 infants obtained through University Hospital, stimuli were presented at 20-, 40-, and 60-dB SL. The average number of milliseconds latency change per decibel of intensity change over the 40-dB range, was .039 for the infants and .044 for the adults. The infants were divided into five groups of seven each to perform a one-way analysis of variance repeated measures design on the latency–intensity trading values. There was no significant difference between the groups. The same analysis of the newborn latency intensity function, over the 30-dB range in which reliable responses could be elicited, showed a .022 ± .008 msec decibel value, which differs significantly from the adult (.040) value over the same intensity region.

An additional consideration relative to stimulus intensity is an estimate of the infants' thresholds. The average minimum intensity required to elicit a response from the newborns was 27 dB SL, as compared to the minimum intensity for adults of 10 dB (Hecox & Galambos, 1974b). The 17-dB difference between adult and newborn thresholds could account for no more than .4 msec latency change since each decibel produces about .02 msec latency shift.

It is interesting to note that such small latency shifts with intensity changes have been demonstrated to occur in adults, only in the presence of high frequency hearing impairment, and not in the case of hearing losses characterized by "flat" audiograms (Hecox and Galambos, 1974b; Galambos & Hecox, in press). No systematic attempt was made to estimate the thresholds of the older infants, although all of them responded at the 20-dB SL level.

E. Frequency Specificity

On the basis of von Bekesy's classic experiments (1960) we know that the presentation of an acoustic signal initiates a traveling wave which propagates from base to apex along the basilar membrane. The place of maximum amplitude displacement is a function of signal frequency such that high frequency signals produce waves whose peaks are nearer the oval window than those produced by low frequency stimuli. Thus, the frequency content of a signal results in the activation of a specific set of neural elements. "Frequency specificity" will be used to refer to this relationship between the space–time pattern of basilar membrane activation and the properties of the neural response it evokes.

One method of investigating frequency specificity depends on the use of continuous noise maskers of varying cutoff frequencies and bandwidths. The frequency spectrum of long duration signals can be more precisely controlled than that of short duration signals, so that continuous stimuli are ideal from the standpoint of physical acoustics. By presenting sufficiently intense noise bands, it is possible to "mask" the response originating from a specific location along the basilar membrane, depending upon what the frequency content of the masker may be. Thus, by preventing the participation of selected regions of the cochlea and observing its effects on the evoked response, it should be possible to define the frequency limits of the region of activity.

The presentation of a click, with its broad frequency spectrum, imparts motion to a considerable portion of the cochlear partition. By presenting noise maskers whose high frequency limit is fixed at 20 kHz and whose low frequency cutoff is variable, it is possible to prevent the contribution of successively longer and more apical portions of the basilar membrane to the observed response. The more apical the edge of the masker, the greater the latency of the resulting response and the smaller its amplitude, reflecting the increased traveling wave delay and fewer units available for activation (Hecox & Galambos, 1974b).

To investigate the hypothesis, suggested by the results of experiment 3, that the prolonged latencies and smaller time–intensity values exhibited by the infants, may be due to the selective impairment of high frequency responsivity, masking conditions as described above were presented to infants of varying ages. The results of such measurements for three infants are shown in Figure 5.12 along with an adult comparison. The most striking feature of these graphs is the narrowed region in which the masker had an effect. This is particularly true for the high frequency masking conditions, in which there is very little change in response latency until the high frequency cutoff reaches 2 kHz. A similar picture emerges from an examination of amplitude changes as a function of masker frequency. The younger the infant, the less effective are the high frequency components of the masker, suggesting that the infant responses are being produced in a more apical region of the cochlea than are adult responses (Figure 5.13). We conclude therefore that the progressive shortening of wave V latency with age, is due in part, to a systematic shift basalwards in the frequency region from which the response is generated.

F.   Comments

The purpose of this section has been to more precisely redefine the nature of the immaturity exhibited by the infant brainstem evoked potential and to suggest some possible physiological mechanisms responsible for its change with age.

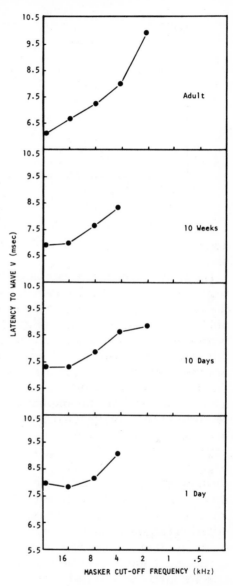

Figure 5.12. Effect of hi-pass noise on wave V latency. The relationship between the low frequency cutoff of a high frequency masker and the latency of wave V is shown for a 60-dB SL monaural click, at several ages. Each point represents the average of three replications of summed responses to 2048 stimuli. Conditions were presented in balanced ascending–descending order. The masker intensity was adjusted at a level sufficient to mask a 60-dB SL click when its bandwidth was 20–20kHz. The spectrum level of the noise masker was not altered during a session, only its bandwidth.

The results of the measurements in this chapter demonstrate that each of the waves in the brainstem evoked response exhibits a gradual shortening of latency with increasing age. It appears that both central and peripheral maturational processes are probably involved with the shortening of latency, since waves I, III, and V show age-dependent changes, and the age at which wave I attains

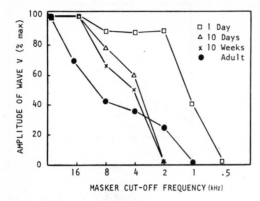

Figure 5.13. Same conditions as Figure 5.12 except that amplitude and not latency is the dependent variable.

adult latency is at least 5 months before it is attained by waves III or V.

The effect of repetition rate upon the reliability with which these responses may be elicited does not appear to interact with age for the values sampled here; thus the prolonged latencies of infancy are unlikely to be due to fatiguability. The thresholds of the neonates were elevated 17 dB in comparison with those of adults, which is in fair agreement with the 10-dB value obtained by Lieberman, Sohmer, and Szabo (1973) for the same experiment. The amount of threshold elevation being demonstrated in these studies is significantly smaller than the amount encountered with cortical evoked responses (Taguchi, Picton, Orpin, & Goodman, 1969; Barnet, 1964), heart rate (Lipton, Steinschneider, & Richmond, 1966), or behavioral measures (Hardy, Dougherty, Hardy, 1959; Kessen, Haith, & Salapatek, 1971). This does not necessarily imply that previous techniques were in error in their estimates of threshold. More likely, there exists a series of thresholds corresponding to the various levels of the nervous system responsible for the generation of the criterion response. Each of these levels surely has its own timetable of maturation, proceeding in a caudorostral direction. Thus the thresholds obtained via brainstem or electrocochleographic methods are lower than thresholds obtained via cortical evoked potentials (Taguchi et al., 1969; Barnet, 1964).

To the extent that a behavioral response depends upon a specific neuroanatomic locus, there may also be a series of behavioral thresholds reflecting the state of maturation of those structures giving rise to the response.

The results of the masking conditions and the abnormally small latency shift with intensity changes exhibited by the youngest infants in this series, argues for the existence of a reduced responsivity in the high frequency region. In light of the base to apex sequence of maturation demonstrated histologically in several mammalian species (Alford & Ruben, 1967; Pujol & Marty, 1970; Anggard, 1965; Sher, 1971), this finding is somewhat surprising, for it suggests that there is a gradual widening of responsivity in both the high and low frequency regions. However, the histological findings of Bredberg (1968) tend to support the electrophysiological inference drawn in this chapter, since the most basalward portion of his human newborn cochlear material was not mature. There are a number of explanations for the reduced responsivity of the high frequency region. First, the middle ear transfer function may be less efficient at high frequencies, thus acting as a low pass filter, as a function of age. A second alternative is that the most basal portion of the cochlea is completed by birth but the brainstem neural structures responsible for high frequency responsivity are not yet mature. The third possibility is that cochlear development is not completed in the high frequency region at birth. The information obtained in these experiments is insufficient to distinguish among these possibilities, although the prolonged latency of wave I suggests that retrocochlear processes cannot account for all of the observed latency shift. We can firmly conclude, however, that the space–time pattern of basilar membrane motion in response to click stimuli results in a frequency specificity clearly distinguishable in infants and adults. The parametric investigation of these differences should provide additional information on the precise frequency regions involved in the generation of the brainstem evoked response as a function of age. Additionally, the measurement of bone-conducted responses as a function of age, should permit the separation of the contribution of middle and inner ear processes to the observed developmental changes.

ACKNOWLEDGMENTS

The author would like to thank Dr. Donald Krebbs of the San Diego Speech and Hearing Center for providing test facilities, Dr. Carol White for providing technical assistance, and Dr. Robert Galambos for his continued guidance in the execution of many of the experiments described in this chapter. The encouragement and generous support of the editors of this volume is also gratefully acknowledged.

REFERENCES

Aldrich, C. A new test for hearing in the newborn: The conditioned reflex. *American Journal of Diseases of Children*, 1928, *35*, 36–37.

Alford, B. R., and Ruben, R. J. Physiological, behavioral, and anatomical correlates on the development of hearing in the mouse. *Annals of Otology, Rhinology and Laryngology*, 1967, *72*, 237.

Anggard, L. An electrophysiological study of the development of cochlear functions in the rabbit. *Acta Oto-Laryngologica* (Stockholm), Suppl. 203, 5, 1965.

Ballenger, J. J. *Diseases of the nose, throat, and ear*. Philadelphia: Lea and Febriger, 1969.

Barnet, A. EEG Audiometry in children under 3 years of age. *Acta Oto-Laryngologica*, 1964, *72*, 1–13.

Barnet, A., and Goodwin, R. Averaged evoked electroencephalic responses to clicks in the human newborn. *Electroencephalography and Clinical Neurophysiology*, 1965, *18*, 441–450.

Bartoshuk, A. Response decrement with repeated elicitation of human neonatal cardiac acceleration to sound. *Journal of Comparative and Physiological Psychology*, 1962, *55*, 9–13. (a)

Bartoshuk, A. Human neonatal cardiac acceleration to sound: Habituation and dishabituation. *Perceptual and Motor Skills*, 1962, *15*, 15–27. (b)

Bast, T. H., and Anson, B. J. *The temporal bone and the ear*, Springfield, Illinois: Thomas, 1949.

Bechterew, W. Uber die innere Abteilung des Strichkorpers und des achten Hirnnerven. *Neurologica Centralblatt*, 1885, *3*, 145.

von Bekesy, G. *Experiments in hearing*. New York: McGraw-Hill, 1960.

Bezold, F. *Die Corrosions-Anatomie des Ohres*. 1882.

Boudreau, J. C., and Tsuchitani, C. *Auditory system in sensory neurophysiology*. New York: Van Nostrand Reinhold Co., 1973.

Bredberg, G. Cellular pattern and nerve supply of the human organ of Corti. *Acta Oto-Laryngologica*, 1968, Suppl. 236.

Brödel, M. *Three unpublished drawings of the anatomy of the human ear*. Philadelphia, Pennsylvania: Saunders, 1946.

Brogden, W. J., Girden, E., Mettler, F. A., & Culler, E. Acoustic value of the several components of the auditory system in cats. *American Journal of Physiology*, 1936, *116*, 252–261.

Bunge, R. P. Glial cells and the central myelin sheath. *Physiological Review*, 1968, *48*, 197–251.

Coats, A., & Dickey, J. Nonsurgical recording of human auditory nerve action potentials and cochlear microphonics. *Annals of Otology*, 1970, *79*, 844–852.

Cooper, E. R. A. The development of human auditory pathway from the cochlear ganglion to the medial geniculate body. *Acta Anatomica*, 1948, *5*, 99.

Davis, H. Slow cortical responses evoked by acoustic stimuli. *Acta Oto-Laryngologica*, 1965, *59*, 179.

Davis, H. The cocktail hour before the serious banquet. In A. Möller (Ed.), *Basic mechanisms in hearing*. New York: Academic Press, 1973.

Davis, H., & Zerlin, S. Acoustic relations of the human vertex potential. *Journal of the Acoustical Society of America*, 1966, *39*, 109–116.

Davis, H. *et al.* Acoustic trauma in the guinea pig. *Journal of the Acoustical Society of America*, 1953, 25.

Demetriades, T. The cochleo-palpebral reflex in infants. *Annals of Otology*, 1923, *32*, 894–903.

Diamond, I. T., & Neff, W. D. Ablation of temporal cortex and discrimination of auditory patterns. *Journal of Neurophysiology* 1957, *20*, 300–315.

Flechsig, P. *Anatomie des Menschlichen Gehirns und Ruckenmarks auf Myelogenetischer Grundlage*, Vol. I. Leipzig, 1920.

Gacek, R. Neuroanatomy of the auditory system. In J. Tobias (Ed.), *Foundations of modern auditory theory*, Vol. II. New York: Academic Press, 1972.

Galambos, R. Neural mechanisms of audition. *Physiological Review*, 1954, *34*, 497.

Galambos, R. Neural mechanisms in audition. *Laryngoscope, 68*, 1958.

Galambos, R., & Hecox, K. Clinical applications of the human brainstem evoked potential to auditory stimuli in J. Desmedt (Ed.), *Cerebral evoked potential in man*, in press.

Galambos, R., Hecox, K., Hillyard, S., Picton, T., Furman, G., & Leigh, M. Human brainstem electrical responses to acoustic signals. *Journal of the Acoustical Society of America*, 1973, *53*, 362. (Abstract).

Galambos, R., Schwartzkopff, J., & Rupert, A. L. Microelectrode study of superior olivery nuclei. *American Journal of Physiology*, 1959, *197*, 527–536.

Gazzaniga, M. *The bisected brain*. New York: Appleton, 1970.

Gersuni, G. V. Temporal organization of the auditory function. In G. Gersuni (Ed.), *Sensory processes at the neuronal and behavioral levels*. London: Academic Press, 1971.

Goldstein, R. Electroencephalic audiometry. In J. Jerger (Ed.), *Modern developments in audiology* (2nd ed.). New York: Academic Press, 1973. Pp. 407–436.

Green, D., & Swets, J. *Signal detection theory and psychophysics*. New York: Wiley, 1966.

Hamilton, W. J., Boyd, J. D., & Mossman, H. W. *Human embryology*, 3rd ed. Baltimore, Maryland: Williams & Wilkins, 1962.

Hardy, J., Dougherty, A., & Hardy, W. Hearing responses and audiologic screening in infants. *Journal of Pediatrics*, 1959, *55*, 382–390.

Hecox, K. Developmental, acoustical, and pathological dependence of brainstem evoked responses. Doctoral dissertation, University Microfilm, Ann Arbor, Michigan, 1975.

Hecox, K., & Galambos, R. Brainstem auditory evoked responses in human infants and adults. *Archives of Otolaryngology*, 1974, *99*, 30–33. (a)

Hecox, K., & Galambos, R. Frequency specificity of the human brainstem evoked response. *Journal of the Acoustical Society of America*, 1974, *56*, 563. (b)

Hecox, K., Squires, N., & Galambos, R. The effect of stimulus duration and rise-fall time on the human brainstem auditory evoked response. *Journal of the Acoustical Society of America*, 1975, in press.

Hursh, J. B. Properties of growing nerve fibers. *American Journal of Physiology*, 1939, *127*, 140–153.

Jerger, J. J., Weikers, N. J., Sharbrough, F. W., & Jerger, S. Bilateral lesions of the temporal lobe, a case study. *Acta Oto-Laryngologica* (Stockholm), 1969, Suppl., *258*, 1–51.

Jewett, D. L. Volume conducted potentials in response to auditory stimuli as detected by averaging in the cat. *Electroencephalography and Clinical Neurophysiology*, 1970, *28*, 609–618.

Jewett, D. L., & Romano, M. N. Neonatal development of auditory system potentials averaged from the scalp of rat and cat. *Brain Research*, 1972, *36*, 89–100.

Jewett, D. L., Romano, M. N., & Williston, J. S. Human auditory evoked potentials: Possible brainstem components detected on the scalp. *Science*, 1970, *167*, 1517–1518.

Jewett, D. L., & Williston, J. S. Auditory evoked far fields averaged from the scalp of humans. *Brain*, 1971, *94*, 681–696.

Johnstone, B. M., & Boyle, A. J. T. Basilar membrane vibration examined with the Mossbauer technique. *Science*, 1967, *158*, 389–390.

Keith, W. Impedance audiometry in infants. *Archives of Otolaryngology*, 1973, *97*, 465–467.

Kessen, W., Haith, M. M., & Salapatek, P. Human infancy: A bibliography and guide. In P. Mussen (Ed.), *Carmichael's manual of child psychology*, Vol. I. New York: Wiley, 1971.

Kikuchi, K., & Hilding, D. A. The development of the organ of Corti in the mouse. *Acta Oto-Laryngologica* (Stockholm), 1965, *60*, 207.

Kirikae, I. *Structure and function of the middle ear*. Tokyo: Tokyo Univ. Press, 1960.

Langman, J. *Medical embryology*. Baltimore, Maryland: Williams & Wilkins, 1963.

Langworthy, O. R. Development of behavior patterns and myelination of the nervous system in the human fetus and infant. *Carnegie Contributions to Embryology*, 1933, 443, *139*, 1–57.

Lev, A., and Sohmer, H. Sources of averaged neural responses recorded in animal and human subjects during cochlear audiometry (electrocochleogram). *Archiv für Klinische und Experimentelle Ohr.—Nas—Kehlk. Heilk.* 1973, *201*, 79–90.

Liebermann, A., Sohmer, H., and Szabo, G. Cochlear audiometry (electrocochleography) during the neonatal period. *Developmental Medicine and Child Neurology*, 1973, *15*, 8–13.

Lilly, D. Acoustic impedance at the tympanic membrane. In J. Katz (Ed.), *Handbook of clinical audiology*. Baltimore, Maryland: Williams & Wilkins, 1972.

Lipton, E. L., Steinschneider, A., & Richmond, J. B. Autonomic function in the neonate: VII. Maturational changes in cardiac control. *Child Development*, 1966, *37*, 1–16.

Littler, T. S. *The physics of the ear*. Oxford: Pergamon Press, 1965.

Marty, R., and Thomas, J. Réponse electro-corticale à la stimulation du nerf cochléaire chez le chat nouveau-né. *Journal of Physiology* (Paris), 1963, *55*, 165.

Masterton, B., & Diamond, I. Hearing: Central neural mechanisms. In E. C. Carterette & M. P. Friedman (Eds.), *Handbook of perception*, Vol. III, *Biology of perceptual systems*. New York: Academic Press, 1973.

McCandless, G., & Best, L. Evoked responses to auditory stimuli in man using a summing computer. *Journal of Speech and Hearing Research*, 1964, *7*, 193.

Mendel, M. I., & Goldstein, R. Stability of the early components of the averaged electroencephalographic response. *Journal of Speech Research*, 1969, *12*, 351–361.

Metz, O. Threshold of reflex contractions of muscles of middle ear and recruitment of loudness. *Archives of Oto-Laryngology*, 1952, *55*, 536–543.

Meyer, D. R., & Woolsey, C. N. Effects of localized cortical destruction on auditory discriminative conditioning in cat. *Journal of Neurophysiology*, 1952, *15*, 149–162.

Monod, N., & Garma, L. Auditory responsivity in the human premature. *Biologia Neonate*, 1971, *17*, 292–316.

Mountcastle, V. (Ed.). *Inter-hemispheric relations and cerebral dominance.* Baltimore, Maryland: Johns Hopkins Press, 1962.

Myslivecek, J. Electrophysiology of the developing brain—Central and Eastern European contributions. In W. Himwich (Ed.), *Developmental neurobiology.* Springfield, Illinois: Thomas, 1970.

Peiper, A. *Cerebral function in infancy and childhood.* New York: Consultants Bureau, 1963.

Picton, T. W., & Hillyard, S. A. Human auditory evoked potentials. II: Effects of attention. *Electroencephalography and Clinical Neurophysiology*, 1974, *36*, 191–199.

Picton, T. W., Hillyard, S. A., Krausz, H. I., & Galambos, R. Human auditory evoked potentials. I: Evaluation of components. *Electroencephalography and Clinical Neurophysiology*, 1974, *36*, 179–190.

Portmann, M., & Aran, J. M. Electrocochleography. *Laryngoscope* (St. Louis), 1971, *81*, 899–910.

Portmann, M., Aran, J., & LaGourque, P. Testing for "recruitment" by electrocochleography. *Annals of Otology, Rhinology and Laryngology*, 1973, *82*, 36–43.

Preyer, P. Psychogenesis. *Dt. Rundschau*, 1880, *23*, 198–221.

Pujol, R., & Hilding, D. Anatomy and physiology of the onset of auditory function. *Acta Oto-Laryngologica*, 1973, *76*, 1–10.

Pujol, R., & Marty, R. Postnatal maturation in the cochlea of the cat. *Journal of Comparative Neurology*, 1970, *139*, 115–126.

Raab, D., & Ades, H. Cortical and midbrain mediation of a conditioned discrimination of acoustic intensities. *American Journal of Psychology*, 1946, *59*, 59–83.

Rapin, I., & Graziani, L. Auditory evoked responses in normal, brain damaged, and deaf infants. *Neurology* (Minneapolis), 1967, *17*, 881–894.

Regan, D. *Evoked potentials in psychology, sensory physiology and clinical medicine.* London: Chapman and Hall, 1972.

Retzius, G. Sur Entwichlung der Zellen des Ganglion spirale acustici und zur Endungsweise des Gehornerven bei Saugetieren. *Biological Untersuch.* N.F., 1884, *6*, 7.

Robertson, E., Peterson, J., & Lamb, L. Relative impedance measurements in young children. *Archives of Oto-Laryngology*, 1968, *88*, 162–168.

Rorke, L. B., & Riggs, H. E. *Myelination of the brain in the newborn.* Philadelphia: Lippincott, 1969.

Rose, G., & Ellingson, R. J. Ontogenesis of evoked responses. In W. Himwich (Ed.), *Developmental neurobiology.* Springfield, Illinois: Thomas, 1970.

Ruben, R. J. Development of the inner ear of the mouse: A radioautographic study of terminal mitoses. *Acta Oto-Laryngologica*, 1967 (Stockholm), Suppl. 220.

Sher, A. The embryonic and postnatal development of the inner ear of the mouse. *Acta Oto-Laryngologica*, 1971 (Stockholm), Suppl. 285.

Skinner, P. Electroencephalic response audiometry. In J. Katz (Ed.), *Handbook of clinical audiology*. Baltimore, Maryland: Williams & Wilkins, 1972.

Sohmer, H., & Feinmesser, M. Routine use of electrocochleography (cochlear anatomy) on human subjects. *Audiology*, 1973, *12*, 167–173.

Spoendlin, H. *The organization of the cochlear receptor*. Basel: Karger, 1966.

Steinschneider, A., Lipton, E., & Richmond, J. Auditory sensitivity in the infant: Effect of intensity on cardiac and motor responsivity. *Child Development*, 1966, *37*, 233–252.

Streeter, G. L. The histogenesis and growth of the otic capsule and its contained periodic tissue spaces in the human embryo. *Carnegie Contributions to Embryology*, 1918, *7*, 5–54.

Streeter, G. L. On the development of the membranous labyrinth and the acoustic and facial nerves in the human embryo. *American Journal of Anatomy*, 1906, *6*, 139–166.

Stubbs, E. M. The effect of the factors of duration, intensity, and pitch of sound stimuli on the responses of newborn infants. Univ. of Iowa Studies on Child Welfare, 1934, *9* (No. 4), 75–135.

Suzuki, T., Kamijo, Y., & Kiuchi, S. Auditory tests of newborn infants. *Annals of Otology*, 1964, *73*, 914–923.

Suzuki, T., and Taguchi, K. Cerebral evoked responses to auditory stimuli in young children during sleep. *Annals of Otology* (St. Louis), 1968, 77, 102–110.

Swets, J. (Ed.) *Signal detection and recognition by human observers*. New York: Wiley, 1964.

Taguchi, K., Picton, T., Orpin, J., & Goodman, W. Evoked response audiometry in newborn infants. *Acta Oto-Laryngologica* Suppl. (Stockholm), 1969, *252*, 5–17.

Teas, D., Eldredge, D., & Davis, H. Cochlear responses to acoustic transients. *Journal of the Acoustical Society of America*, 1962, *34*, 1438–1459.

Terkildsen, K., Osterhammel, P., & Husin't Veld, F. Electrocochleography with a far field technique. *Scandinavian Audiology*, 1973, *2*, 141–148.

Tonndorf, J. Cochlear mechanics and hydrodynamics. In J. Tobias (Ed.), *Foundations of modern auditory theory*, Vol. I. New York: Academic Press, 1970.

Wedenberg, E. Auditory tests on newborn infants. *Acta Oto-Laryngologica*, 1956, *46*, 446–461.

Weitzman, E., Fishbein, W., & Graziani, L. Auditory evoked responses obtained from the scalp electroencephalogram of the full term human neonate during sleep. *Pediatrics*, 1965, *35*, 458–462.

Weitzman, E., & Graziani, L. Maturation and topography of the auditory evoked response of the prematurely born infant. *Developments in Psychobiology*, 1968, *1*, 79–89.

Weitzman, E. D., & Kremen, H. Auditory evoked responses during different stages of sleep in man. *Electroencephalography and Clinical Neurophysiology*, 1965, *18*, 65–70.

Wever, E. G., & Lawrence, M. Transmission properties of the middle ear. *Annals of Otology*, 1950, *59*, 5–18.

Whitfield, I. C. *The auditory pathway*. London: Edward Arnold, 1967.

Witelson, S., & Pallie, W. Left hemisphere specialization for language in the newborn: Neuroanatomical evidence of asymmetry. *Brain*, 1973, *96*, 641–646.

Wood-Jones, F., & Won, I. C. The development of the external ear, *Journal of Anatomy*, 1934, *68*, 525–533.

Worden, F., & Galambos, R. Auditory processing of biologically significant sounds. *Neurosciences Research Program Bulletin*, *10*, Feb. 1972.

Yakovlev, P. I, & Lecours, A. R. Myelogenetic cycles of regional maturation of the brain. In A. Minkowski (Ed.), *Symposium—Regional development of the brain in early life*. Oxford: Blackwell, 1967.

Yntema, C. L. An experimental study of the origin of the cells which constitute the seventh and eighth cranial ganglia and nerves in the embryo of *Amblystoma Punctatum. Journal of Experimental Zoology*, 1937, *75*, 75.

Yoshie, N. Auditory nerve action potential responses to clicks in man. *Laryngoscope*, 1968, *78*, 198.

chapter 6: Speech Perception in Early Infancy[1]

PETER D. EIMAS
Brown University

I. INTRODUCTION

Since the publication of *Syntactic Structures* (1957) and *Aspects of the Theory of Syntax* (1965) by Chomsky, psychologists have, in ever increasing numbers, turned their research efforts toward the study of language, and with similar enthusiasm, toward the study of language acquisition. Bloom (1970), Braine (1963a, b, 1971), and of course Roger Brown and his associates (e.g., Brown, 1970) have made considerable progress in describing the acquisition of the child's earliest grammars—that is, the grammars that are in evidence between the ages of approximately 18 months and 5 years. The basic empirical data for the construction of these grammars, as well as for the corresponding theories of language acquisition (e.g., McNeill, 1966, 1970a, b; Slobin, 1971), have come almost exclusively from the child's conversations with psychologists. However, as even casual observation reveals, the production of utterances

[1] Preparation of this chapter and the author's research reported herein were supported in part by grant HD 05331 from the National Institute of Child Health and Human Development.

that are strictly rule governed, that is, that are based on an internalized formal grammar, does not really mark the beginnings of language acquisition. There are at least 12 to 18 months of experience in hearing language and perhaps 6 to 12 months of experience in producing many of the sounds and prosodic features of language, prior to the first meaningful and orderly productions.

Although many linguists and psychologists have recognized the importance of this initial period of language acquisition, it is of interest to note that their research endeavors were again primarily devoted to production rather than perceptual processes (see, for example, Jakobson, 1968; Irwin, 1957; Lewis, 1936; and Menyuk, 1971). Despite this early lack of interest in perceptual processes related to the acquisition of language, systematic investigations of the infant's ability to perceive speech have begun in the past few years. The full importance of this early perceptual experience with speech is now widely appreciated, as is most clearly evidenced by the following remarks of Friedlander (1970):

> Whether one chooses to accept Chomsky's contention that the capacity to apprehend and utilize complex grammatical structures is innate, or Lenneberg's reliance on biological foundations to explain the development of language, the fact remains that the infant's experience at hearing language spoken is an indispensable prerequisite for his own eventual ability to speak it [p. 20].

The goals of these recent investigations of infant speech perception have been to uncover (a) the receptive capacities of the young infant for speech, (b) the ontogeny of speech perception in a linguistically relevant manner, (c) the processes and mechanisms underlying the infant's perception of speech, and most important of all, (d) the manner in which later language competence is related to and develops from this early perceptual experience. Progress, albeit somewhat limited, has been made toward each of these goals; the limitations are especially evident with regard to understanding how the infant's perceptual experience with speech during the initial year of life relates to the development of mature language skills.

The plan of this chapter is to describe in detail a series of studies that pertain to the infant's receptiveness for the segmental units of speech, his ability to perceive phonetic feature contrasts, and the manner in which this perception occurs. Next, data will be presented that relate to the problem of the perceptual mechanisms that are involved in the perception of speech by infants (and adults)—a process that, as will be shown, is highly sophisticated and well developed in the human organism as young as 1 month of age. Finally, there will be a brief review of the infant's ability to perceive suprasegmental features of language and an attempt to relate the findings on early speech perception to the development of full linguistic competence.

II. INFANT STUDIES

A. Perception of Voice Onset Time

One method of describing the consonantal sounds of any language is in terms of the articulatory gestures and maneuvers that are necessary for their production. One such classificatory scheme (Gleason, 1961) involves two major dimensions: the manner of articulation and the place of articulation. The former refers to such characteristics of production as the presence or absence of voicing, nasal resonance, and friction. Place of articulation, on the other hand, refers to the locus of maximum constriction, or in the case of the stop consonants [b, d, g, p, t, k], the locus of complete closure. The stop consonants [b, d, g] are considered voiced in that their production is characterized by regular periodic pulsing of the vocal folds at or very near the time of the release of air pressure. The remaining stop consonants [p, t, k] are classified as voiceless in that periodic pulsing is delayed following the release of pressure. Within these two categories of stop consonants, the individual sounds are distinguished with respect to place of articulation. The bilabial stops [b] and [p] are generated with a complete closure at the lips, whereas the apical stops [d] and [t] are produced with closure formed by placing the tip of the tongue against the hard palate. The velar stops [g] and [k] are marked by closure of the vocal tract at the region of the velum, as a consequence of the back of the tongue pressing against the velum or soft palate.

Investigations of the production and perception of the stop consonants in adult listeners have revealed a number of vary interesting phenomena. For the moment we will be concerned only with investigations of voicing distinctions among the stop consonants. The voicing dimension in the stop consonants is universal or very nearly so. Moreover, although the distinctions made along the voicing continuum are not phonetically identical in all languages, the cross-language research of Lisker and Abramson (1964) has indicated that the manner in which diverse languages make use of this dimension is not arbitrary, but rather very much restricted. They investigated the production of voicing distinctions in 11 languages, many of which were from quite distinct language groups, and found that, with relatively minor exceptions, the various phonetic tokens fell at only three modal values along a single continuum. Lisker and Abramson named this continuum voice onset time (VOT), and defined it in articulatory terms as the time between the release burst and the onset of periodic pulsing of the focal folds or voicing. It is the case that not all languages make use of the three modal values of voicing. English, for example, uses only two locations, a short lag in voicing and a relatively long lag in voicing. The former signals the voiced stop consonants, whereas the latter signals the voiceless stops. The third category, marked by a relatively long voicing lead and found in Thai, for example, is not found in English. Of particular interest for linguists concerned with language universals is the fact that all of the languages which Lisker and Abramson studied make use of the middle category, short voicing lag. The acoustic consequences for the two voicing distinctions found in English are shown in Figure 6.1: These, as described in the preceding material, correspond to the short and long voicing lags characteristic of the voiced and voiceless stop consonants, respectively.[2]

Lisker and Abramson (1970; Abramson and Lisker, 1970, 1972) have also investigated the perception of the acoustic consequences of variations in voice onset time by speakers of several languages. Series of synthetic speech patterns that varied only in VOT were constructed by means of a computer-controlled parallel resonance synthesizer. Variations in VOT can be realized acoustically by varying the onset of the first formant relative to the onset of the second and third formants and by having the second and third formants excited by a noise source rather than by a periodic source during the time interval when the first formant is absent. Adult listeners of Thai, Spanish, and English were presented the synthetic speech patterns for identification and discrimination.

---

[2] It is important to note that the acoustic cues underlying the voicing distinctions discussed in the present chapter apply to sound segments in absolute initial position. Although, as Lisker and Abramson (1964) have commented, voice onset time does separate voicing categories in sentences in an adequate manner, there is some effect of embedding the various voicing distinctions in continuous speech. We have, as a consequence, limited our research to date to voicing distinctions in absolute initial position where voice onset time is relatively insensitive to contextual effects (Lisker and Abramson, 1967).

Figure 6.1. Spectrograms of synthetic speech showing two conditions of voice onset time (VOT): slight voicing lag, represented by [ba] in the upper figure and long voicing lag, represented by [pa] in the lower figure. The symbols F—1, F—2, and F—3 represent the first three formats, that is, the relatively intense bands of energy in the speech spectrum. [Courtesy of L. Lisker and A. S. Abramson. From Eimas *et al.* Speech perception in infants. *Science*, January 22, 1971, *171*, 303–306. Copyright 1971 by the American Association for the Advancement of Science.]

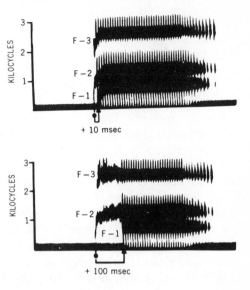

The perception of this dimension was found to be nearly categorical in that the listeners' ability to discriminate continuous variations in VOT was very little better than their ability to identify the individual sound patterns absolutely. That is to say, the listeners could discriminate two values of VOT when these VOT values signaled different phonetic contrasts, the voiced and voiceless stops in English, for example. However, they were virtually unable to discriminate the same difference in VOT when the two VOT values signaled acoustic variations of the same phonetic contrast. Thus, the discriminability functions of these listeners were marked by peaks at the region of the phonetic boundary (or boundaries, as in Thai) and by troughs of near chance performance for those stimuli which were identified as belonging to the same phonetic category. In a more recent study with kindergarten and second-grade children, Wolf (1973) again found essentially categorical perception of this dimension. In addition (as is probably true for the Lisker and Abramson data), she found that the obtained discriminability functions could be very closely predicted from the extreme categorical assumption (Studdert-Kennedy, Liberman, Harris, & Cooper, 1970) that listeners can discriminate two stimuli only to the extent that they can be assigned to different phonetic categories. Categorical perception is typically not found with nonspeech sounds that vary continuously along such continua as intensity and frequency. Listeners are able to discriminate many more stimuli than they are able to identify absolutely and, most important, the discriminability functions do not show the same peaks and troughs characteristically obtained in the perception of voice onset time (Eimas, 1963; Miller, 1956).

More recent investigations by Dorman (1972) have revealed that the behavioral characteristics of categorical perception are mirrored by the activity of the brain as measured by the averaged evoked potential. Using as his measure the difference between the maximum negativity wave occurring 75 to 125 msec after stimulus onset (N1) and maximum wave of positivity occurring between 175 and 225 msec (P2), he found no change in the N1–P2 magnitude when listeners were presented with a within-phonetic-category change in VOT. However, there were large and reliable changes in the N1–P2 difference when the shift stimulus signaled a different voicing category. The difference in VOT was, of course, the same in both conditions. The categorical perception of VOT in particular and of the stop consonants in general has been assumed to be a function of the special processing which the sounds of speech undergo and hence to be a special characteristic of perception in a speech or linguistic mode (Liberman, Cooper, Shankweiler, & Studdert-Kennedy, 1967; Studdert-Kennedy *et al.*, 1970; and for additional, but related evidence of the special processing of speech, see Studdert-Kennedy and Shankweiler, 1970; Wood, Goff, & Day, 1971).

Given the categorical and presumably linguistic manner in which voice onset time is perceived and the universal, or at least very nearly universal, manner in which voice onset time distinctions are produced, it seemed reasonable to assume that there might exist special, biologically determined processes of perception for this acoustic dimension (see also Lieberman, 1970, for a more detailed discussion of the relationship between the processes of speech production and speech perception; and Stevens, 1972). As a consequence, we further reasoned that if evidence for at least the beginnings of speech perception in a linguistic mode were to be found in infants, it would be likely to be obtained with speech sounds that differed along the voice onset time continuum. Thus, in our first experiment (Eimas, Siqueland, Jusczyk, & Vigorito, 1971), we compared the perception, more exactly the discriminability, of speech sounds that varied by a fixed difference in VOT, under two experimental conditions: in one condition the two stimuli were from different adult phonetic categories [b] and [p], in this study, whereas in the second condition, the two stimuli to be discriminated were from the same adult phonetic category [b] or [p]. Evidence indicating a discontinuity in the discriminability of VOT, that is, greater discriminability of two values of VOT that signal different adult phonetic categories, permits the inference of categorical perception, and presumably at least the beginnings of speech perception in a linguistic mode.

The experimental methodology for all of our infant studies has been a modification of the reinforcement procedure developed by Siqueland (Siqueland, 1969; Siqueland & DeLucia, 1969). Each infant is treated individually. After placement in a reclining infant's seat, the infant is given a blind nipple to suck, which is held gently by one of the experimenters, and a baseline rate of high-amplitude, nonnutritive sucking is obtained. The high-amplitude criterion is that amplitude which yields a sucking rate of approximately 20 to 30 responses per min, typically about 50% of the infant's total sucking output. Thus, the amplitude criterion varied from infant to infant. However, as a result of this variation, the variability in the baseline sucking rate was greatly reduced, and in addition the mean and individual baseline sucking rates were such that rates could change in either direction over the course of the experiment without the contamination of floor and/or ceiling effects. After establishment of the criterional amplitude and baseline rate of sucking, the presentation and intensity of a synthetic speech pattern is made contingent upon the infant's rate of high-amplitude sucking. The nipple on which the child sucked was connected to a positive pressure transducer which transduced each of the infant's sucking responses to a polygraphic record as well as to a digital record of all criterional high-amplitude sucking responses. Criterional responses activated a power supply that increased the intensity of the auditory feedback, from an inaudible level to approximately 75 dB, which was 13 dB over the background level of stimulation of 62 dB, caused primarily by the ventilation system. For all infants and irrespective of the criterion amplitude a sucking rate of two responses per second maintained the auditory feedback at maximum intensity, a level that produced few startle responses and that adult listeners judged as a comfortable level of stimulation. After the initial study, this procedure was modified as follows. Each criterional sucking response produced one presentation of the synthetic pattern (.5 sec in duration) plus .5 sec of silence. However, not every high-amplitude sucking response resulted in presentation of the stimulus. Each response recycled the timing apparatus. Thus, if the infant produced a series of responses, each of which was separated by less than a second, he would not receive the full 1 sec of stimulus presentation (.5 sec of speech and .5 sec of silence) for each sucking response. This limitation was imposed in order to prevent the occurrence of auditory feedback at durations greater than 1 sec after the last response. With both reinforcement procedures, continuous high-amplitude sucking produced the continuous presentation of the speech pattern, each individual presentation of the sound stimulus being separated by .5 sec of silence.

The presentation of an auditory stimulus in this manner (either rate of response contingent or simple response contingent) typically results in an increase in the infant's rate of sucking, when compared with the baseline rate. After continued presentation of the initial stimulus, most infants show a decrement in the rate of responding, presumably as a result of the decrement in the reinforcing properties of the initial novel stimulus (cf., Sokolov, 1960; Berlyne, 1966). When the rate of sucking had diminished by 20% or more for 2 consecutive min, compared with the minute immediately preceding the first decrement, the auditory feedback stimulus was changed without interruption. A different synthetic speech pattern was made contingent on high-amplitude sucking. The second stimulus was presented for 4 min, after which the experiment was ended. Our control subjects were treated in the same manner with one exception: After the initial diminution in sucking rate, no change was made in the auditory stimulus. The experiment was, of course, continued for 4 additional min with the original feedback pattern. Either an increase in response rate associated with the change in stimulation greater than that shown by the control subjects or a decrease of lesser magnitude than was shown by the control subjects was taken as inferential evidence that the infants perceived the two stimuli as different.

The subjects in the first experiment were 26 infants 1 month old, and 26 infants 4 months old, drawn from the population in the greater Providence, Rhode Island area. The infants were randomly assigned to treatments with the restriction that an equal number of male and female infants were assigned to each treatment. As in most of our experiments with infants, the percentage of infants who completed testing was approximately 40 to 50 and this percentage did not differ reliably across conditions. The primary reasons for discontinuing the use of an infant in the experiment were crying, refusal to accept the nipple, and falling asleep. The latter state is easily identified by the characteristic sucking pattern associated with sleep. A few infants were eliminated when they produced no sucking responses for an extended period of time and, of course, a few infants were lost because of experimenter error or apparatus failure. Almost all of the infants who were eliminated from the experiment were eliminated prior to the shift in stimulation.

The stimuli for the first voicing experiment were six synthetic speech patterns, three of which were perceived by adult listeners as the voiced stop [b] plus the vowel [a] and three of which were perceived as the voiceless stop [p] plus the vowel [a]. The stimuli differed from each other in VOT only. The VOT values were -20, 0, $+20$, $+40$, $+60$, and $+80$ msec. The negative sign indicates that the first formant and periodic pulsing began before the release burst, that is, before the onset of the second and third formants. Identification functions from adult listeners (Eimas & Corbit, 1973; Lisker & Abramson, 1970) have indicated that, with the series of bilabial stop consonants, VOT values below the value of $+25$ msec are consistently identified as the voiced stop [b], whereas VOT values greater than $+25$ msec are perceived as the voiceless stop [p]. At each age level there were three groups of infants differentiated by the nature of the change in stimulation. Group D with 16 infants received two stimuli to be discriminated from *different* adult phonetic categories. The actual stimuli had VOT values of $+20$ and $+40$. Group S, also with 16 infants, received two stimuli from the *same* adult phonetic category, either [b] or [p], and the actual VOT values were either -20 and 0 msec or $+60$ and $+80$ msec. In Group S, half of the listeners heard the two acoustic variations of [b], while the remaining infants heard the two [p] variations. The third group, O, with 20 infants, served as a control group and received a single stimulus randomly selected from the six stimuli. The control group functions to counter any possible argument that the increment in response rate associated with a change in stimulation may in fact be artifactual in that, in infants, changes in response rate tend to be cyclical in nature. Inasmuch as the acoustic differences between stimuli for Groups S and D were identical, 20 msec of VOT, comparisons of between- and within-phonetic-category discrimination (based on adult categories, of course) are unbiased by stimulus differences.

Figure 6.2 shows the minute-by-minute response rates for the 5 min before and the 4 min after the shift in stimulation for each of the three groups at both age levels. There was a significant increase in the response rate compared with the baseline level of responding, after initiation of response-contingent feedback ($p < .01$ in each

instance). As expected from the nature of the experimental procedure, there was also a reliable decrement in performance during the
2 min prior to stimulus shift (again $p < .01$ in each instance). An
analysis of variance of the average rate of responding during the 5
min prior to shift revealed nonsignificant differences for treatments
(i.e., Groups D, S, and O) and a nonsignificant age-by-treatments
interaction. The 4-month-old infants did respond at a higher rate
($p < .01$). However, this in no way violates the major conclusion of
no systematic differences between treatment groups prior to the
initiation of experimental treatments.

As inspection of Figure 6.2 indicates for the 4-month-old infants,
the response rate following the change in stimulation (or the point
in time at which stimulation would have occurred in the case of
Group O) is differentiated by the nature of the shift in stimulation.
When the mean response rate for the 2 min before shift was
compared with the mean response rate for the 2 min or 4 min after
shift, the performance of Group D indicated a reliable increment in
high-amplitude sucking ($p < .01$). Analysis of the same measures
for Group S revealed a nonsignificant decrement in performance. In
the control condition, there was a fairly substantial decrement in
the rate of sucking during the initial 2 min of the interval corresponding to the shift period in the experimental groups. However,
the decrement was significant ($p < .02$) only when the data from the
entire 4 min of "postshift" responding were considered. The same
analyses for the 1-month-old infants revealed essentially the same
findings. The only difference of any note was that the 1-month
infants from Group S showed a nonsignificant increment in performance.

In Figure 6.3, the recovery data are summarized for both age
groups. An analysis of these data, the mean response rate for the
first 2 min after shift minus the mean response rate for the 2 min
immediately prior to shift, revealed a significantly greater recovery
in Group D than in Group S which, in turn, did not differ
significantly from the control group. Although data shown in Figure
6.3 indicate a greater tendency toward categorical perception in the
4-month-old infants, the age-by-treatments interaction failed to
even approach the .05 level of significance.

These results strongly indicate that infants as young as 1 month
of age are not only responsive to speech and able to make rather
fine discriminations, but that they are also capable of perceiving
voicing distinctions in a manner approximating categorical perception. That is to say, infants are better able to discriminate a given

difference between two values of voice onset time when they signal different adult phonetic contrasts (that is, different voicing distinctions) than when they signal acoustic variations of the same phonetic contrast or voicing distinction. This form of perception, indicative of the processing of speech in a linguistically relevant

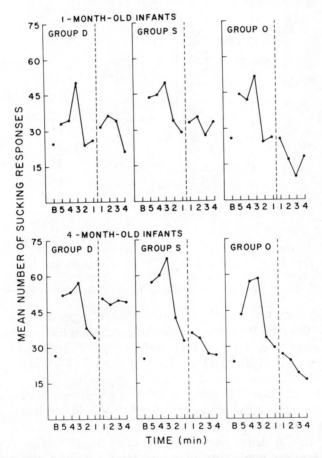

Figure 6.2. Mean number of sucking responses as a function of time and experimental conditions for 1- and 4-month-old infants. The dashed line indicates the occurrence of the stimulus shift or in the case of the control groups (O), the time at which the shift would have occurred. The letter B represents the baseline rate. Time is measured with reference to the moment of stimulus shift and indicates the 5 min prior to and 4 min after shift. The stimuli were the synthetic stops [b] and [p]. [The data from the 4-month-old infants are from Eimas *et al.* Speech perception in infants. *Science*, January 22, 1971, *171*, 303–306. Copyright 1971 by the American Association for the Advancement of Science.]

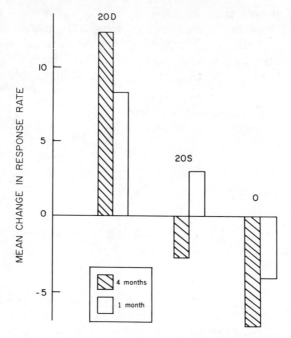

Figure 6.3.   The mean change in response rate as a function of experimental conditions. The data are shown separately for the 1- and 4-month-old infants. [From Eimas *et al.* Speech perception in infants. *Science*, January 22, 1971, *171*, 303–306. Copyright 1971 by the American Association for the Advancement of Science.]

manner, occurs ". . . with relatively limited exposure to speech, as well as with virtually no experience in producing these same sounds and certainly with little, if any, differential reinforcement for this form of behavior [Eimas *et al.*, 1971, p. 306]."

Given the unexpectedly early age at which linguistically relevant processing of speech begins, and the implications such data have for the biological foundations of speech, we believed it important to replicate our findings. In order to add to the generality of the findings, the decision was made to investigate the perception of VOT differences again, but now in the context of a different set of consonants, the apical stops [d] and [t]. The experimental procedures were the same as those in the Eimas *et al.* study with the exception that the presentation of the auditory feedback was now made response-contingent rather than rate-contingent; that is, high-amplitude sucking responses resulted in presentation of the auditory stimulus at maximum amplitude, regardless of the rate of sucking. The subjects were 20 infants 2 and 3 months old, 10 of whom were randomly assigned to what corresponded to Group D in the first experiment, and 10 were assigned to the equivalent of Group S. Both groups were equated for sex and age. The stimuli were again six synthetic speech patterns prepared by Lisker and Abramson which varied only in VOT. The individual VOT values were -30, $+10$, $+20$, $+50$, $+60$, and $+100$ msec. Adult listeners consistently identify the first three stimuli as [d] plus the vowel [a] and the last three as [t] plus the vowel [a]. The infants were randomly assigned to two experimental groups: Group D, in which the two stimuli to be discriminated came from different adult phonetic categories (VOT values of $+10$ and $+60$ msec), and Group S in which the two stimuli were acoustic variations of the same phonetic contrast (VOT values of -30 and $+20$ msec or $+50$ and $+100$ msec). In both instances, the difference in VOT was 50 msec.

Figure 6.4 shows the minute-by-minute response rate for the 5 min prior to shift and the 4 min after shift. The effects are quite similar to those of the Eimas *et al.* (1971) study. First, there were no differences between groups during the 5 min prior to shift in auditory feedback. Both groups showed a reliable increase in response rate after the introduction of response-contingent feedback, as well as a decrement in response rate in the 2 min before shift. When the mean response rate during the 2 min prior to shift was compared with the average rate during the 2 (or 4) min after shift, the analysis showed a reliable increment ($p < .01$ in both instances) for Group D and a nonsignificant decrement for Group S ($p < .10$ in both instances). As would be expected, the magnitude of

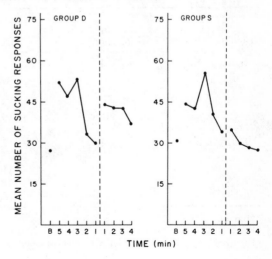

Figure 6.4.   Mean number of sucking responses as a function of time and experimental conditions. Time is measured with reference to the moment of stimulus shift and is indicated by the dashed line. The stimuli were the synthetic apical stops [d] and [t].

recovery was reliably greater for Group D than for Group S ($p < .01$ for both measures, i.e., the first 2 or the total 4 min of shift). It is worth noting the similarities in the recovery data for the two experiments. In the [b, p] study, Group D showed an increment of 10.3 responses per min during the first 2 min of the shift period compared with the 2 min prior to stimulus shift, whereas in the [d, t] study, the increment in response rate was 10.4 responses per min. Using the same response measure, Group S showed no change in the response rate and a decrement of 5 responses per min in the [b, p] and [d, t] studies, respectively. The reader will recall that the difference in VOT was 20 msec in the first experiment and 50 msec in the second experiment. It would appear then that recovery is not related to the absolute difference in VOT but rather is related to whether or not the two stimuli signal different adult phonetic contrasts. In a series of earlier, unpublished studies, which compared the discriminability of 100-msec and 60-msec differences in VOT, when the two stimuli to be discriminated signaled the bilabial voiced and voiceless stops, no differences were found in magnitude of recovery. Nor, interestingly, were the recovery magnitudes for a difference of 60 or even 100 msec greater than the recovery magnitude for a VOT difference of 20 msec obtained in the Eimas *et al.* (1971) study, provided only that both stimuli belong to different categories. Table 6.1 shows the mean change in response rate for

TABLE 6.1   THE MEAN INCREMENT IN RESPONSE RATE DURING THE FIRST TWO MINUTES OR ENTIRE FOUR MINUTES AFTER A CHANGE IN AUDITORY FEEDBACK

Response measure	Age (in months)	Difference in VOT in milliseconds		
		20[a]	60[b]	100[b]
Initial 2 min	1	8.3	10.6	7.6
		(8)[c]	(10)[c]	(10)[c]
	4	12.3	8.0	14.2
		(8)	(10)	(10)
	mean	10.3	9.3	10.9
Entire 4 min	1	5.6	8.8	5.3
		(8)	(10)	(10)
	4	11.5	7.2	13.1
		(8)	(10)	(10)
	mean	8.5	8.0	9.2

[a] From Eimas *et al.*, 1971.
[b] From unpublished studies by Eimas.
[c] The numbers in parentheses are the numbers of infants in each subgroup.

the first 2 min after a change in stimulation and for the entire 4 min of postshift testing. Analyses of variance performed on these data revealed no significant main effects or interactions.

Moffitt (personal communication) has also obtained evidence for the categorical perception of voicing contrasts. Trehub and Rabino-vitch (1972), using the sucking response and response-contingent auditory feedback, have demonstrated that infants at 17 weeks of age were able to detect the difference between synthetic versions of [b] and [p] and between natural speech samples of [b] and [p] as well as of [d] and [t]. However, they did not compare within-phonetic-category discriminability with the synthetic speech and hence their data do not provide additional evidence related to the nature of speech perception in nonarticulate infants.

As has been mentioned previously, there is a third voicing distinction, characterized by a relatively long voicing lead, that is phonemic in Thai, for example, but is not phonemic in English. Thus the production of stop consonants with long voicing leads would be a relatively rare phenomenon in English (Lisker & Abramson, 1964). Given this lack of exposure or experience in hearing this distinction, it is of considerable interest to determine whether infants who are raised in an environment where this distinction is not phonemic are able to perceive this voicing contrast, and if so, to determine the nature of the perception. In a preliminary study, 18 infants 2 and 3 months old were assigned to two groups, of 9 infants each. For one group, the two stimuli to be discriminated had VOT values of -100 msec and -40 msec, whereas in the second group the two VOT values were -40 and $+20$ msec. The stimuli were from the series of synthetic apical stops. We had selected these values on the basis of identification data of Thai speakers presented by Lisker and Abramson (1970), which indicated that the boundary between the prevoiced and the voiced stops fell at approximately -20 msec. However, the results of our experiment indicate that this is not the case. Although there were no significant differences in the magni-tude of recovery, there was a tendency for greater recovery when the VOT values were -100 and -40 msec. Moffitt (personal communication) has pilot data indicating greater recovery when the two stimuli to be discriminated have VOT values of -60 and -20 msec than when they have values of -40 and 0 msec. It would seem, then, that the real boundary is somewhere around -50 msec. In an attempt to test this hypothesis, 34 infants 2 and 3 months old were randomly assigned to two groups. In one group, S, the two stimuli to be discriminated had VOT values of -70 msec and -150

msec and presumably were both examples of the prevoiced phonetic category. The second group, D, were presented stimuli with VOT values of + 10 msec and − 70 msec. These stimuli were assumed to lie on either side of the phonetic boundary separating the voiced and prevoiced stop consonants. All stimuli were from a series of synthetic apical stops. The experimental procedures were the same as those previously used. The results from this study were equivocal: Although the infants in Group D showed a reliable ($p < .01$) recovery of the sucking response during the initial 2 min after the shift in stimulation (a mean gain of 7.2 responses per min) and the infants of group S showed a nonsignificant increment of 2.2 responses per min ($p < .10$), the difference between the two groups failed to attain an acceptable level of significance ($p > .10$). Thus, at this time we are able to conclude only that there is a strong suggestion that infants are able to discriminate the voiced–prevoiced distinctions in a manner approximating the categorical nature of perception characteristic of adult listeners.

In summary, investigation of the young infant's ability to perceive differences in voicing strongly indicates that he is readily able to perceive such differences and, more importantly, that he perceives changes in voicing in a nearly categorical manner. The latter we have taken as strong inferential evidence for perception in a linguistic mode. In a later section, we will discuss the mechanisms that are responsible for this form of perception—mechanisms that we believe to be a part of the structural endowment of the human organism.

B.   Perception of Place Contrasts

Research over the past two decades on the perception of speech in adult listeners has revealed a sufficient cue for the perceived phonetic distinctions among the voiced [b, d, g] and voiceless stop consonants [p, t, k]; (for a detailed review of this research, see Liberman *et al.*, 1967). This cue is the second-formant transition; variations in the starting frequency and direction of change reflect the underlying differences in articulatory movements in the production of these sounds. As Liberman *et al.* (1967) have noted, the second-formant transition ". . . is a major cue for all the consonants except, perhaps, the fricatives [s] and [š], and is probably the single most important carrier of linguistic information in the speech signal [p. 434]." Figure 6.5 illustrates in schematic form the first,

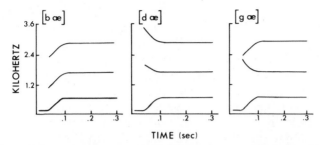

TIME (sec)

Figure 6.5. Schematic representations of the three synthetic speech patterns, [bæ], [dæ] and [gæ], illustrating variations in the second- and third-formant transitions which are sufficient for the perceived distinction among the voiced and voiceless stop consonants and which reflect variations in place of articulation.

second, and third formants and their transitions for the voiced stops [b], [d], and [g] in the context of the vowel [æ].[3] When adult listeners are presented series of synthetic speech sounds that vary continuously in the starting frequency and extent of the second-formant transition, the resulting identification and discriminability functions indicate that the perception of this dimension is categorical. As was true for the perception of voicing contrasts, adult listeners are able to sort the acoustic patterns into three phonetic categories with a high degree of consistency. In addition, the discriminability functions reveal that the ability to discriminate these sounds is only slightly better than the ability to identify them absolutely (e.g., Mattingly, Liberman, Syrdal, & Halwes, 1971; Eimas, 1963; Liberman *et al.*, 1967; Studdert-Kennedy, 1970).

Moffitt (1971) published the first experimental study on the perception of place distinctions in infants. Using heart rate as the dependent measure and a habituation followed by release-from-habituation procedure, he found that infants approximately 6 months of age were able to discriminate two synthetic speech patterns which adult listeners consistently perceived as [b] and [g]

[3] Although variations in the second-formant transition alone are sufficient for the perceived distinctions among the voiced and voiceless stop consonants, the inclusion of a third formant with a varying transition lends greater realism to the resulting sound patterns. Moreover, the perception of two- and three-formant patterns by adult listeners is essentially the same, both being categorical in nature. Consequently we, as well as Morse (1972), have elected to use the more realistic stimuli. The stimuli shown in Figure 6.5 are schematic representations of three of the synthetic stimuli constructed by Pisoni (1971), several of which, including the pattern [dæ] depicted in the figure, were used in our studies of place discrimination by infants.

plus the vowel [a]. These patterns varied only in the second formant transition. Morse (1972) in a similar, although more elaborate, study investigated the infant's ability to perceive variations in the second- and third-formant transitions under two experimental conditions: (1) when these acoustic variations were presented in a speech context, that is, when they distinguished the voiced stops [b] and [g]; and (2) when they were presented in a nonspeech context. The nonspeech context is realized by eliminating the entire first formant and the steady-state portions of the second and third formants. What remains are the second- and third-formant transitions, which adult listeners perceive as either a rising or falling "chirp." Thus, in the two conditions the critical stimulus information is the same; the only difference is that in one situation adults perceive the patterns as speech, whereas in the other condition the acoustic patterns are perceived as nonspeech chirplike sounds.

The experimental procedures used by Morse were virtually the same as those of the Eimas *et al.* (1971) study. The subjects were approximately 2 months of age. When compared with a control group of infants who received only a single stimulus, both experimental groups of infants produced a greater number of sucking responses during the 4 min after the shift in stimulation. The sucking rates for the two experimental groups did not differ. However, Morse also examined the individual recovery records for the experimental infants. He found that the data for those infants who discriminated the nonspeech sounds were bimodally distributed and, in addition, straddled the recovery data of the infants who received the synthetic speech sounds. That is, the infants who received the nonspeech patterns recovered either more or less than any of the infants who heard the two synthetic speech patterns. On the basis of this evidence, Morse has contended that the perception of the speech stimuli was in a linguistically relevant manner. Essentially his argument rests on the similarity between his findings with infants and the results of a study by Mattingly *et al.* (1971). Reanalysis of the Mattingly *et al.* study revealed that adults discriminated second-formant transitions in isolation (i.e., non-speech chirps) either better or worse than they discriminated the same transitions in a speech context. Given that adult listeners process speech linguistically (as opposed to a purely auditory processing) plus the analogous findings from his study and the Mattingly *et al.* study, Morse drew the conclusion that infants were also able to process or perceive distinctions in a linguistically relevant manner.

However, as Morse notes, more direct evidence for the linguistic processing of speech is obtainable from comparisons of the categorical nature of the discriminability functions for the speech and nonspeech stimuli. Although measures of nonspeech discriminability provide interesting data for a number of reasons, they are not necessary for conclusions concerning the manner in which speech is processed, that is, whether in a linguistic or an auditory mode. Prodded by Morse's provocative argument for the linguistic processing of place cues, we undertook to investigate this problem by comparing the discriminability of variations in second- and third-formant transitions when they signaled different phonetic contrasts and when they signaled acoustic variations of the same phonetic contrast. Greater discriminability in the former case would, as noted previously, be evidence for categorical perception and, as we have assumed, for perception in the speech mode.

The subjects of this experiment were 48 male and female infants, 2 and 3 months of age. They were randomly assigned to three treatment groups, equated for number, age, and sex. As in the original study on the discriminability of voicing, one group, D, received stimuli from different phonetic categories, whereas in this experiment, the two stimuli of the second group, S, were acoustic variations of the same phonetic contrast [d]. Finally, there was a control group, C, which received only one stimulus and thus served again to counter any possible arguments that the increment in responding associated with a shift in stimulation was due to the cyclical nature of the infants' sucking patterns. The stimuli were three synthetically produced speech sounds, two of which were perceived by adult listeners as [d] plus the vowel [æ] and the third as [g] plus the vowel [æ]. The three stimuli differed only in the starting frequency and direction of the second- and third-formant transitions. The differences in starting frequencies for the two stimuli of Group D closely approximated the same differences for Group S. It should be noted that adult listeners were able to discriminate the stimuli presented to Group D better than 80% of the time, whereas the two stimuli administered to Group S were differentiated at a level only slightly better than chance. For greater detail concerning the construction and perception of these stimuli by adult listeners, the reader is referred to a doctoral dissertation by Pisoni (1971).

The experimental procedures of this study were the same as those used in the first voicing study with infants, with the exception that the presentation of the reinforcing stimulus was response-contingent; that is, each high-amplitude sucking response resulted in a single presentation of the speech stimulus at maximum intensity.

In general, the results, which are shown in Figure 6.6, parallel the earlier findings on the discriminability of voicing contrasts. An analysis of the date for the 5 min prior to a shift in stimulation revealed no reliable differences among the three groups. As is apparent from inspection of Figure 6.6, presentation of a response-contingent speech stimulus produced an increase in the rate of sucking compared with the baseline rate. In addition, there was, as expected from the nature of the experiment, a substantial decrement in the sucking rate during the 2 min before the stimulus shift, presumably as a function of the infant becoming satiated to the reinforcing properties of the once-novel stimulus. An analysis of the postshift sucking rates (mean response rate for the initial 2 or entire 4 min of postshift stimulation minus the mean response rate for the 2 min prior to shift) revealed significant effects due to treatments, but only when the data for the entire 4 min were used

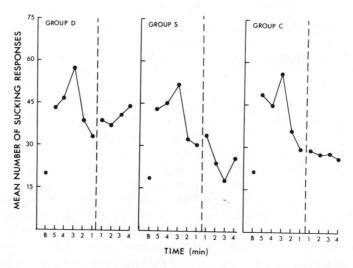

Figure 6.6.   Mean number of sucking responses as a function of time and experimental conditions. Time is measured with reference to the moment of stimulus shift, which is indicated by the dashed line. The stimuli were the synthetic voiced stops [d] and [g].

$(.05 > p > .01)$. Individual comparisons showed that Group D, with a mean increment of 4.1 responses per min, differed reliably from both Group S and Group C, which did not differ from each other. In both of these latter groups the mean rate of sucking declined during the postshift phase of testing: 6.1 and 4.8 responses per min for Groups S and C, respectively.

The major difference in the pattern of results for this study is the relatively slow manner in which the rate of sucking recovered when the second or shift stimulus signaled a difference in place of articulation. In all of the VOT studies, a reliable increment in sucking was evident within the first 1 or 2 min of change in the value of the voicing feature (i.e., a change in the phonetic category). It is possible that differences in the acoustic cues signaling place distinctions are more difficult to detect and process and, as a result, recovery of the sucking response is slowed. However, we do not have data that bear directly on this point. It is of interest to note that, in a replication of this study, we obtained the same pattern of results: There was reliably greater recovery for Group D than for either Group S or Group C, but only when the data for the entire 4 min of the postshift phase were considered. There was also greater recovery by Group D in the final 2 min than in the initial 2 min of shift, as was true in the first study. The data of the replication study must be interpreted with some caution, however, at least with regard to the categorical nature of the perception. The absolute differences in the starting frequencies of the third-formant transitions were not equated for Groups D and S, the difference being greater for Group D than for Group S. However, given the fact that the pattern of results was so similar in the two studies, it seems unlikely that the greater recovery by Group D was solely a function of the larger difference in the starting frequency of the third-formant transition.

On the basis of these findings, evidence has again been obtained in support of the hypothesis that at least the beginnings of categorical perception are present in infants before the onset of speech production. Discriminability was greater when the acoustic variation signaled a change in place of articulation than when the acoustic variation signaled variants of the same place of articulation. We have taken this particular discontinuity in discriminability to be evidence for perception in a speech mode, and thus have supported Morse's (1972) contention that infants are able to process place distinctions, as well as voicing distinctions, in a linguistically relevant manner.

III. THEORETICAL CONSIDERATION

The discovery that infants as young as 1 and 2 months of age are capable of processing some of the segmental units of speech in a manner that is linguistically significant indicates that infants have some knowledge of the phonetic structure of language. Specifically, they must have knowledge of at least some of the phonetic features. The problem is to ascertain the nature of this knowledge and the manner in which the infant comes to possess it.

With regard to the nature of this knowledge, it would seem reasonable to examine existing theories of speech perception that were developed to meet the demands and characteristics of speech and speech perception by adult listeners. In this way, we might discover the capacities, information, and knowledge that are necessary for the perception of speech, and more specifically for the perception of phonetic features by infants. However, this course of action encounters certain difficulties, inasmuch as the application of these models to the perceptual data of infants requires, in the writer's opinion, inordinately complex knowledge on the part of the infant. This is the case since most models of adult speech perception are based on very complex mediational systems of processing. One of the reasons for the complexity of the speech perception models is that the transformation of the acoustic energy signaling speech to the perceptual event does not appear to be a simple conversion. As has been discussed most notably by Liberman and his colleagues (Liberman, 1970; Liberman *et al.*, 1967; Mattingly and Liberman, 1969; Studdert-Kennedy, 1970) speech is a very complex code:

> We use the term code, in contrast to cipher or alphabet, to indicate that speech sounds represent a very considerable restructuring of the phonemic "message." The acoustic cues for successive phonemes are intermixed in the sound stream to such an extent that definable segments of sound do not correspond to segments at the phoneme level. Moreover, the same phoneme is most commonly represented in different phonemic environments by sounds that are vastly different. There is, in short, a marked lack of correspondence between sound and perceived phoneme. This is a central fact of speech perception [Liberman *et al.*, 1967, pp. 431–432].

Although Liberman does not exclude the possibility that a purely auditory decoder exists, he and his associates believe that a more plausible argument can be made for the perception or decoding of the highly encoded segments of speech by processes that are involved in the production of speech. This motor theory of speech perception is not a simple peripheral model, but rather assumes that the perception of speech signals is mediated in some manner by central, neural events. These neural events may be at the level of invariant motoric commands to the articulatory system (see also Cooper, 1972, for a more recent discussion of the processes of speech production and perception). At minimum, a model of this nature, if applied to the infant's ability to differentiate phonetic features, would demand that the infant has in some way acquired knowledge which would permit the transformation of abstract phonetic features into articulatory commands. Inasmuch as our infant listeners have had limited, if any, experience in the consistent articulation of phonetic distinctions, such knowledge must be part of the native endowment of the human organism.

Similar conclusions are necessary when we attempt to extrapolate other models of speech perception to accommodate the infant data on speech perception. Consider, for example, the analysis-by-synthesis model of Stevens and Halle (1967) and Stevens and House (1972). In this model, perception of a linguistic segment occurs when the stored image of the received sound is matched by an internalized representation of the sound, synthesized by the listener. In brief, the sequence of events occurs as follows. Upon reception of the sound, an auditory analysis is performed and the auditory pattern is stored in a temporary memory. On the basis of this auditory analysis and contextual information, the listener formulates an abstract representation of the sound. The representation is assumed to be composed of features or sets of features that can be converted to instructions to the articulatory mechanism by phonological rules. In perception, the features are converted into articulatory instructions, but rather than these instructions then being converted into motor commands (which in the production of speech actually activate the articulatory system and thereby generate sound), an internalized or computed auditory pattern is generated and compared with the stored auditory pattern. If the two patterns match, then the hypothesized abstract representation is assumed to be correct and is read out to higher centers of integration. As is true for the motor theory, perception requires knowledge of phonological rules, capable of mapping abstract phonetic features into articulatory events. Once more we are left with the disquieting conclusion that if this model is to be applicable to the behavior of the young infant, he must enter this world with considerable knowledge of the phonological component of language.

Even if one restricts the demands placed upon these models to explaining the detection of a change in a single feature, as is in fact the case in the infant studies previously described, it would seem that these models would still require knowledge of the rules for the conversion of phonetic features into articulatory maneuvers or commands, albeit for features taken one at a time. Before assuming knowledge of this considerable complexity as an inherent characteristic of the human infant, we have attempted to explain the results of our infant studies by another means, namely, by linguistic feature detectors. These detectors are assumed to be especially tuned to restricted ranges of acoustic information that signal phonetic features. Although we realize that mechanisms of this nature most likely do not completely eliminate the problems associated with the perception of highly encoded information, we do believe that the data pertaining to the beginnings of speech perception (as well as to much of the adult data) may be accommodated with a feature detector system. Whether theoretical models based exclusively on detector systems tuned to very complex patterns of stimulation can eventually explain all of the facts of speech and its perception is at present a question answerable only by future research.

There are several lines of evidence, in addition to the results of our investigations of the perception of speech by infants, that led us to believe that linguistic feature detectors might exist, especially for the relatively invariant acoustic cue of VOT. First, there is the finding that the categorical perception of this dimension is characteristic of a number of languages (Abramson & Lisker, 1970, 1972). Second, when one compares the perception of this dimension in listeners ranging in age from a few months to adulthood, the degree of categorical perception does not appear to be age-related, which is to say, it appears to be unaffected by experience with language, of either a perceptual or a productive nature. Thus, we find that infants, young children, and adults are virtually unable to distinguish differences in VOT when they signal the same voicing contrast, whereas all of these listeners are readily able to distinguish differences in VOT when the two VOT values are examples of different voicing distinctions. We realize that it is difficult to make absolute comparisons when there exist large differences in methodology, but the fact remains that a pattern of results exists that is indicative of poor discriminability for within-phonetic-category differences and high discriminability for between-phonetic-category differences for listeners of all ages. Third, there are the results of

Lisker and Abramson (1964) that revealed marked constraints on the manner in which voicing distinctions are produced in a wide variety of languages. These findings, in addition to the evidence that indicates that voicing distinctions are universal or very nearly so, have led us to the conclusion that specialized perceptual structures might well exist. Moreover, it seems reasonable to assume that these structures might take the form of feature detectors that are differentially tuned to the acoustic consequences of the primary modes of production. Other investigators of the processes of speech perception have likewise speculated upon the existence of feature detectors, arguing in effect that the selection of phonological features reflects the structural constraints imposed upon the mechanisms involved in both the production and the perception of speech (see, for example, Abbs and Sussman, 1971; Cole and Scott, 1972; Lieberman, 1970; Stevens, 1972; Studdert-Kennedy, 1970).

In order to obtain evidence for the existence of linguistic feature detectors, Eimas and Corbit (1973) used a selective adaptation procedure, similar to that used by investigators of the human visual system in their search for complex visual feature detectors (e.g., Blakemore & Campbell, 1969; Blakemore & Sutton, 1969). We reasoned that if feature detectors mediate the perception of voiced and voiceless stop consonants, then repeated presentation of one of the voicing distinctions would fatigue or adapt the detector for this voicing distinction, and consequently reduce the sensitivity of the detector. In this manner, the assignment to phonetic categories of a series of stimuli differing only in VOT should be altered: Fewer stimuli should be assigned to the adapted category, especially those stimuli at the region of the phonetic boundary where both detectors may be sensitive to the same VOT values. Evidence for this line of reasoning was obtained by comparing the identification functions for two series of stop consonants, the apical stops [d, t] and bilabial stops [b, p] under two conditions: In the first condition, listeners were in an unadapted state, whereas in the second condition, the identification functions were determined after selective adaptation of the two modes of voicing found in English. Selective adaptation was accomplished by the repeated presentation of a good exemplar from one of the modes of voicing.

The subjects for the first experiment were three university students who were paid for their voluntary participation. Because of the taxing nature of the experimental procedures, it was necessary to use adult listeners. We have as yet found no way to match the methodological demands of the selective adaptation procedure with the behavioral characteristics of infants (or for that matter of young children) and with the ethical considerations regarding the testing of children so as to be able to obtain meaningful data.

The stimuli were two series of 14 synthetic speech sounds, the members of each series differing from one another in VOT alone. The bilabial series had VOT values ranging from − 10 msec to +60 msec, while the apical series had values from 0 msec to +80 msec. The two series differed in the starting frequencies and direction of the second- and third-formant transitions. These variations, as previously noted, were sufficient for the perceived distinctions among the voiced and voiceless stops, i.e., between [b] and [d] and between [p] and [t]. All stimuli were perceived as a consonant plus the vowel [a].

Identification functions with listeners in an unadapted state were obtained by presenting the 14 stimuli of each series separately and in a random manner until 50 judgments were obtained for each stimulus. Each stimulus was 450 msec in duration and the interval between stimuli was 3 sec. Identification functions were then obtained for each series after adaptation with [b] (VOT value = − 10 msec), [d] (VOT value = 0 msec), [p] (VOT value = +60 msec), and [t] (VOT value = +80 msec). Thus there were in all eight adaptation conditions, four with each of two series of stimuli. On any single day, only one of the adaptation conditions was administered. Ten identification judgments were made to each of the 14 stimuli of the two series after adaptation with each of the four adapting stimuli.

An adaptation session was conducted as follows: Listeners first heard 2 min (150 presentations) of the adapting stimulus, with each stimulus separated by 350 msec of silence. Next, 70 adaptation trials were presented. Each trial began with 1 min of the adapting stimulus, followed by 500 msec of silence and then a single, randomly determined stimulus to be identified. After 5 sec of silence, the next trial began.

The results for a single listener are shown in Figure 6.7. In each of the eight conditions, adaptation produced a sizable shift in the locus of the phonetic boundary. Furthermore, the direction of the shifts was perfectly consistent: In all instances, the phonetic boundary moved closer to the adapting stimulus, indicating that a greater number of identification judgments were assigned to the unadapted mode of voicing. Thus, after adaptation with a voiced stop ([b] or [d]), the listener produced a greater number of identification responses belonging to the voiceless category. This was most

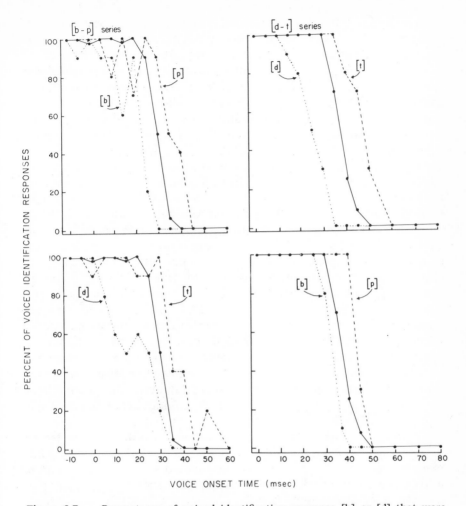

VOICE ONSET TIME (msec)

Figure 6.7.   Percentages of voiced identification response [b] or [d] that were obtained with and without adaptation for a single subject. The functions for the [b–p] series are on the left and those for the [d–t] series are on the right. The solid lines indicate the unadapted identification functions and the dotted and dashed lines represent the identification functions after adaptation. The phonetic symbols indicate the adapting stimuli. [From Eimas and Corbit, 1973.]

marked for stimuli near the original phonetic boundary. Adaptation with a voiceless stop, on the other hand, consistently produced a greater number of identification responses belonging to the voiced category. Again, this effect was most pronounced for stimuli situated adjacent to the original boundary.

The findings for the remaining two listeners were virtually identical with those shown in Figure 6.7. There were 24 instances of attempted adaptation, eight for each of three subjects. In each of these instances, adaptation caused a shift in the locus of the phonetic boundary toward the adapting stimulus. The mean shift in the locus of the boundary was 8.0 msec, although it should be noted that adaptation with a voiceless stop consonant produced a greater shift than adaptation with a voiced stop, 10.0 msec versus 6.1 msec.

Of particular importance was the finding that the shifts in phonetic boundary occurred even when the adapting stimulus and the stimuli to be identified were from different series. Moreover, for all listeners, the mean magnitude of the boundary shift was only slightly (less than 2 msec) contingent upon the adapting stimulus and identification series belonging to the same class of stop consonants. This cross-series effect rules out explanations based on adaptation of the sound pattern as a phonetic unit as well as explanations based on simple contrast effects or shifts in response criteria. It is difficult to understand, given these explanations, how alterations in the perception of a bilabial stop as an entire sound unit, [b] for example, would affect perception of the apical stops. Similarly, it is difficult to explain shifts in the phonetic boundary for a series of apical stops as a consequence of a change in the response criterion or adaptation level resulting from the repeated presentation of a bilabial stop consonant. Indeed, Sawusch and Pisoni (1973) have presented evidence indicating that phonetic boundaries are relatively stable despite experimental manipulations that according to adaptation level theory or decision theory would be expected to produce a notable shift. The evidence strongly indicates that what were in fact selectively adapted were detectors for those complex portions of the sound patterns that both series had in common, namely voice onset time.

A second experiment by Eimas and Corbit (1973) likewise provided strong evidence for the existence of feature detectors. Inasmuch as numerous studies have shown that the ability to discriminate two synthetic speech sounds varying only in VOT is closely related to the ability to assign differential phonetic labels, adaptation, which results in a shift in the phonetic boundary, should primarily result in a shift in the peak of the discriminability function. That is, if selective adaptation actually changes the sensitivity of the mechanism mediating the perception of one of the voicing contrasts, the alteration of the underlying mechanism should be evidenced not only in the identification functions but also in the discriminability functions. To test this prediction, discriminability functions for the bilabial stops were obtained from three adult listeners before and after adaptation. The psychophysical procedure of ABX was used, in which the listeners' task was to indicate whether the third stimulus, X, was identical to the first stimulus, A, or the second stimulus, B. Sets of stimuli to be discriminated were arranged by pairing each stimulus of the series with the stimulus 10 msec removed. Given that the series consisted of 11 stimuli separated by 5 msec of VOT, there were thus nine different pairs and four permutations of each pair for a total of 36 ABX trials. To obtain the discriminability functions when listeners were in an unadapted state, the various permutations of the ABX triads were presented randomly, separated by 5 sec of silence. To measure the effects of adaptation, the same procedure for obtaining identification functions after adaptation was used with the exception that, in place of a single stimulus to be identified, a randomly selected ABX triad was presented for discrimination. The adapting stimulus was a synthetic [p] with a VOT value of +60 msec. The results, shown in Figure 6.8, were unequivocal: All three listeners showed a marked shift in the peak of the discriminability function. Moreover, the shift in the discriminability functions matched almost perfectly the shift in the identification function.

Figure 6.8. The mean discriminability function for three listeners. The points are plotted midway between the two values of voice onset time being discriminated. The solid line represents the discriminability function without adaptation and the dashed line represents the discriminability function after adaptation with [p]. The arrows indicate the locus of the phonetic boundaries with (dashed arrow) and without (solid arrow) adaptation with [p]. [From Eimas and Corbit, 1973.]

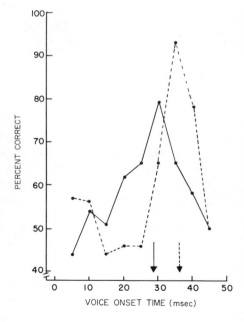

In a later series of studies, Eimas, Cooper, and Corbit (1973) investigated some of the properties of these linguistic feature detectors. By demonstrating that the shift in the phonetic boundary could be obtained when the adapting stimulus was presented to one ear and the stimuli to be identified were presented to the other, unadapted ear, they were able to infer that the primary site of the detector was centrally rather than peripherally located. A second experiment revealed that these detectors were part of the specialized speech processor, the existence of which has been well established by studies with aphasics (Geschwind, 1970), by studies with normal adults in dichotic listening situations (e.g., Studdert-Kennedy & Shankweiler, 1970), and by measures of average evoked potential when speech and nonspeech sounds are processed (Molfese, 1972; Wood, Goff, & Day, 1971). Evidence for this conclusion came from a comparison of the effects of adaptation when the voicing information was presented in a speech context and when it was presented in a nonspeech context. The latter condition was realized by eliminating the final 400 msec or steady-state portion of the synthetic speech pattern. Although the remaining initial 50 msec contains all the voicing information necessary to denote a voiced stop, this brief pattern is not usually (nor was it) perceived by listeners as speech. The phonetic boundary shifted reliably after adaptation with the full synthetic pattern, but was left virtually unchanged after adaptation with the brief pattern. Thus, the linguistic information of voicing in these patterns was not extracted. It is apparently the case that considerably more information than the presence or absence of voicing and rapidly changing formant transitions are necessary for the activation of the speech processor (cf. Mattingly et al., 1971).

The evidence from our studies of selective adaptation of voicing contrasts has established with reasonable confidence the existence of linguistic feature detectors. The problem remains to explain how these detectors might mediate the perception of voicing contrasts and thereby account for the data from both adult and infant listeners. To accomplish these ends, Eimas and Corbit (1973) offered the following set of assumptions:

(a) There exist detectors that are differentially sensitive to a range of VOT values with greatest sensitivity (as might be measured, in principle, by the output signal of the detector) occurring at the modal production value for a particular voicing distinction (Lisker & Abramson, 1964). (b) Some VOT values excite both detectors, but, all other things being equal, only the output signal with the greater strength reaches higher centers of processing and integration. (c) The phonetic boundary will lie at the VOT value that excites both detectors equally, all other factors being equal. (d) After adaptation, the sensitivity of a detector is lessened; that is, the output signal is weakened or decreased. Furthermore, for purposes of simplicity, the signal strength is assumed to decrease equally for the entire range of VOT values to which the detector is sensitive. From this it follows that selective adaptation shifts the phonetic boundary by shifting the point of equilibrium along the VOT continuum. If we further assume (e) that no distinction is made by higher-order processing elements between two output signals from the same detector, that is, no distinction is made when the same detector is excited by two different values of VOT, then the peaked discriminability functions are readily accounted for [p. 108].

To explain the infant's ability to differentially discriminate VOT differences, we need assume that these detectors are operative shortly after birth, perhaps being made functional by merely experiencing speech. Thus, the presentation of a speech signal with voicing information will excite the appropriate detector. The repeated presentation of the same voicing information will result in adaptation of the appropriate detector. The adaptation or lessening of the output signal of the detector may well be responsible, either directly or indirectly, for the lessening of the reinforcing properties of the speech signal and the concomitant decrement in response rate to obtain the stimulus. The introduction of a second stimulus that excites the same detector will not be registered as a different or novel stimulus, and hence there will be no recovery of the response to obtain the second stimulus. However, the introduction of a second stimulus that excites a different detector will produce a new or novel experience and result in increased responding to obtain the novel event. To account for the data suggesting the infant's ability to discriminate the prevoicing contrast in a nearly categorical manner, one need only assume the existence of a third voicing detector. However, whether such a detector actually exists is a question answerable only by the results of future research with appropriate subjects.

In a recent article by W. E. Cooper (1974), evidence has been obtained indicating that feature detectors underlie the perception of phonetic contrasts based on differences in place of articulation. However, inasmuch as the acoustic cues for place are highly encoded, that is, there are marked variations in the direction and starting frequency of the second- and third-formant transitions as a function of the vowel context, we are unable to state at present the exact nature of the information that is analyzed by these detectors. First, it is conceivable that detector analyzers operate upon invariant, but as yet not fully understood, acoustic information. On the other hand, there may be multiple sets of analyzers for place cues, each of which operates in a particular context. Admittedly, this is not a very parsimonious system, but similar analyzing systems appear to exist for complex visual information (cf. McCollough, 1965). Finally, place-cue detectors might operate on or analyze higher-level, more abstract sources of linguistic information. The latter alternative obviously presents problems, in that we are unable to specify the exact nature of this abstract information as well as how it might be made available to very young infants. The first two alternatives permit detector systems comparable to those hypothesized for the analysis of voicing information and as such might be available to mediate the perception of place contrasts in infants.

In summarizing our research to date, we are able to conclude that very young infants are certainly sensitive to the segmental sound units of speech. Moreover, they are able to make relatively fine discriminations of both voicing and place cues in a manner that approximates the categorical nature of speech perception found in adult listeners. This processing of speech in a linguistic mode is, we strongly believe, accomplished by means of linguistic feature detectors that are a part of the inherent structure of the human organism. It is the operation or excitation of these detectors that provides in an automatic and relatively simple manner the linguistic information in the form of phonetic features which the infant is capable of utilizing in the perception of speech.

IV. PERCEPTION OF SUPRASEGMENTAL UNITS

There is, relatively speaking, a substantial literature concerned with the development of the infant's capacity for the perception of suprasegmental units of language, that is, for the perception of such factors as stress and intonation, and there are, as well, several reports regarding the age at which infants are supposedly able to differentiate speech from nonspeech acoustic signals (e.g., Lewis, 1951; Wolff, 1969). One of the more recent and prolific contributors to this general area of research has been Friedlander (1968, 1969, 1970). Using a simple, two-choice operant procedure to obtain a measure of choice, Friedlander has shown that infants approximately 1 year of age have very decided preferences for voice inflections and differing degrees of redundancy and can discriminate the mother's voice from that of a stranger. Similarly, Turnure (1969) has shown that infants at 3 months of age are sensitive to distortions in the mother's voice and are able to differentiate between the mother's voice and a strange voice by 9 months of age. Research on the perception of suprasegmental units and related aspects of speech has been summarized by a number of writers, including Lewis (1951), Kaplan and Kaplan (1971), and Morse (1972), and so will not be given extensive coverage in this report.

In examining the literature on the development of these aspects of speech perception, one notes rather widespread agreement (e.g., Fry, 1966; Kaplan & Kaplan, 1971) with the generalization put forth by Lewis (1951). He has contended that the ability to differentiate differences in suprasegmental features, such as stress and intonation, ontogenetically precedes the ability to differentiate differences in segmental units. Obviously, the more recent work on the perception of segmental units of speech by infants, much of which has been described previously in this chapter, has cast serious doubt on this generalization. In addition, as Morse (1972) has noted, the earlier evidence upon which this conclusion was based, was marked by a number of deficiencies, ranging from poor definitions of the stimulus and response to inadequacies in measurement and experimental design. However, Kaplan (1969) has presented evidence that 8-month-old infants were able to differentiate normal intonation patterns, whereas 4-month-old infants were unable to do so. The stimulus was the natural speech utterance, "See the cat," with either a rising or falling intonation contour. The response measure was change in heart rate associated with the introduction of a second (novel) intonation pattern after habituation to the first pattern. On the other hand, Morse (1972) found that infants between the ages of 1 and 2 months were able to discriminate two synthetically produced CV (consonant–vowel) syllables ([ba]) that differed only in the terminal fundamental frequency contour. In one stimulus, the fundamental frequency rose from 120 Hz to 194 Hz, while the second stimulus was constructed with a fundamental frequency contour that fell from 120 Hz to 70 Hz. The reasons for these contradictory findings are unclear, given the rather large differences in stimuli, response measures, ages, and general experimental procedures. What does emerge, in fact, when all of the infant speech perception data are considered, is the generalization that the human infant begins to process speech at a very early age. Furthermore, this processing includes suprasegmental features as well as segmental features, and, most importantly, this perceptual processing clearly functions so as to derive information that has linguistic significance.[4]

V. SIGNIFICANCE OF EARLY SPEECH PERCEPTION

The significance of the infant's ability to perceive and discriminate differences in phonetic features in a speech mode lies in the fact that this form of perceptual processing indicates the infant's competence to recognize and process speech as speech. In order to accomplish this, the infant need not be aware that there exist two classes of acoustic events, speech and nonspeech; all that is necessary is that there are functional speech processing mechanisms available for the extraction of some, though not necessarily all, of the linguistic information in the speech signal. In this manner, the recognition and analysis of speech may proceed automatically and without conscious awareness, provided only that the acoustic signal contains sufficient linguistic information (i.e., phonetic features, for the purposes of this discussion) to activate the speech processing mechanisms (cf. Eimas, Cooper, & Corbit, 1973). This ability to recognize speech and to subject it to a linguistic analysis (phonetic analysis in the case of the very young infant) has certain advantages for the infant in the process of acquiring a human language. First and foremost, it certainly hastens the acquisition process and indeed may even make language possible. Without these inherent abilities, a long and tedious course of tuition would be necessary, in order for the infant to learn to differentiate speech as a special class of acoustic signals requiring additional analyses for the extraction of linguistic information. Indeed, it is difficult to

----

[4] The issue, of course, remains as to whether there is an ontogenetically determined order for the emergence of phonetic features in production as Jakobson (1968) has hypothesized. Although this topic is beyond the scope of the present chapter, it is of interest to note that more recent and controlled research by Port and Preston (1972) has revealed evidence indicating a developmental sequence in the order of occurrence of voicing contrasts as measured by voice onset time. Of particular interest is the finding that the first contrast to appear is the middle mode of voicing (short voicing lag) that corresponds to the English voiced stops. This voicing distinction, as noted previously, has appeared in all of the languages studied by Lisker and Abramson (1964) and moreover it is the category that Eimas and Corbit (1973) found to be more resistant to adaptation.

imagine just what form of training or experience would be necessary to achieve these ends.[5]

Second, with the ability to process phonetic features, the infant possesses a means for segmenting an essentially continuous acoustic input into discrete elements. It is generally accepted that full language competence requires the knowledge that language is composed of discrete elements in addition to grammars or sets of rules governing their permissible combinations. That the infant automatically analyzes speech into at least one form of discrete units, that is, phonetic features, would seem to serve well the requirement that the potential language user recognize the discrete nature of language, despite its continuous packaging. Indeed, this form of analysis, in occurring at the very beginnings of the language acquisition process, precludes the infant from having to *learn* that language is composed of discrete elements and, as a consequence, must likewise hasten the acquisition process.

Another possible and interesting advantage of the young infant's ability to recognize and attend to speech is its effect upon the social bonding between parents and offspring. In a very provocative paper, Mattingly (1972) has argued that speech may have functioned early in man's prelinguistic evolutionary history as a sign stimulus for the release of a variety of social behaviors, not the least of which was the fostering of mutual recognition among parents and their children. Such behavior would have helped to establish and maintain the social bonding between infants and their caretakers with the consequence that there would be more opportunity for social interaction, at least some of which on the part of parents would be linguistic in nature. If speech were still to serve this function, as well as being a remarkably efficient vehicle for the transmission of information, then speech itself would be one means by which the infant maintains close contact with those who are most likely to provide him with maximum linguistic input and experience.

In summary, the early recognition and analysis of speech in a linguistic mode can be viewed as processes that provide linguistic

[5] The Molfese data are particularly interesting in that they provide evidence for the lateralization of language as early as the first week of life. In line with this conclusion is the study by Witelson and Pallie (1973) which revealed that the planum temporale (the language-mediating surface of the temporal lobe) is larger in the left hemisphere than in the right hemisphere for adults *and* neonates. Thus, the anatomical, electrophysiological, and behavioral data all indicate a capacity for the processing of speech by the very young infant.

experience and knowledge about the very nature of language—
knowledge that the very young human organism would find inordinately difficult to learn, to say the least, and without which language in its human form would not be possible.

ACKNOWLEDGMENTS

I wish to thank Dr. A. M. Liberman for his suggestions and critical comments over the past several years regarding many of the issues discussed in this paper. I am also grateful to Dr. Franklin S. Cooper for his generosity in making the facilities of the Haskins Laboratories continuously available for the preparation of stimulus materials.

REFERENCES

Abbs, J. H., & Sussman, H. M. Neurophysiological feature detectors and speech perception: A discussion of theoretical implications. *Journal of Speech and Hearing Research*, 1971, *14*, 23–36.

Abramson, A. S., & Lisker, L. Discriminability along the voicing continuum: Cross-language tests. In *Proceedings of the Sixth International Congress of Phonetic Sciences*, Prague, 1967. Prague: Academia, 1970. Pp. 569–573.

Abramson, A. S., & Lisker, L. Voice-timing perception in Spanish word-initial stops. In *Status report on speech perception*, January-June, SR 29/30, 1972. New Haven, Connecticut: Haskins Laboratories. Pp. 15–25.

Berlyne, D. E. Curiosity and exploration. *Science*, 1966, *153*, 25–33.

Blakemore, C., & Campbell, F. W. On the existence of neurons in the human visual system selectively sensitive to the orientation and size of retinal images. *Journal of Physiology*, 1969, *203*, 237–260.

Blakemore, C., & Sutton, P. Size adaptation: A new aftereffect. *Science*, 1969, *166*, 245–247.

Bloom, L. *Language development: Form and function in emerging grammars.* Cambridge, Massachusetts: M. I. T. Press, 1970.

Braine, M. D. S. The ontogeny of English phrase structure: The first phase. *Language*, 1963, *39*, 1–13. (a)

Braine, M. D. S. On learning the grammatical order of words. *Psychological Review*, 1963, *70*, 323–348. (b)

Braine, M. D. S. On two types of models of the internalization of grammars. In D. I. Slobin (Ed.), *The ontogenesis of grammar*. New York: Academic Press, 1971. Pp. 153–186.

Brown, R. *Psycholinguistics.* New York: The Free Press, 1970.

Chomsky, N. *Syntactic structures.* The Hague: Mouton, 1957.

Chomsky, N. *Aspects of the theory of syntax.* Cambridge, Massachusetts: M. I. T. Press, 1965.

Cole, R. A., & Scott, B. Phoneme feature detectors. Paper presented at the meetings of the Eastern Psychological Association, Boston, Massachusetts, April, 1972.

Cooper, F. S. How is language conveyed by speech? In J. F. Kavanagh & I. G.

Mattingly (Eds.), *Language by ear and by eye.* Cambridge, Massachusetts: M. I. T. Press, 1972. Pp. 25–45.

Cooper, W. E. Adaptation of phonetic feature analyzers for place of articulation. *Journal of the Acoustical Society of America*, 1974, *56*, 617–627.

Dorman, M. F. Auditory evoked correlates of speech sound discrimination. In *Status Report on Speech Perception*, January-June, 1972, SR 29/30. New Haven, Connecticut: Haskins Laboratories. Pp. 111–120.

Eimas, P. D. The relation between identification and discrimination along speech and nonspeech continua. *Language and Speech*, 1963, *6*, 206–217.

Eimas, P. D., Cooper, W. E., & Corbit, J. D. Some properties of linguistic feature detectors. *Perception and Psychophysics*, 1973, *13*, 247–252.

Eimas, P. D., & Corbit, J. D. Selective adaptation of linguistic feature detectors. *Cognitive Psychology*, 1973, *4*, 99–109.

Eimas, P. D., Siqueland, E. R., Jusczyk, P., & Vigorito, J. Speech perception in infants. *Science*, 1971, *171*, 303–306.

Friedlander, B. The effect of speech identity, voice inflection, vocabulary, and redundancy on infants' selection of vocal reinforcement. *Journal of Experimental Child Psychology*, 1968, *6*, 443–459.

Friedlander, B. Identifying and investigating major variables of receptive language development. Paper presented at the meetings of the Society for Research in Child Development, Santa Monica, California, 1969.

Friedlander, B. Receptive language development in infancy. *Merrill-Palmer Quarterly*, 1970, *16*, 7–51.

Fry, D. B. The development of the phonological system in the normal and deaf child. In F. Smith & G. A. Miller (Eds.), *The genesis of language.* Cambridge, Massachusetts: M. I. T. Press, 1966. Pp. 187–206.

Geschwind, N. The organization of language and the brain. *Science*, 1970, 170, 940–944.

Gleason, H. A. *An introduction to descriptive linguistics* (Rev. ed.). New York: Holt, 1961.

Irwin, O. C. Phonetical description of speech development in childhood. In L. Kaiser (Ed.), *Manual of phonetics.* Amsterdam: North-Holland, 1957. Pp. 403–425.

Jakobson, R. *Child language, aphasia, and phonological universals* (translated by A. Keiler). The Hague: Mouton, 1968.

Kaplan, E. L. The role of intonation in the acquisition of language. Unpublished doctoral dissertation, Cornell University, 1969.

Kaplan, E. L., & Kaplan, G. The prelinguistic child. In J. Eliot (Ed.), *Human development and cognitive processes.* New York: Holt, 1971. Pp. 358–381.

Lewis, M. M. *Infant speech.* London: Kegan Paul, 1936.

Lewis, M. M. *Infant speech.* London: Routledge, 1951.

Liberman, A. M. The grammars of speech and language. *Cognitive Psychology*, 1970, *1*, 301–323.

Liberman, A. M., Cooper, F. S., Shankweiler, D. P., & Studdert-Kennedy, M. Perception of the speech code. *Psychological Review*, 1967, *74*, 431–461.

Lieberman, P. Towards a unified phonetic theory. *Linguistic Inquiry*, 1970, *1*, 307–322.

Lisker, L., & Abramson, A. S. A cross-language study of voicing in initial stops: Acoustical measurements. *Word*, 1964, *20*, 384–422.

Lisker, L., & Abramson, A. S. Some effects of context on voice onset time in English stops. *Language and Speech*, 1967, *10*, 1–28.

Lisker, L., & Abramson, A. S. The voicing dimension: Some experiments in comparative phonetics. In *Proceedings of the Sixth International Congress of Phonetic Sciences*, Prague, 1967. Prague: Academia, 1970. Pp. 563–567.

Mattingly, I. G. Speech cues and sign stimuli. *American Scientist*, 1972, *60*, 327–337.

Mattingly, I. G., & Liberman, A. M. The speech code and the physiology of language. In K. N. Leibovic (Ed.), *Information processing in the nervous system*. New York: Springer-Verlag, 1969. Pp. 97–117.

Mattingly, I. G., Liberman, A. M., Syrdal, A. K., & Halwes, T. Discrimination in speech and nonspeech modes. *Cognitive Psychology*, 1971, *2*, 131–157.

McCollough, C. Color adaptation of edge-detectors in the human visual system. *Science*, 1965, *149*, 1115–1116.

McNeill, D. Developmental psycholinguistics. In F. Smith & G. A. Miller (Eds.) *The genesis of language*. Cambridge, Massachusetts: M. I. T. Press, 1966. Pp. 15–84.

McNeill, D. The development of language. In P. H. Mussen (Ed.), *Manual of child psychology*. New York: Wiley, 1970. Pp. 1061–1161. (a)

McNeill, D. *The acquisition of language*. New York: Harper, 1970. (b)

Menyuk, P. *The acquisition and development of language*. Englewood Cliffs, New Jersey: Prentice-Hall, 1971.

Miller, G. A. The magical number seven, plus or minus two: Some limits on our capacity for processing information. *Psychological Review*, 1956, *63*, 81–97.

Moffitt, A. R. Consonant cue perception by twenty- to twenty-four-week-old infants. *Child Development*, 1971, *42*, 717–731.

Molfese, D. L. Cerebral asymmetry in infants, children, and adults: Auditory evoked responses to speech and noise stimuli. Unpublished doctoral dissertation, The Pennsylvania State University, 1972.

Morse, P. A. The discrimination of speech and nonspeech stimuli in early infancy. *Journal of Experimental Child Psychology*, 1972, *14*, 477–492.

Pisoni, D. On the nature of categorical perception of speech sounds. Unpublished doctoral dissertation, University of Michigan, 1971.

Port. D. K., & Preston, M. S. Early apical stop production: A voice onset time analysis. In *Status Report on Speech Perception*, January–June, 1972, SR 29/30. New Haven, Connecticut: Haskins Laboratories. Pp. 125–150.

Sawusch, J. R., & Pisoni, D. B. Category boundaries for speech and nonspeech sounds. Paper presented at the meetings of the Acoustical Society of America, Los Angeles, California, 1973.

Siqueland, E. R. The development of instrumental exploratory behavior during the first year of human life. Paper presented at the meetings of the Society for Research in Child Development, Santa Monica, California, 1969.

Siqueland, E. R., & DeLucia, C. A. Visual reinforcement of nonnutritive sucking in human infants. *Science*, 1969, *165*, 1144–1146.

Slobin, D. I. *Psycholinguistics*. Glenview, Illinois: Scott Foresman, 1971.

Sokolov, E. N. Neuronal models and the orienting reflex. In M. A. B. Brazier (Ed.), *The central nervous system and behavior*. New York: Josiah Macy, Jr., Foundation, 1960. Pp. 187–276.

Stevens, K. N. The quantal nature of speech: Evidence from articulatory–acoustic data. In E. E. David, Jr., and P. B. Denes (Eds.), *Human communication: A unified view*, 1972. Pp. 51–66.

Stevens, K. N., & Halle, M. Remarks on analysis by synthesis and distinctive features. In W. Wathen-Dunn (Ed.), *Models for the perception of speech and visual form*. Cambridge, Massachusetts: M. I. T. Press, 1967. Pp. 88–102.

Stevens, K. N., & House, A. S. Speech perception. In J. Tobias (Ed.), *Foundations of modern auditory theory*, Vol. 2. New York: Academic Press, 1972. Pp. 3–62.

Studdert-Kennedy, M. The perception of speech. In *Status report on speech perception*, July–September, 1970. New Haven, Connecticut: Haskins Laboratories. Pp. 15–48.

Studdert-Kennedy, M., Liberman, A. M., Harris, K. S., & Cooper, F. S. Motor theory of speech perception: A reply to Lane's critical review. *Psychological Review*, 1970, *77*, 234–249.

Studdert-Kennedy, M., & Shankweiler, D. P. Hemispheric specialization for speech perception. *Journal of the Acoustical Society of America*, 1970, *48*, 579–594.

Trehub, S. E., & Rabinovitch, M. S. Auditory–linguistic sensitivity in early infancy. *Developmental Psychology*, 1972, *6*, 74–77.

Turnure, C. Response to voice of mother and stranger by babies in the first year. Paper presented at the meetings of the Society for Research in Child Development, Santa Monica, California, 1969.

Witelson, S. F., & Pallie, W. Left hemisphere specialization for language in the newborn. *Brain*, 1973, *96*, 641–646.

Wolf, C. G. The perception of stop consonants by children. *Journal of Experimental Child Psychology*, 1973, *16*, 318–331.

Wolff, P. H. The natural history of crying and other vocalizations in early infancy. In B. M. Foss (Ed.), *Determinants of infant behavior*, Vol. IV. London: Methuen, 1969. Pp. 81–109.

Wood, C. C., Goff, W. P., & Day, R. S. Auditory evoked potentials during speech perception. *Science*, 1971, *173*, 1248–1251.

Author Index

Subject Index